To all our comrades

on the fighting front

The VOICE of NORWAY

❈

By HALVDAN KOHT and
SIGMUND SKARD

AMS Press, Inc.
New York
1967

PREFACE

"If there is anyone who still wonders why this war is being fought, let him look to Norway. . . . And if there is anyone who doubts the democratic will to win, again I say let him look to Norway. He will find in Norway, at once conquered and unconquerable, the answer to his questions."

The words are those of President Roosevelt. This book is written with the purpose of showing the truth of these words, the profound reasons why Norway may be put forward as an instance of the ideals and the realities which more than thirty nations have united to defend and to uphold.

At the present moment, Norway seems stricken, crippled, and bleeding under the savage heels of merciless German Nazis and their perverse Quisling henchmen. But the Norwegian nation does not admit defeat. Her spirit will survive.

And even if the barbarous conquerors of the Norwegian soil should succeed in torturing to death every free man and woman in the land (they never will succeed!), the Norwegian nation, by her civilization, her literature and art, her social and political achievements, has left an immortal heritage that will live on as an incentive for future generations.

Her struggle for freedom and law, for national organization and individual liberty, is the universal struggle of all progressive nations. But the Norwegian struggle has a particular character due to the indomitable virility of the people and the strange vicissitudes of their history, their sharp decline and their striking recoveries. Here is a genuine Nordic people, stubbornly fighting for the true Nordic ideals, asserting herself in vigorous individualities and holding together in community of interest and faith.

We do not intend to present in this book a complete picture of the political and intellectual rise of Norway. We have chosen to take as our standpoint two fundamental ideas, basic of all Western

[vii]

PREFACE

civilization, those of law and liberty, just those ideas that a new-awakened barbarousness has risen against and attempts to crush, trying even to persuade the world that the opposite ideas, arbitrariness and dictatorship, represent the true spirit of Nordic race.

We do not claim that the Nordic nations, more than others, have by nature a particular will to build their society on the ideas now endangered by Nazi aggresssion. But we may be justified in asserting that history has worked to develop in them an eminently constructive unity of love of freedom and respect for law, making them the natural champions of the highest ideals of future national and international life.

It happens that Norway is the one of the Nordic nations which for years has shared the struggle of the United Nations against the enemies of our common civilization. This situation has placed Norway in the vanguard of Nordic progress, and her history and literature may well serve as a fitting example of what civilization has at stake in a struggle that stretches from Kirkenes in our homeland to the Cape of Good Hope and from the Aleutians to Australia.

CONTENTS

CONTENTS

Part I

FREE MEN BUILD
THEIR SOCIETY

INTRODUCTION

With law shall we build our land, not with lawlessness lay it waste.
So reads the introduction to Norway's ancient code of laws. So
read those of Denmark and Sweden as well. A common principle
of Scandinavian society, fundamental to all the nations of the
North, has found expression in these words.

The codes as we have them were written in the thirteenth century. But the formula is certainly much older, as appears from its
poetic, alliterative form. The principle it proclaims lies at the base
of Scandinavian history as far back as we are able to discern.

I

When the nations of Southern Europe first made the acquaint-
ance of the people from the North, they thought them a gang of
wild barbarians. They saw them first as rapacious, murdering Vikings, who mercilessly swooped down upon the civilized countries of Europe. Terror-stricken they prayed: "Free us, Lord, from
the frenzy of the Northmen!" One should not minimize this aspect
of the Viking raids, but at the same time it must be remembered
that there were other important aspects. From a historical point
of view, some of these are, indeed, more important. On the one
hand we have all that the Vikings learned abroad and the impulses
they brought with them in art, politics, and religion. On the other
hand we have their own constructive activities in these foreign
lands.

It is a notable fact that wherever the Vikings went they set to
work establishing ordered kingdoms or commonwealths, and that
many of these became the lasting foundations of social or political
life. Norwegians settled Iceland and the Faroe Islands, conquered
and settled the Shetland and the Orkney Islands, the Hebrides and
parts of northern Scotland. They established kingdoms at Dublin

[1]

and on the Isle of Man. Danes, together with Norwegians, made themselves masters of the Danelaw in England and of Normandy in France. Danish Vikings even reigned for a time in the Netherlands. In the East, Swedish Vikings founded the kingdom of Russia, and some Polish historians even think it likely that the kingdom of Poland may have been established by Scandinavian, specifically Danish, Vikings.

In all these settlements or conquests the law was supreme.

An old French poem about the Vikings who invaded France tells an anecdote which reveals the impression they left on their contemporaries in the country they conquered. It is said that a messenger from the king of France came to ask for their chief, and he got the proud answer: "We have no chief, we are all equals." Of course that was not literally true. But the answer tells us something about the spirit of the invaders. They felt themselves to be free men, and what they really obeyed was the law.

Nothing could illuminate this mentality better than the fact that the settlers of Iceland established no executive authority whatever in their commonwealth. They created a parliament, termed the *Althing* or General Assembly, which some years ago (1930) celebrated its millennial anniversary. The Althing was a meeting of all free landholders for legislative and judicial purposes. But there was no national sovereign. The law alone was the master of free men.

The Icelanders took the same kind of organization along to their settlement in Greenland.

In the Faroe Islands there was a chief who eventually fell under the authority of the king of Norway. But at his side there was always a general assembly, here called the *Lagthing* (or "Law Thing"), possibly older even than the Icelandic Althing, and still in existence.

On the Isle of Man to this very day the fundamental constitution is a heritage from the time of Norwegian rule, which centers around a people's assembly called *Tynwald*, that is, "*Thing* Plain."

Just as the Icelanders often referred to their territory as their "law," and as, in the same way, some districts in Norway were named "laws," so the Viking domain in England was called the

INTRODUCTION

Danelaw. It is significant that in no part of England was the proportion of free farmers or yeomen as high as there. And it means not a little that the very word "law" in English is a Scandinavian loan word—philologists may dispute whether it is of Danish or Norwegian origin. The importance of the Danish-Norwegian conquest of Normandy, not only to the duchy itself but even to the development of the political system that came to rule both England and France, is well known to all students of medieval history. An American historian has demonstrated this to the world better than anyone else.[1] Legend ascribed to the first Viking duke of Normandy so perfect a rule of law that every man might travel safely across his domain—something one could not do at that time in the other provinces of France. A piece of gold lost on the highroad might be found again untouched by anybody.

The founding of the Russian empire was equally important in Eastern Europe. According to the Russian chroniclers the Swedish Vikings were called in by the inhabitants to establish law and peace in the country.

Thus, in a wide circle embracing almost all the neighboring countries, the northern peoples made their influence felt as a power in state building and left their mark on the history of all Northern Europe. Only Germany escaped the activities of the Vikings, perhaps to her own lasting disadvantage.

II

Simultaneously with the establishment of all such Scandinavian state organizations abroad, the kingdoms of Denmark, Norway, and Sweden were set up at home. They were founded by royal conquerors. But it is a noteworthy fact that in Norway, at any rate, there were already in existence several unions of provinces based simply on the common maintenance of law, before the whole country was united into one kingdom. And one of the main tasks of the new national kings was to organize the common law.

[1] Charles H. Haskins, *Norman Institutions* (1918), and *The Normans in European History* (1915).

[3]

INTRODUCTION

Anyone who has read or seen Ibsen's magnificent historical drama, *The Pretenders*, will recall the programmatic idea announced in it: "Norway has become a kingdom; it shall be made a nation." He will also have grasped the almost insurmountable difficulties of the task by reason of the tremendous inherent forces which opposed themselves to such national unity. Norway at that time, a thousand years ago, had a population of certainly less than a million, perhaps not much over half a million, spread over a large territory filled with natural obstacles to communication and nation-wide coöperation. Present-day Norway has an extent of about 125,000 square miles, or as much as all of New England plus New York and New Jersey. Ancient Norway was considerably larger. It would be impossible to give any exact figure in square miles, because the northern parts of the country had what geographers in recent times have called "open frontiers." The Norwegian kings collected taxes from the nomadic Finns or Lapps far into what is now Swedish Lapmark and as far east as the White Sea. Even in the south there were no fixed boundary lines, since the frontiers consisted of vast forests or uninhabited mountain plateaus. In fact, definite boundaries were not drawn up until the middle of the eighteenth century; in the farthest north, not before the nineteenth century.

Perhaps one may gain a more concrete idea of the extent of this country by observing that from north to south it covers a distance of more than thirteen degrees of latitude, or approximately the distance from the northernmost point of Maine to the southernmost point of North Carolina. If one should swing Norway around its southernmost cape, the northern end would extend south of Venice. It is easy to imagine the variety of living conditions within such an extensive area and the difficulties of tying a sparse people together over such distances.

In addition, the nature of the country has done almost everything in its power to cut people off from one another. The whole Scandinavian peninsula is virtually a large tableland of which Sweden includes almost all the lower plains, Norway all the mountains.

INTRODUCTION

In one of Bjørnson's many hymns to Norway these words appear:

A land towers up to the everlasting snow,
'Tis but in the clefts that life seems to grow.

The high and rocky, often ice-clad, mountains may offer to the eye innumerable vistas of superb beauty. But for the sustenance of the people they leave but narrow valleys, set between forbidding barriers. Only in the southeastern parts of the country and inside the Trondheimsfjord may one find broader settlements. In fact, almost two thirds of the Norwegian area is completely unproductive and unfit for cultivation. At the very most, some 10 to 15 percent of it is in one way or another cultivable. Valuable forests cover a fourth of the area. The remainder is naked mountains and barren heath.

On the other hand, Norway is favored to an unusual degree by her climate. Although situated between the latitude of 58 and 71 degrees, or about as far north as Alaska, it has warmer summers than any other country in the same latitude, and even at the coldest places the winters are not excessively cold. Whether the reason is the Gulf Stream, or whether the prevailing southwestern winds may claim most of the credit, it is a gratifying fact that along the whole coast, from the farthest north, the sea never freezes, and it offers the people the richest fisheries in the world. Woods grow in the northernmost counties; barley ripens as far north as latitude 70°, and wheat up to latitude 66°, corresponding to land far north of Hudson Bay; fine strawberries are cultivated and gathered in latitude 67°; potatoes grow everywhere. In most places the soil is of the very best quality, and very few countries surpass Norway in their yield per cultivated acre. The extent of such area is, however, too small to produce at best more than half of the grain needed for the population. Only in meat and dairy products is the country self-supporting.

However, nothing is easily won in Norway. Whatever is obtained from land or sea is won by hard toil, compelling man to use all his powers and often risk even his life. What pioneer and frontier life was to Americans, the daily struggle for existence through innumerable generations has been to the Norwegians. It has fostered a hardy and stubborn race. It has bred in every man a will of his own, one that does not bow readily to that of other people. But, at the same time, it has given him a deep understanding of the laws of nature and taught him the necessity of mutual help. It has created minds that are independent, but also profoundly loyal and adaptable to social duties.

While these are the basic traits of Norwegian character, there are glaring differences of mind and manners throughout the country. The physical variations of race cannot account for such differences. Though the small, black-haired people may predominate in many districts of the west and the tall blond ones in the east, in all parts of the country the two extremes have mixed and have assumed local characteristics. Indeed, the isolation of every local community (within which, on the other hand, the inhabitants generally live very close together) has given a kind of particular nationality to each one of them.

One may think the people of the east characteristically Norwegian in their proud reticence; but just as Norwegian are the talkative and impressionable people of the north, the vivid though somewhat prudent ones of the west, the good-natured, humorous ones of the south. Within these groups again there are startling variations. In some districts everybody seems to be a poet; in some, decorative arts are common property; in others all seem educated for practicing law; in still others historical interests prevail. There is no end of varieties. And every district is conscious of its particular character, looking at its neighbors with a certain ridicule, contempt, or forbearance. It would be possible to make up a psychological description of all the local groups of Norway based upon the sayings of neighbors about each other, and it would not be flattering, though very amusing. In sum, it would attest to the wealth of contrasts and to the proper pride of all the local divisions within the Norwegian nation. How would it be possible to unite them into a nation?

FOUNDING the KINGDOM

I

All the local kingdoms, earldoms, and other minor political units of Norway were first brought under one master by the armed forces of King Harold Fairhair, by inheritance the ruler of some southeastern districts. On the basis of computations by Icelandic annalists of the twelfth century and of researches of Norwegian historians of the nineteenth century, it has been customary to place the decisive victory of Harold in the year 872. It seems probable that this event should rather be dated a decade or two later. In any case we can take it for granted that Norway was a united kingdom before the end of the ninth century. It is thus one of the oldest kingdoms in Europe.

The history and achievements of the founder of the kingdom are interwoven with legends. His extraordinary personality made a vivid impact on the imagination of the people. They believed he had been fostered and helped by trolls, by that mystical mountain spirit who was the original guardian of Norway. They remembered the Fairhair as the severe and majestic ruler whose frowns brought everybody to obedience.

He may have been influenced by Carolingian ideas, though perhaps not directly, since in his day the empire of Charlemagne was dissolved. The influence may have come through the medium of the young kingdom of England, where Alfred the Great, inspired by French ideas, was then establishing a new nation. As a matter of fact, King Harold allied himself with Alfred's grandson, the great King Æthelstane, who conquered the Danelaw. In the 920's, Harold sent his son Hákon to be educated at the court of Æthelstane, and the Norwegians felt pride in naming this Hákon the "foster son of Æthelstane."

The kings of Norway and England had a common interest in

[7]

fighting the Vikings who imperiled the peace of their realms. The royal oath of the king of Norway charged him with two obligations. One was the defense of the country against foreign aggression, the other was the maintenance of law and peace within the boundaries. Piracy was forbidden. The fact that there was at this time a lull in the Viking raids on England was due not only to the strong resistance now encountered but also to the pacification of Norway and Denmark under powerful kings.

For a century and a half, the fate of the kingdom of Norway remained uncertain. At times the country was split once more under several rulers and at other times the whole country or parts of it was even under the domination of foreign (mostly Danish) kings. The last of these foreign masters was the powerful King Canute (1028–35), who boasted of having won, besides Denmark, England, Norway, and a part of Sweden. But the descendants of Harold Fairhair always claimed the kingdom as their legal inheritance. They fought for it, and time and again retook it.

One of them was the celebrated athlete and warrior Olaf Trygvason, who ruled Norway for the five last years of the tenth century. He had been a Viking, but had received the Christian baptism in England, and sword in hand he enforced Christianity in Norway. After his fall the kingdom was split. A second Olaf, who also had been a great Viking, conquered it again. He had been baptized at the court of the duke of Normandy and he was the real organizer of the Christian Church in Norway. During his prolonged stay in Normandy he must have learned much about the art of ruling a country. He brought the ideals of Charlemagne with him. But he fell in defending his kingdom against King Canute, in the battle of Stiklestad, July 29, 1030. He was made the national saint of his country; the anniversary of his death became the great national festival. And the Norwegian chiefs who once had opposed his severe government were now so deeply imbued with the national idea that they rebelled against foreign domination. From that day in 1035 when Olaf's young son Magnus, named after Charlemagne, was enthroned as king, the unity and independence of Norway remained unimpaired.

FOUNDING the KINGDOM

II

Before the unification of Norway several counties had joined into larger units under a common law, such an organization being called simply "law." One embraced the fjord districts in the west, another the districts around the great lake Mjøsa in southeastern Norway, a third all the districts around the Trondheimsfjord. Each such "law" had a common meeting place where the people gathered once a year in a *Thing* to hear the laws recited and have their disputes adjudged.

The foremost people of the districts formed the courts. Subordinate courts functioned in the parishes and in the shires. Each parish formed a religious unity, centered around a temple. The shires, too, had such religious centers. They also had their military chief. All of them, however, chiefs and priests as well as common people, were equally bound by the laws, which had been developed by tradition through centuries.

The organization of larger "law" districts, a comparatively recent event going hardly further back than the ninth century, was the result of expanding intercourse and the need of legal unity among neighboring counties. It seems to have been achieved by friendly agreement, and such "laws" had no common political or military chief. The national kings, however, gave new impetus to this development and systematically implemented the legal organization of the country.

The great organizer among the early kings was no doubt the second King Olaf, who after his death was celebrated as Saint Olaf. His life was not altogether saintly. He was a warrior and a lover of women. But he was also a missionary king who did not tolerate any remnants of pagan belief or ceremony. Assisted by his English bishops and clergymen, he established definite Christian rituals and had all temples replaced by churches. He had seen the strict government of the duchy of Normandy and he wanted his own kingdom brought into firm order. It was undoubtedly his achievement that a new "law" was founded embracing the coast districts of southeastern Norway. It is more uncertain whether he extended the limits of the older "laws"; we do know that since his time all the shires of Norway were assigned to one or another of the existing "laws." In this way, a long step was taken toward national legal unity. In fact, in the whole extensive country only four distinct laws were recognized. The northernmost districts, which because of the distances could not well be united with the "law" of the Trondheim counties, received the law book of this district.

By a contemporary notice—indeed in a poem by the skald and adviser of King Olaf, Sigvat Thordson—we are told that he gave laws to the country. We may assume that these laws dealt mainly with the rules of Christianity and Church. But there was in them at least one provision of a purely humane order, the rule that in every law district, later extended to every shire, a serf should be given his freedom at all annual *Thing* assemblies. In ecclesiastical tradition Olaf was praised for having fulfilled the duty of every Christian king by giving the same justice to high and low. Yet he certainly did not change the Norwegian laws that fixed the payment of fines according to the social rank of the offended party. The tradition expresses the fame he won, confirmed by contemporary sources, as an unsparing defender of law and justice. His death fighting for his royal claims and the independence of the country consecrated his life and activity. He not only became the sanctified symbol of national unity, but "the laws of Saint Olaf" became in the popular mind the foundation of all civic rights.

The OLD NORSE SYSTEM
of LAW

At the beginning of the thirteenth century there existed in Trondheim, the ecclesiastical and in certain respects the royal capital of Norway, a law book that according to tradition was written in the days of King Magnus the Good, son of Saint Òlaf. This tradition may very well be true. It would not even seem unlikely that some laws had been put into writing by Saint Olaf himself and his English clergymen. However, the law texts that have come down to our day do not reach further back than the end of the twelfth century, and internal evidence indicates that they can hardly have been recorded earlier than the beginning of that century. Nevertheless they contain many laws, virtually a whole complex of rules, that date back to the eleventh century and even earlier times. Thus we are able to trace the legal conceptions that have lain at the base of Norwegian society since the establishment of the kingdom. Though expressed in rules for specific cases, they form a coherent system that may well bear comparison with Roman law; they are elaborated with strict logic and often with a subtlety of thinking that evokes admiration. They almost made a nation of lawyers.

The laws prevailing in the various districts of Norway were in a quite particular sense the intellectual property of every inhabitant. They had to be publicly recited in all the annual assemblies of every law district, so that every man would have them impressed on his memory and at the same time be able to see that they were fully and correctly rendered. Men who were renowned as "wise" or "scholarly" (those two terms were expressed by a single word in ancient Norwegian) were selected for the task of law recital and they undoubtedly did much to gather the laws into the perfect system which now presents itself to us. They were called "lawmen," and it was they who undertook the writing of the law books that are preserved to our day. From the end of the twelfth century they were regularly appointed by the king and took an oath saying: "I shall announce to the people of my law district the law that was first established by Saint Olaf and later was agreed to by his descendants as valid between the king and the nation."

The terms of this oath demonstrate that the law was the property of the citizens in the sense, too, that it was conceived as an agreement between people and king. The king was not only the defender of law within his kingdom, but he himself was in duty bound to obey the law. Otherwise he would forfeit his royal power. This is explicitly stated: "No man shall attack another in his home, neither the king nor any other man. If the king does this, the arrow shall be sent forth through all the shires, and men shall go upon him and slay him, if they are able to seize him; if he escapes, he shall never be allowed to return to the land."

The fundamental principle of social and political life was expressed in the sentence that "Whoever shall deny law to another shall not enjoy law." Respect for the law was the condition of a membership in society. "The beginning of our law," it is said, "is that every one of our countrymen shall be inviolate in his rights and his person, both within and without the kingdom." "All free men," the law continues, "shall enjoy security in their homes and also in traveling to, or returning from, the distant parts of his farm." The man who ventured to break the peace of the country and the rights of his countrymen put himself outside the law.

The Norwegian laws, like those of all other Teutonic peoples, contained an elaborate system of fines as punishments or as compensations for injuries inflicted upon fellow citizens. But there were crimes that could not be paid for in this way. Such crimes included manslaughter in sacred places like churches and places of justice, all cases of murder or arson, of treason or rebellion, of inland piracy, and of sorcery, even some cases of theft or robbery. It may be noted that all these crimes belonged to the category of those that could not possibly be paid for by fines even in pagan times, the temples at that time being just as sacred as were churches later; even sorcery was a damnable crime to enlightened pagans of the Viking age. The very fact of such crimes put a man outside the law and beyond its protection. He had no more part in social peace and safety. He was no more a member of his native society; he was its enemy like the wolf or the bear and must not be helped by anyone; and he had no means of escaping the wrath of his former fellow countrymen except by fleeing the country.

Does that mean that any one of them was entitled to kill him? Yes, but on one essential condition: the man who took it upon himself to kill an outlawed criminal would immediately have to apply for legal confirmation of his act. He had to address himself to the representatives of society to obtain justification for having taken the law into his own hands. For, in the ancient conception, the enforcing power was in the hands of society itself. Of course, in practice society could but rarely act corporately. That might happen when the people assembled in court would pursue the violator of the sacredness of a place of justice. Otherwise the law recognized a group of citizens as representative of society, and one of the old law books substantiates this rule by saying: "Five men make a body."

The vital matter is that society was a party to all crimes or violations of law or rights. Therefore, in principle, no private revenge could be allowed. We often hear that the families of a man sought revenge for his being killed or otherwise offended. But, officially at least, society condemned such behavior. The law required every crime or claim to be decided by court and judgment.

The other side of this principle was that every citizen shared the responsibility of seeing the common decisions of society fulfilled. He was part of the enforcing power, and every one of its decisions or acts had an individual appeal to him. He was active in shaping such decisions, whether by legislation or by judgment in court.

Every free man had the right, indeed the duty, to meet at the general assembly, or *thing*, of his parish, to vote there the rules of common interest and to sit in court and judge violations of the law. Then he might go to the *thing* of the larger folkland or shire for the same purpose. And finally he might assist at the annual *Lagthing* (or "Law *Thing*"), the supreme authority of the whole law district.

Quite naturally it became customary that only a certain number of representatives should assemble at the *Lagthings* or, at any rate, take part in the decisions there. And even that a group of these representatives should be selected to sit as a court. As the king ever more firmly established himself as the mainstay of the social and political will of the nation, the royal officials of the district came to take care of all such elections and appointments. This was not, however, felt as a loss of popular sovereignty. For obviously the royal officers could not proceed arbitrarily in their exercise of such functions; they would have to select those men who by tradition and social position must be the natural representatives of their countrymen.

Traditional ideas, or what we would call public opinion, reigned to an extent that in our times is felt only in moments of the highest emergency. In *things* and in courts there was never a question of voting and deciding by majority. The general presumption was that every decision would finally be unanimous. There could be no real dissension as to what was law and justice. Everybody conceived the law as an autonomous power, objective and divine, to which all must bow equally.

Historians have expressed different opinions as to how far members of a society like that of ancient Norway could be called truly free individuals. Of course, we cannot transfer our ideas of liberty to those past times. Legally every free man and woman was completely free. There were serfs or thralls; but they were swiftly disappearing, so that from the middle of the thirteenth century the laws no longer took them into consideration. All were free. They could not all have the same influence in society; the owners of large estates would be more powerful than common farmers, and mere small holders, like the owner of a poor cottage, did not rank much higher than hired laborers. But legally the latter were free to order their life according to their own desires. They would not, however, readily think of overstepping the boundaries set for them by social tradition.

In general, the power of traditional law was not felt as a coercion of the mind. It was accepted quite naturally and voluntarily, and did not impair the feeling of acting in freedom. In ancient Norway, as in any other country and at any time, there would be strong minds and weak minds. We may well be justified in assuming that the conditions of settlement imposed by the geographic conditions of Norway, the fact that every farmer, whether working a small or a large holding, was living by himself, not in village communities, helped to foster independent ways of acting and thinking. More positively we may state that men who went abroad for commerce or for war, or who entered the royal service, came into touch with new conditions and acquired new ideas. From the Viking age cases are reported of chiefs who broke away from all religious bonds and set their trust in their individual powers.

In the highest ranks of society a freer individualism no doubt developed, and new demands of state and church affected the conception of law. But on the whole, social solidarity remained the strongest force in life.

Every man served the law, and in every matter of violation or dispute he had to seek redress by law and judgment. Criminals, that is men who broke the law in their relations with other people, were sentenced to amends or fines according to the enormity of their crime and the social rank of the person offended. They were expected to comply with the sentence inflicted upon them. In principle, they would be outlaws if they refused to pay, and this menace would generally force their compliance.

Since, however, part of the fines had to be paid to a representative of society, the king or his officials, the execution of sentences became a part of the king's duties. Very early we hear that the king is having thieves and robbers decapitated or mutilated, and later royal prisons were established. In cases of so gross a crime as homicide, it became the legal practice that the king would accord a patent of residence in the country to a criminal who had paid his fines.

Ancient law knew no difference of procedure between civil and criminal cases. In all of them the question involved a violation of legal rights, and such a violation was always a crime against society as a whole. Every right a man possessed was considered valid until challenged by somebody, and then society would not interfere except on complaint of the offended party. Even in economic matters no one was his own executor. Said the old law: "None of us shall take goods away from another, nor shall we be guilty of taking the law in our own hands; every man is entitled to legal judgment in what concerns his possessions."

A man might well help himself to his goods from thieves and robbers. But if he took the law into his hands in other cases, the offended party might appeal to the court. He did not have to wait for the regular meeting of the *thing* or the court; he was entitled to have the *thing* summoned to give a judgment on his complaint.

Thus society was an active instrument of the law, always ready to act. It was, however, a natural consequence of the establishment of a national royal power—whose main task it was to maintain general peace and justice—that the king increasingly took care of the administration of law. I have mentioned how he controlled the execution of sentences and even took the execution into his own hands, how he influenced the composition of *thing* courts and appointed the lawmen. These latter by degrees became real judges, and increasingly they came to replace the *Lagthings*. The popular courts still functioned for centuries, in fact as late as the seventeenth century. But the scope of their activity was steadily diminishing. The interests of the national body politic were constantly enlarging themselves and encroaching upon traditional individual rights. On the other hand, the individual was detaching himself from ancient ties, partly owing to the very extension of society.

Originally man was not merely a separate being. He was the representative of a family or, more than that, of a clan or kin. In some cases the old Norwegian laws take into account the kinship unto the twelfth degree. The most important task of the kinsfolk was to defend the legal rights of every one of them; but that was a task which passed ever more completely into the hands of the public authorities. Far more enduring was the relation of the kin to a man's real estate.

As a matter of fact, the farm was not at the free disposal of the proprietor. He was, in a way, merely managing it on behalf of the family. In particular, he could not alienate it at his own pleasure. If he found himself compelled to sell it, he was obliged to offer it first to his kinsfolk. If he sold it to someone not related, the nearest heirs were entitled to take it back. In Roman law, the rights of the heirs appeared as a limitation on the proprietor's right of devising. In Norwegian law, the right of heritage (*odal*) was primary and absolute. It was intended to keep the estate or farm in the hands of the family through successive generations. This right was a matter of common law, regarded as a social institution hallowed by centuries of tradition.

With the passing of time and the increasing importance of trade, the right of odal had to be protected and circumscribed by a framework of processual rules, but also limited as to its scope in time and extension of kindred. It was, however, so firmly rooted in the social consciousness of the Norwegian nation as to maintain itself through all later times, and when Norway won its free constitution in 1814, the stipulation was explicitly made that the right of odal should never be abolished.

Meanwhile, both state and church, each in its own way, had been active in transforming the traditional notions of personal and family rights. The state organized the citizens for military purposes; the church had moral claims on its parishioners. In both cases, the new institutions promoted economic demands, in different forms of taxing. They even changed the laws. Both state and church acquired the right of expropriating pieces of land for public use. Both of them succeeded in seeing implemented the sentence of death or outlawing with the right of confiscating all the property of the criminal, including the real estate. The church obtained an abridgment of the absolute right of inheritance in so far as a man was allowed to donate or devise a certain amount of his property to the benefit of ecclesiastical institutions, no more than a tenth of his inherited property, a fourth of what he himself had acquired.

On the other hand, although the church was allowed to collect tithes from all people, the parishioners would not grant her the full tithe for her free disposal. They adopted an agreement to the effect that they would retain a fourth of the tithe for the support of the poor in their district. That was a social obligation that they wanted to take care of themselves.

In many ways law was changing. But, despite all such changes, the idea of law and of social solidarity kept its firm hold on the people. It remained the foremost obligation of all public authorities and institutions that they should defend and maintain the law in all domains of society.

The KINGS and the LAW

I

These law-abiding people, loyal to their kings, discharging their duties to royal and ecclesiastical officers, to neighbors and to the poor, had a pride in their own country, in their chiefs and in themselves, a pride that strengthened their will to defend their law against foreign aggressors, a pride that was nourished by the memories of past feats. Honor was a passion with them. From one generation to another they told each other stories about the bravery of kings and warriors.

What had they not heard about the first King Olaf, the Trygvason? He was defeated in a battle with the Danes and the Swedes and some treacherous compatriots, but only because he was lured into a trap, accompanied by nine ships against a whole navy. How proud and superior he was in the meeting with certain death! Did he not scorn his enemies? When hearing that the Danes were mustering against him, he said: "We are not afraid of those cowards; there is no courage in Danes." And about the Swedes he said: "Those horse eaters ought better to sit at home and lick their feast bowls than try themselves against our arms." Only when he heard about the Norwegian earl who laid his ships against him, did he say: "There will be a hard fight, for they are Norsemen like ourselves." Finally, when all his ships had been cleared of men and he stood almost alone on the high deck of his royal ship, he would not allow his enemies to slay him but sprang overboard into the sea and disappeared. No one could ever be sure whether he drowned or eventually escaped. There was a rumor that someone had recognized him as a monk in the Holy Land; perhaps he had still been able to serve God.

And the second Olaf, the Saint, the whole country was full of legends about him. Everywhere one might find wells that he had caused to spring forth, or roads he had broken through hard cliffs, or churches he had forced trolls to help him build. He was the great benefactor of the people, the father of their laws. But he, too, had been a valiant fighter for the independence of the country. In his last battle (1030), meeting a superior army led by half-pagan and self-willed chiefs, he showed an undaunted courage, worthy the champion of God's cause and that of the fatherland, and his men followed him with faithful enthusiasm, falling by his side. That battle seemed the very foundation of a new Norway, a Christian and united nation.

His son, Magnus, who was made king by the national uprising against the tyranny of King Canute (1035), won the surname the Good and was beloved by the whole nation. He even became the king of Denmark and he led both Danes and Norwegians to victory against the Slavonic enemies who threatened to invade and conquer their lands.

The younger brother of Saint Olaf, Harold Hardrada, who succeeded Magnus on the throne, in his youth served the Byzantine emperor as chief of his Scandinavian guard and fought his wars from Sicily to Syria. Innumerable stories were told about his bravery and his cunning. He was really a man of the great world, married to a princess of Russia, a brother-in-law of the kings of Hungary and France, a lover of the arts and himself a poet. When the emissary of the archbishop of Bremen came to demand his subjection, he cried out in wrath: "There is no archbishop in Norway but me." Although he defeated the Danes in one battle after another, he was not able to maintain his rule over their country, and he fell at Stanford Bridge while attempting to conquer England (1066). His defeat, however, was ascribed to his reckless contempt of danger and death, battling a vastly superior force without a thought of fleeing.

And what about his grandson, King Magnus Bareleg? His watchword was: "The goal of a king is honor, not longevity." He wanted to extend his kingdom; he conquered the Hebrides and the Isle of Man and added them to the other western isles that had been

Norwegian provinces more than a century. When he fell in an ambush in Ireland (1103), he died with a jest on his lips.

His son, Sigurd, won fame and surname from his crusade to the Holy Land (1108–11), defeating the Saracens in Portugal and in the Mediterranean and helping to conquer Sidon for the kingdom of Jerusalem. His followers came home boasting that he had comported himself like the ruler of a great power. Popular tradition asserted that the royal title later assumed by the Norman duke of Sicily was originally conferred on him by King Sigurd; and Constantinople, the meeting place of East and West, was made the scene of adventures in which the king of Norway proved the equal of the mighty emperor.

All such stories were a part of the inheritance of the Norwegian people. They felt themselves to be free men, imbued with a strong sense of honor, and they would remain a free nation. When, in the 1160's, the powerful Danish King Waldemar had made an attempt to conquer Norway, he finally dropped the plan, admitting that he could persuade none of his magnates to settle in Norway, because, he was reported as saying, there lived a hard and unruly people.

Unruly, yes, but only in relations with foreign masters. They obeyed the law, but only their own law, the laws of Saint Olaf. Therefore they could not be made slaves.

II

When, in 1872, for the millenary of the Kingdom of Norway, the modern national poet Bjørnson celebrated the memory of Sigurd the Crusader in a popular drama, he made one of his skalds praise his feats by a song proclaiming:

> The glaive of battle reflects a splendor,
> An honor that strengthens the people's work.

The idea of these lines may be more a poetical vision than a result of practical experience, although it seems proved that the

liberation of peasants in the eighteenth century and the transformation of Norwegian tenants into property holders in the
nineteenth century, coincided with an increase of their production. Anyhow, the honor inherent in peaceful work was vividly
felt even in ancient Norway.

It is significant that people loved to quote two versified lines
composed by King Sigurd himself—as a matter of fact, the only
poetry he ever attempted, since, unlike his ancestors Harold Hardrada and Magnus Bareleg, he was not a poet. These lines said:
"Farmers I love best, the land being settled and the peace standing
firm." And the people later recalled his reign as the happiest period they had experienced for a long time past.

There was another tradition, contrasting the warlike Sigurd
with his peaceable brother Eystein, who reigned together with
him, and this tradition was elaborated in dramatic form, making
the two brothers for the entertainment of their men compare
themselves to each other: Sigurd praising his crusading feats,
Eystein telling about what he achieved sitting at home. Manifestly,
the tale of this emulation of the brothers is intimately in sympathy with the efforts of Eystein, helping the peaceful progress of
the nation by enforcing law and by building roads, harbors, hos-
tels, churches; he had the last word in the dispute and so came out
of it with the greatest honor.

In many other cases the sagas of the kings give precedence to
the work of peace. They represent the Swedish lawman Thorgny
as a great hero because on behalf of the people he compelled his
king to make peace with Saint Olaf; and he has always remained
a symbol of Scandinavian peace. Plainly the sagas are approving
when they tell how the men of Magnus the Good made him conclude a treaty of peace and friendship with the king of Denmark
instead of conquering that country. They are proud of the son and
successor of Harold Hardrada, the third King Olaf, who obtained
the double surname of "Farmer" and "the Peaceful." They as-
cribe to him the first foundation of coöperative religious gilds in
the country. And the queen of Magnus Bareleg, the Swedish
princess who was given to him in pledge of durable peace between

Norway and Sweden, was honored with the surname, "the Bride of Peace."

The spirit that manifested itself in such a way had its background in the life and work of the people. As a matter of fact, the period from the ninth century to the first half of the fourteenth was an age of material progress hardly matched by any other until the eighteenth and nineteenth centuries. Much new land was cleared and new farms spread into the common lands and woods far up the hills and in distant valleys. In this period the whole of Norway was settled. We may realize the pride and joy that accompanied this movement by observing the names which were given to the new farms; often they bore the names of the men who had cleared them, and now and again they could even afford a jesting or playful name.

III

At the same time the organization of the nation was advancing in great strides, notably after the second half of the twelfth century. In the middle of the century (1152) the Church of Norway obtained an archbishop of her own, residing in Trondheim, and her privileges and jurisdiction were defined. Toward the close of the century a remarkable king, Sverrir (1177–1202), came into power by defeating the king supported by the church. He vindicated by legal arguments the subordination of the church to the royal authority, thus asserting the unity of the state government. In this conception he was in advance of his times, and his successors had to make their compromise with the church, leaving her free in ministering to the moral needs of the nation and in her canonical self-government. On the whole, however, despite some transitory conflicts, the coöperation between king and church remained very cordial, and, throughout the Middle Ages, the Church of Norway was one of the strong elements in upholding the national unity of the people.

King Sverrir was more completely successful in organizing civil government. His was what historians often like to call a "modern" personality. Though in fact a brilliant strategist and a military leader who evoked the most ardent devotion of his men, he liked to jest deprecatingly about his personal lack of courage. He disdained to give any other proof of his pretended royal birth than the assertion that Saint Olaf had presented himself to him in visions. In his fight against ecclesiastical supremacy he based his policies on those of the national saint. After defeating his rival to the throne, the grandson of Sigurd the Crusader, he sat down and dictated his own saga in order to influence public opinion in his favor, and he addressed himself to the people in a learned pamphlet against the bishops. Such speeches of his as are preserved show him a masterful polemical orator, particularly in a sarcastic vein. He undoubtedly found his inspiration in the great contemporary rulers of Europe, Emperor Frederick Barbarossa in Germany, Philip Augustus of France, Henry II of England, and, more especially, he kept in close alliance with the Anglo-Norman empire, from which he even secured troops for his warfare.

He incited his men to battle by pointing to the titles and riches of the noblemen opposing him, promising them the inheritance of the slain foes. In fact, he did annihilate a large part of the old nobility and in their stead he placed his own officers in posts of administration throughout the country. Thus he founded a new nobility, attached to the king and more truly national in its activities. At the same time he laid the beginnings of a more stable central government led by a chancellor. And he it was who started appointing the lawmen by royal authority. He even began concluding treaties with foreign powers to secure shipping across the sea, the first one being made with Scotland (about 1185).

One of his nearest successors, his grandson King Hákon Hákonson, often called the Old, reigned for almost half a century (1217–63). He was characterized as "modest" by the Anglo-Norman historian Matthaeus Parisiensis, who visited him for a time. With him we see the personality of the king more and more disappear behind the regular functions of government and act through the royal chancery and the Council of the Realm. Until that time there had often been rivalries and even wars between different pretenders to the throne. Now it became established by law that only one man might be entitled to inherit the royal crown, namely the oldest legitimate son of a king (King Hákon himself was illegitimate) provided he was not deemed absolutely unfit to reign. Thus the unity of the nation was made secure, and even Iceland and Greenland acknowledged the king of Norway as their sovereign.

During the reign of Hákon, foreign commerce showed a marked increase, for in these times German merchants came sailing in their own ships, bringing and taking away more goods than the ships of the Norwegians had been able to transport. King Sverrir had not liked the Germans because at first they brought mostly wines and other luxuries. But when they began importing grains and, after a while, even organized a more regular export of Norwegian fish, they grew more useful to the country. Then it proved ever more urgent to conclude treaties that gave to the foreign merchants a basis of law, and through negotiations with German cities such treaties were made from the middle of the thirteenth century. Treaties for the same purpose were concluded with England, too, and these were the first of their kind in northern Europe.

King Hákon maintained relations with many foreign sovereigns. He exchanged ambassadors and gifts with the Emperor Frederick II, Louis IX of France, and Henry III of England. He made treaties with the grand prince of Novgorod for the regulation of frontier conditions in the far north. He gave his daughter in marriage to a prince of Castile. Norway now really entered the European family of nations.

Perhaps partly inspired by the example of some of these sovereigns, he gave impetus to an extensive legislative activity. This was continued in a still more ambitious way by his son, King Magnus, who was justly honored with the surname of the Law Mender. He got the consent of all the *Lagthings* to revise the laws of the country, and in the 1270's he persuaded them to adopt the revised laws. King Magnus thus established a common body of laws for the whole kingdom and Norway was at that time the only nation in Europe that had such a national code. Seventy years later Sweden, while it was united with Norway, followed the Norwegian example. But no other nation in Europe achieved a similar work throughout the whole Middle Ages.

Essentially, the revision of the law by King Magnus consisted in the adjustment of all existing discrepancies between older laws, and this was in itself a difficult and delicate task. In addition, however, he, or his commission of legal experts, elaborated in more detail many of the principles formerly established. In practice the criminal law had been considerably humanized as early as the reign of King Hákon. The sentence of death had largely been replaced by imprisonment, particularly in the case of crimes of theft. In the new law code considerations of humanity were made a leading rule.

In the section regarding judges it was stated that in all criminal cases four fundamental rules—or "sisters" as they were termed in the allegorical style so dear to the clerical taste of the age—should preside at the decisions of the court, namely: mercy and truth, justice and peaceableness. In the first place this meant a departure from the legal formalism that had been the bane of all ancient trials, and the idea was positively enforced by a provision saying: "That is the reason judges are appointed, that they shall measure causes and crimes and temper [this Latin word is employed in the Norse text] the sentence according to the gravity of the case as in their conscience they may find it truest for God." In the second place it introduced into the law the idea of mercy, even putting it foremost among the four fundamentals and strengthening it by adding: "God will punish severely those who judge wrongly, but still more severely those who give too hard sentences."

All such rules increased the judicial authority of the royal officials. The *Lagthings* were maintained as the courts of the country; but the "tempering" of sentences would naturally be rather a matter for the appointed judges than for the popular jury. And the prisons to which criminals could be sent were built by royal initiative and belonged to the king.

The very establishment of a common code of laws inevitably led to an increase of royal legislative power. It was explicitly provided that the king should have the authority to "mend the laws." Of course he would have to lay new laws before the *Lagthings*, but because they remained local assemblies and were never united on a national basis, they were not in a position to refuse their agreement or even to propose amendments. In practice, their adoption of laws was reduced to the registration of royal decrees.

On the whole, the laws of King Magnus implied a strengthening of the central government. The sphere and the activities of this government were defined in a particular law that termed itself the Code of the *Hird,* or the Body-Guard, but which, in fact, was what we now would call a constitution—as far as I am aware, the oldest written constitution of any nation, dating from the 1270's.

It is significant that in this important document the old legislative powers of the people are not mentioned by a single word. Neither is anything said about the powers of taxation; these latter, however, were guaranteed by the common law book, which provided that the king should have no authority to impose new taxes but by assent of the people. The constitution maintained and enlarged the royal oath that defined the duties of the king toward his subjects. Thus, in principle, he was responsible to the nation for his administration. But the people had no legal means to carry this responsibility into practice.

The constitution of King Magnus was solely occupied with the executive power, the dynasty and the administration of the country. From that object it derived its name. The *Hird* (originally a loan word from the Anglo-Saxon), or the Royal Body-Guard, had developed into the body of the whole administration, civil and military, of the country, and thus the rules of the *Hird* became the rules of the national government. While this code strengthened the position of the king, at the same time, however, it introduced, or confirmed, important feudal elements of administration.

Norway never became completely feudalized, in particular, in so far as the great mass of the people never lost their personal freedom, whether they owned their own farms or cultivated the soil of other proprietors. Proprietors of large estates, the noblemen of the realm, never acquired jurisdiction over their tenants or cotters. An increasingly feudal character obtained in the relations between the king and his high officers, the barons as they now were called in imitation of the English title.

Fundamental in this aspect was the fact that by degrees, since the close of the twelfth century, the national military service was commuted into an annual tax, while the barons were charged with keeping armed men at their service for the assistance of the king. They were paid by being authorized to collect for themselves a part of the royal revenues, and very soon we see their position defined as possessors of the royal fiefs. They felt themselves vassals in the general European style.

The Code of the *Hird* established definite rules for the royal succession, making the principle of inheritability more absolute than before. Still the new king would have to seek and receive the homage of the people in the *Lagthings*. But, if there was no legal heir, the nobility and the clergy would have the power to select the new king.

Further, it was explicitly stated that the king had to exert his legislative and administrative functions with the advice of his wise or good men, that is the Council of the Realm which, from now on, became an ever more regular institution, composed of the foremost of the vassals, the bishops, and the royal officials. For the most important matters the king was expected to summon a "parliament" of all the noblemen and bishops of the kingdom. In such ways the power of the nobility was organized in more fixed forms than ever before, and the Code gave exact rules about every class of royal officers, their appointment, their duties, their rank, etc. A special agreement which King Magnus made in one of his parliaments, in the year 1273, regarding the military obligations and rights of the vassals, was embodied in the Code.

In another parliament, in 1277, he agreed to a final "compromise" with the Archbishop of Trondheim regarding the privileges of the church. This document became a part of the particular ecclesiastical laws that constituted the church as a partly independent power, standing beside and coöperating with the king.

The KINGS and the LAW

The "compromise" of 1277 remained valid until the end of the Middle Ages when the church, by the Lutheran Reformation, was absorbed by the state.

King Magnus's code of civil law was in force still longer, indeed for fully four centuries. In all essentials, particularly as to land property and tenure, it embodied the old conceptions of society and law characteristic of the Norwegian people. And the people strove, stubbornly and consciously, to maintain this sacred inheritance of their ancestors. It was their best weapon in their struggle for freedom.

The CRISIS of NATIONAL FREEDOM

I

As the nobles organized their social and political power ever more firmly, they became more strongly engrossed by their class interests and were inclined to place them above all other considerations—a phenomenon that has parallels in all countries and all ages. On the one hand, they began to conceive of the king as reigning essentially on their behalf, and they wanted to use the royal authority for their particular benefit. On the other hand, they constituted themselves more sharply as a definite group, separate from the lower classes and determined to make these serve the exclusive profit of their masters. Conflicts ensued on both sides.

The kings, even when selected to serve as tools of the nobility, generally tried to regain their independence; and in the struggle for power, which sometimes developed into downright war, the noblemen of all three Scandinavian kingdoms, from the last decades of the thirteenth century, began to unite their forces for the common goal. Class solidarity gradually grew stronger than the national idea, and it was strengthened by a mutual infiltration, through marriages and migrations, of noble families across national boundaries. Thus, frequently, noblemen in one country developed economic interests as well as family connections in another, and since the Norwegian nobility was by far the least numerous and the least wealthy in the ensemble, it was absorbed by the brother class of Denmark and Sweden and in this way gradually denationalized.

Another result was the establishment of political unions of the Scandinavian kingdoms in such a way that Norway had kings in common sometimes with Sweden (after 1319), sometimes with

Denmark (after 1380), sometimes with both of them (after 1389). During the fourteenth and the fifteenth centuries, whenever a new union king was elected, it was explicitly agreed and sworn that each kingdom should be ruled and administered according to its particular laws and by its own national officers. But especially after the masterful Queen Margaret, sometimes called "Sir Queen" by foreigners, Danish princess, Norwegian queen, educated in Sweden, had succeeded in uniting all three kingdoms (1389), the royal rulers tended to treat their empire as one state. In practice this would mean Danish superiority, and it provoked resistance both in Norway and Sweden. But as the Norwegian nobility gradually lost its particular national traditions and interests, Norway obviously became the weaker party in all these combinations and rivalries. In the sequence of events, her nobility helped rather than opposed the amalgamation of government.

Although the unions had originally been achieved by the election of the Norwegian royal heirs as kings of Denmark and Sweden, the kings preferred to reside in Denmark. They summoned the Council of Norway to meet down there, or they even asked their Danish Council for advice in Norwegian matters. Foreign noblemen came to be placed in Norwegian fiefs and entered the Council of Norway.

The decline of national interests in the government of Norway manifested itself plainly in the abandonment of the old Norwegian provinces. King Magnus the Law Mender had already been forced by war to cede the Hebrides and the Isle of Man to the king of Scotland (1266). In the middle of the fifteenth century the first king of the Oldenburg house, Christian I (the "bottomless purse," as he was called), mortgaged the Shetland and Orkney Islands to Scotland; and his successors pledged themselves in vain to recover the islands—they never seriously tried to fulfill their promise. At the same time, the sailing to Greenland, an obligation of the king, completely stopped, and the Norse population there, left to itself, ignominiously degenerated and became extinct. Of the whole western dominion of Norway only the Faroe Islands and the union with Iceland were maintained.

CRISIS of NATIONAL FREEDOM

As long as Catholicism reigned in the North, all the western islands, even the alienated ones, still remained under the jurisdiction of the Archbishop of Trondheim, and he was in fact the last leader and champion of Norwegian independence. But the church as a national power was crushed by the Lutheran Reformation, and Norway was made—in the terms of the day—a "pantry fief" of the Danish nobility, handed over to foreign exploitation.

II

During this whole period when the nobility was tightening its grip on the government of the country, from the closing years of the thirteenth century, documents preserved to our day tell of growing complaint on the part of the farmers and peasants against encroachments on their rights by the noblemen in their capacity of landed proprietors and royal officials. We hear that the noble masters tried to extort all kinds of new taxes and duties from their subordinates, sometimes in the form of additional rents, sometimes as "presents" for the favor of defending their rights in court. Through the medium of their assemblies in the *thing*, the people repeatedly put their cause before the king, and they summed up their complaints in the charge that the noblemen did not behave according to "law and justice," a term essentially synonymous with the English term of "common law." From one district they wrote to the king: "We have run your sheriff out of this shire, and we are firmly determined, if you order him back, to abandon our lands and seek an abode at some other place." As a matter of fact, the laws stated emphatically the obligations and the rights of the land tenants, and new duties could not be established except in extra-legal ways. Their defense, then, was in the law.

The kings generally ordered that the laws had to be observed. But as they rarely came to the country, their power and even their interest in enforcing the law weakened. When the people did not succeed by legal means in resisting the economic and political pressure of the noblemen, they rebelled by force. In particular, the years 1436–38 saw an extensive uprising in the southeastern districts under the leadership of a man of the gentry, Amund Sigurdson. The Norwegian farmers had no doubt heard about the powerful fight of the Bohemian peasants against nobility and emperor, and they were inspired by the great national upheaval in Sweden under the celebrated Engelbrekt Engelbrektson. Their case was brought before the Council of the Realm, presided over by the old Archbishop Aslak Bolt, a man who sprang from the gentry and was perhaps a kinsman of Amund. He was a hot-tempered man, ardent for justice. He it was who once, angered by the domineering behavior of a Holstein nobleman in Norway, stamped on the deck of his ship, exclaiming: "I'll show how one should grapple with a Holsteiner and a foreigner." Through him the Council negotiated with the rebellious farmers, acknowledged their just demands, and removed the iniquitous foreign lieutenants. But the victory did not prove lasting, and other local insurrections had no better success.

On the whole, the condition of the farmers, particularly that of the tenants, was deteriorating during the last centuries of the Middle Ages. With the coming of the sixteenth century, critical days fell upon them.

III

At that time the Danish nobles strove mightily to consolidate their dominion in Norway. In Sweden the national elements within all classes proved strong enough to reëstablish, virtually since 1448, definitively after 1523, the complete independence of the country. But Norway lost her independent government.

As the union policies had been shaping themselves more firmly in the course of the two preceding centuries, the Council of the Realm had appropriated the right to elect the king of the country. Even then the final acknowledgment of the king had to be made at the general *Lagthings* or even at national assemblies of delegates of the people. But such acknowledgment degenerated into an empty form, and as the Council of Norway affiliated with that of Denmark, the initiative and the power of election virtually passed to the Danes.

This Danish dominance was finally confirmed with the introduction of the Lutheran Reformation (1536). In all the Scandinavian countries, most particularly so in Norway, the Reformation was not the result of a popular movement, but simply an act of placing the church under royal control and her fortune at the disposal of the state. And in the same Danish Assembly of Estates which adopted the Reformation, the nobility persuaded the king to promise that in the future Norway should no longer be an independent kingdom but be incorporated completely in Denmark. The practical meaning of this provision was the unhampered opening up of Norway to the influx of Danish noblemen, and although the formal extinction of Norway as a kingdom was not put into force, the result in practice was the fulfillment of the desires of the nobility.

During the first period of Swedish and Danish infiltration, there continued to exist within the Norwegian nobility a national party that upheld the independence and the traditions of the country. This party may often even have determined the attitude of the Council of the Realm. By the agreement of 1536 the separate Council of Norway was abolished. From now on the nobility of Norway and of Denmark was regarded as a unit; and the Council of the Realm, meeting with the king in Denmark, became, not an organ of Norwegian independence, but the instrument for destroying it. In the interest of independence, and at the same time of the church, the Archbishop of Trondheim made a last stand of resistance, but had to flee the country. The maintenance of national life was left with the common people.

In the long run, the Reformation meant an increase in the royal authority; and in Denmark the king at once appeared as more of a real master to the country than he had been for centuries. Norway, however, was left to the nobility as their part of the bargain. By the seizure of the church lands, the properties of the crown mounted to as much as one third of all cultivated land in the country, and all of it was allotted to the noblemen as their fiefs. Certainly much more than a third of the soil was already in the direct possession of noblemen. Now they got under their control something like two thirds or three fourths of the farm land, and they eagerly set about extending their properties by purchase and other means. At the same time they were anxious to have their privileges and their incomes increased. All the great fiefs were given to Danish noblemen, some of whom had immigrated from Germany; and, contrary to all Norwegian traditions, they struggled to introduce in Norway the customs and rules of their more feudalized home country.

The Norwegian people took their stand on the law. They could not prevent the change in the position of the Council of the Realm. They had to accept the election of the king by the Council of Denmark. They would not, however, recognize this change as the establishment of a new national order. They were told, and they saw it realized in practice, that the laws of inheritance were still followed in the selection of royal successors, and they were content with having the elections presented to them for formal acknowledgment. They used these opportunities for explicitly stating the condition that the ancient laws should be kept in force.

The documents preserved from the local *thing* assemblies of the 1520's and the 1530's, which accepted the Danish kings as kings of Norway, plainly show the spirit of the people. They wanted to be guaranteed that, in future as before, they might "enjoy the law and the good old custom of Norway," "retain the law of Saint Olaf," "our ancient privileges and liberties conceded and given to us by the good old ancestral kings." Sometimes they defined their desires more specifically, declaring that they expected to be charged with no higher taxes and expenses than their ancestors had paid and that they should not be plagued with unmerciful sheriffs. Fundamentally their wish was to maintain the legal basis of the society they lived in; only on that condition could they think of a "quiet and peaceful life." Their fight was a defensive one, and in so far as the law was concerned, they might count on the support of the king.

In more than one regard, the foreign noblemen would have liked to change the laws that hampered their efforts to extend their power and wealth. They wanted to acquire the same jurisdiction with respect to their Norwegian tenants as they were accustomed to exercise in Denmark or Germany. That would have meant the transformation of the free landholders into peasant serfs. But the law protected them against abandonment to the arbitrary rule of the masters of the estates, and in only a very few cases did the king concede to some high fief-holder the right to appoint his own judges; even then the judges had to follow Norwegian law.

The foreign noblemen did not like the Norwegian law of odal, which gave the heirs of a farm the right to reclaim it from the foreign buyer, thus making his possession of it insecure. According to the law, the foreigner himself could never enter into the right of owning land by odal. The immigrant noblemen tried to evade the difficulty by persuading or bribing the sellers of land to renounce for themselves and their heirs the right to raise the claim of odal. Such a stipulation, however, had no legal validity, and the idea of odal was so powerful with the Norwegian farmers as to constitute an effective defense for their inherited property. In a judicial document of the sixteenth century regarding an odal lawsuit, a girl is quoted as having said that "before the farm of my father shall come out of inheritance and fall in the hands of foreigners, I will go round and get hold of money and buy it back." In a petition to the king in Copenhagen, the new nobility of Norway asked for such a change of the odal law as would make it easier to buy up farms. But the king refused, and he even endeavored to put limits upon the acquisition of land by his fief-holders in Norway and by their sheriffs.

It was more difficult for the king and the people to prevent the increase in rents and taxes that went on, not against the law, but outside it. The systematic efforts of the landed proprietors and the fief-holders in this regard were largely successful. To the farmer population in Norway, as to that of other European countries, the sixteenth century became a time of great hardship.

But perhaps in no other country was the resistance so hard and so tenacious, or even so efficient, as it was in Norway. Obscure in their own age, but almost brilliant in the light of after-history, the Norwegian farmers proved what stuff they were made of.

They would never abandon what they thought their right. Since it was foreigners who led the struggle for subduing the people, the resistance took on the character of a national defense. The law was the shield of liberty.

IV

As late as the fifteenth century the farmers who rose against oppression or illegal claims might find leaders in men of the gentry. Some of these leaders even worked their way up to seats in the Council of the Realm and could there defend the cause of the lower classes. In the sixteenth century, however, the gentry lost their part in national affairs. Some few of their number might still be favored with the holding of small fiefs, but they were not summoned to the Council in Denmark. Many of them entered local public service as rectors of churches and as royal lawmen. In such capacities they became members of a new bureaucracy, and they did valuable work in maintaining national law traditions.

Perhaps still more important was the fact that, as a class, the gentry became ever more identified with the better common farmers, the proprietors of odal land. If that meant a decline of the gentry, even to the extent that their descent was forgotten, it involved a portentous strengthening of the farmer class. In the nature of the case the odal man would be the most independent among the members of his class. Often there were no more than one or two of them in a single parish; and in the fights of the farmers during the next centuries, the leadership would chiefly devolve on them.

In the course of the sixteenth century, and far down into the seventeenth, uprisings of farmers occurred again and again. They combined in refusing to pay new taxes or duties, and they appealed to the courts or to the king with their complaints of illegal treatment. More or less regularly, some selected members of the Council of Denmark were sent to Norway to act as a Supreme Court in all important matters, and wherever they came they were flooded with whole bundles of petitions and remonstrances complaining of lieutenants and sheriffs. Quite naturally they usually looked with disfavor on such imputations against their class fellows, and often they simply put aside the representations received. The fief-holders and their sheriffs would not yield to protestations and when, consequently, they tried to extort by force what they felt they were entitled to demand, it repeatedly happened that the people of the parishes put up an armed resistance. That was rebellion, and in the fights that ensued the people were always defeated, their leaders executed, and their properties confiscated.

Within limited circles the people might feel a broad class solidarity and put forward an ambitious program, which did not, however, point further than to the remedy of the evils of the moment. A band of farmers who, about 1540, under a leader armed with a great club, went out to slay the sheriff of their district, announced when examined: "We intended to go all over the world to rouse the common men and march them forth to kill all fief-holders and sheriffs in existence." They were captured and put to death.

In some very flagrant cases of abuse it happened that notorious peasants' fleecers were sentenced to the loss of their positions and even put into prison. And sometimes royal decrees were issued to enjoin on all civil servants the observance of law. On the whole, however, the particular complaints and rebellions led to no practical measures. They were all limited in locale and could not reach a nation-wide importance. But they left a profound influence on the mentality of the people. The memories of these events remained alive for centuries and imbued the people with a strong hate of oppression and a fighting spirit.

On the other hand, the ruling classes were steadily kept in fear of a truly national uprising. At the close of the sixteenth century, the foremost of the Danish noblemen in Norway wrote to the king that the people both north and south had a rebellious spirit. A pamphlet was published that depicted in glaring colors the tyranny of noblemen, sheriffs and other officials and warned against the dangers that might follow. A clergyman, writing at the beginning of the seventeenth century, after having himself experienced stubborn resistance to increased ecclesiastical excises, repeated the judgment of the sagas that the Norwegians were hard and unruly, even reinforcing it by affirming that, from time immemorial and even today, they were "a hard, unruly, wilful, arrogant, rioting, rebellious, and sanguinary people."

To a certain extent such impressions kept tyranny in check, and after a time the king felt strong enough to interfere against the lawlessness of his representatives. Thus, in the long run, the resistance of the people was not in vain.

One feature of their struggle to live undisturbed by new forces and conditions deserves special mention. That was the unwillingness of the people to go warfaring outside the country. During the frequent wars in the sixteenth and seventeenth centuries between the kings of Denmark and Norway on the one side and the kings of Sweden on the other, it occurred almost regularly that the people on both sides of the frontier made secret agreements that they would not attack each other but just keep to the defense of their own country. Such agreements were known as "farmers' peace treaties." They attest the will of Norwegian and Swedish farmers to abstain from all aggression and to allow each man to enjoy his own rights and goods.

We may judge all such acts as lacking in large political understanding, although we might be tempted to think that if all people had acted in the same way, no more wars would have been fought. The farmers, of course, grasped neither the national nor the international implications of their acts. They simply, but deeply, desired to see no disturbance of their peaceful ways of living. According to old tradition, the king was the defender of the national peace, and the people showed themselves brave enough when the country was attacked.

In fact they felt that they were serving the king when they opposed the royal officials. They could not conceive of the king except as the highest guardian of law and the enemy of law breakers. In this regard they were led by a true political instinct. In fighting for their own freedom they were supporting the king in his efforts to throw off the tutelage of the noble class and to build up a government more perfectly organized for the welfare of the whole nation.

FREE BURGHERS and FREE FARMERS

I

In the meantime, new economic and social elements were slowly pushing forward and gradually changing the conditions and the outlook of the nation. Commerce and industry demanded and created new customs, new laws, new forms of political and social organization.

As far back as archaeological research allows us to penetrate the life of the people, the exchange of goods had been going on in Norway, both within the country and with foreign countries. But not before the eleventh century had small cities begun to grow up, built around old market places or new ecclesiastical and royal residences. Special market laws developed and, from the thirteenth century at least, they were gradually transformed into city laws. They still embraced no more than four or five cities; Bergen, on the western coast, was the only one of real commercial importance. In these towns a class of merchants and artisans came into existence.

The conditions of the cities and of commerce were radically changed when, in the latter half of the thirteenth century, the German merchants, particularly those from Lübeck, began to pour into the country. In their broad cargo ships they carried along generous quantities of grain, supplementing the Norwegian bill of fare with a most desirable food. The grain was imported and used not only for baking but also for brewing. At the same time the newcomers started to organize the exportation of fish from Norway, making Bergen the staple place for this article.

In such ways the German merchants were able to further the economic development of the country. One result was that cod fishing in northern Norway was gradually expanded, and the population there spread much farther to the east than ever before. But by virtue of their superior wealth and organization, the Germans tended to crowd out the native merchants. They became particularly powerful in Bergen and in Oslo. In Bergen they even established a separate settlement as a *Contor* of the Hanseatic organization, constituting a state within the state.

By laws and treaties they were permitted to arrive only as importers and exporters and to stay in the cities only during the shipping season, that is, for the summer months. But as early as the close of the thirteenth century, they began to maintain their residence even during the winter, later pleading this custom as a vested right. Ever more constantly they trespassed upon the legal privileges of the native merchants, buying and selling by retail and conquering the local commerce both within and without the cities. In Bergen they asserted their right to obey only their own laws, defying the public authorities.

Numerous conflicts ensued. There were even wars and violences, fighting between the kingdom of Norway and the Hanseatic League, or between the royal commanders in Bergen and the *Contor* people. After the first war, an international arbitration verdict, in 1285, conceded to the German merchants almost unlimited rights of commerce. By special agreements the kings later tried to restrict their activities within the limits of the national laws. While the kings resided abroad, the Council of Norway strove to maintain such national policies. The Germans, however, had powerful weapons at their disposal, the most efficient of them being the threat to stop all importations to Norway, which occasionally was carried into effect. Neither did they shrink from brutal force. A commander in Bergen who had proved a fierce opponent of their usurpations, was attacked at a public *thing* meeting by an armed host of German merchants, numbering, it is said, two thousand men. He fled to one of the monasteries of the city, but the Germans pursued him in there. They slew the bishop and seven priests before the altar and killed sixty other men. Then they set fire to the tower where the commander had sought refuge, and thus forced him out and slew him. This happened in the year 1455, and the deed remained unpunished. For a long time economic forces proved stronger than written laws. During three centuries the Germans virtually controlled the whole of Norwegian commerce and trade.

In the course of the sixteenth century several conditions began to undermine the dominant position of the Germans and ultimately brought them under the law. On the one hand, the Hansa suffered from increasing competition with the growing commerce of England and the Netherlands; it was no longer the master of the North Sea. On the other hand, a new commerce developed in Norway, independent of the Hansa and connected with the demands of the Western nations. The increasing need for lumber in these countries gave a new value to the woods of Norway, and the large-scale export of their production from centers of commerce outside Hanseatic influence laid the foundation of a new class of native merchants. The lumber trade gave the impetus to the first great industry of Norway. Lumber mills were established along almost all the rivers to exploit the limitless water power of the country. At the same time another industry began to develop, iron ore having been discovered in the mountains and a little later even silver and copper. The reduction of the ores could be achieved very cheaply by virtue of the easy access to wood utilized as charcoal. Thus the producers were able to compete in foreign markets.

The simultaneous weakening of the Hansa and the strengthening of the native merchant class led to the final defeat of German economic domination in Norway. As early as the beginning of the sixteenth century the particular privileges of the German merchants in Oslo were annulled, and before the close of the century the monopolies and the independence of the *Contor* in Bergen were crushed. An end was put to all kinds of lawlessness. German merchants were still living and active in the Norwegian cities; in Bergen they even maintained themselves as an exclusive settlement down to the middle of the eighteenth century, and German sermons were preached in one of the churches there until the middle of the nineteenth century. Merchant immigrants from Germany continued to arrive in Norway during all these years. Now, however, they no longer lived outside Norwegian law; they became Norwegian citizens and were absorbed by Norwegian society. At the same time, immigrants were coming from Denmark, the Netherlands, and Scotland. They all brought to the country new energy and initiative in enterprise, and many of their descendants became active leaders in the struggle for national liberty and progress.

II

The cities, both old and new, were largely self-governing corporations, electing their own councils and aldermen. With their increasing wealth they became a new power in the nation, and they demanded consideration as such. The kings found in them a desirable counterbalance to the nobility. In a period of transition they even helped to establish new organs of national self-government. From the 1620's they became a part, sometimes even the most important part, of the Estates of the Realm, which at that time began to be summoned.

When the Estates were called for the acknowledgment of a new king, the farmers always had to be summoned as being by tradition the true representatives of the people. From its inception there had never been any question of dividing the assembly according to social rank. In the sixteenth century, however, the cities began to be recognized as representing a distinct order of the nation, and the national assembly was divided into separate meetings of nobility, clergy, burghers, and farmers. When now the war needs of the state made it urgent to demand new taxes, the government might easily increase the taxes of the farmer population because an essential part of them were settled on crown lands. But it was necessary to negotiate separately with the burghers about all new taxes, and that finally led to the first summons of a national diet for other purposes than giving homage to a new king.

In this first diet, which met in Oslo (recently rechristened

Christiania by order of the king) in 1628, all four orders of the realm were assembled. The chief negotiations, however, were conducted with the burghers and they resulted in the important decision to start the building of a Royal Navy, corresponding to the action of the king a little earlier in the same year for the organization of a national army based on conscription. Both acts strengthened the power of the king.

In the course of the next thirty years, the Estates were repeatedly summoned for the purpose of levying war taxation. Then, however, the farmers were no longer called to meet, and sometimes the burghers even met alone. That was a manifest proof of their increasing political importance, and they offered to the king a new basis for his authority, making him more independent of the nobility.

The king had long been struggling to restore his power as the supreme ruler of the nation, and that indeed was the reason why he failed to fulfill his promise of 1536 to abolish the existence of Norway as a separate kingdom. There was a steady rivalry between the king and the Council of the Realm as to which should represent the sovereignty of the kingdom. With the disappearance of the Council of Norway, the king saw his chance to remain at least the sovereign of that country, the more so since the law of succession by inheritance was more firmly established there than in Denmark. His task must be to transform the noblemen from their position as masters to that of servants of the king and the nation.

From 1572 the king ordinarily appointed a personal representative as his governor in Norway. He always had to name a nobleman, but he strove to find a man on whom he could rely to serve the royal interests. It is instructive to see how the task of the governor was defined: as agent of the king he would have to assist every man of the kingdom, poor or wealthy, in maintaining his rights according to law and justice. Every year he had to go around to the general *Lagthings*, sit in court with the lawmen and the representatives of the people and take care that every man was judged according to the law of Norway. He had to receive all complaints regarding fief-holders or sheriffs, cite them to court, and watch the procedure to see that both parties were justly treated. He was made the general controller of the whole administration of the kingdom.

In the 1620's, simultaneously with the summons of the first tax-granting diets and with the organization of military forces at the service of the king, the royal activities as to government and legislation assumed a still larger scope. Royal ordinances began to organize jurisdiction and administration in all their branches directly under the authority of the king, a strict control of all public officers was instituted, and there was even an attempt to make the sheriffs of the fief-holders royal officials.

These efforts reached their climax in the year 1661. In the preceding year, by a coup in which the representatives of the burghers and the clergy assisted, the king had succeeded in making himself the hereditary sovereign and the absolute monarch of Denmark. In 1661 the Estates of Norway, in full assembly, ceded to him the same power and hereditary rights in their country.

This was the end of all popular representation in national affairs. But the matter essential to the people lay in the abolition of the oppressive domination of the nobility. The king would now, to a much larger extent than ever before, be influenced by considerations of the general welfare of the people, and the burgher class in particular might expect to see their interests taken care of.

As a matter of fact, one of the very first measures adopted by the absolute monarch was a decree establishing and defining the complete monopoly of the city burghers in all commerce and trade of the country. Mercantilistic principles had begun shaping the policies of the government since the first half of the seventeenth century; from now on they dominated.

One of the consequences of these principles, as well as of the establishment of absolutism, was the conception of the whole Dano-Norwegian monarchy as a unity; and the strong royal bureaucracy that now developed, leaning heavily on the burgher class, became completely common to all the lands of the monarch.

The tendency to unification expressed itself most clearly in the new Norwegian Law Book, issued by the king in 1687. It was indeed in most of its chapters directly copied from the new Danish Law Book, issued some few years before, virtually the first national code of Denmark.

The new Norwegian law wiped out the medieval system of outlawry and private fines. In fact, the whole legal and judicial development since the establishment of a national kingdom had been steadily restricting the functioning of this system, which by now had virtually outlived itself. To an increasing extent the idea of society as the upholder of the law had been replaced by that of government, and absolutism completed the development in this direction. It was a loss that the participation of the people in the administration of justice was at the same time ended. The courts were made absolutely royal institutions. Neither could it be considered a progressive measure that the death penalty was extended and that even torture was introduced. It was a decided gain, however, that scattered legislation of the last centuries was codified into a new system, and the new Law Book became the foundation of further legal development.

A highly important exception to the idea of Dano-Norwegian unity was made in only one respect, but that a vital one, namely in regard to the conditions of the farmers. As to the principle of odal and the rights of tenants, the old Norwegian laws were in all essential matters included in the new Law Book. Thus, in its fundamental constitution, the society in Norway was allowed, and must be allowed, to continue its development on an integral national basis.

III

While the government in Copenhagen was enthusiastic about mercantilistic ideas, the representatives it sent to Norway became convinced that their task should be to further the interests of the farmers. This idea was very clearly grasped by the royal governor who was appointed in 1664 and retained this position for thirty-five years. He was U. F. Gyldenløve, who, as the illegitimate son of the king, had great opportunities to give weight to his views.

He was a man of swift intelligence, informal and charming manners, and he made himself extremely popular with the farming population of his new country. In one of his reports he stressed the difference between the state of Norway and that of other countries, as it "here is constituted and maintained by the farmer." He concluded that "the welfare of the farmer is the essential matter, the root and the basis of the preservation of this whole kingdom, and it cannot be maintained except by the affection of the hearts and the minds." He came to love the people, and his judgment of them was quite unlike that of former times: "They who know Norway and the nature of the inhabitants," he wrote, "no doubt must admit that they are a helpful, brave, and faithful nation, which, perhaps, has not many to equal it in the world."

The peculiar situation of Norway within the union with Denmark gave rise to a development that laid the foundation of a remarkable farmers' democracy. Not only, as already noted, was the farmer class strengthened by the absorption of the former gentry, but at the same time, the nobility tended to disappear from the country, not a few of them enjoying the incomes of their fiefs and estates in Norway while they lived as absentees. After the coup of 1660, when all the fiefs were transformed into districts of royal administration, they had still less reason to reside in Norway.

As an upper class, the nobility was to a certain extent replaced by the city burghers. After the exhaustive wars which ended about that time, the government found itself obliged to sell crown lands. Most of the large estates were bought by wealthy burghers. Even before that time, the growth of the lumber industry had made the burghers' grip extend further to include forests in all parts of the country.

This development aroused a storm in the entire farming population. In the beginning of the 1670's the government was flooded with petitions from the farming communities all over the country, and the unanimity of the demands put forward was such that one can hardly escape the impression that there was a universal propaganda behind them. The petitions attempted to persuade the government that the burgher proprietors had acquired their estates so cheaply as to have earned the whole price back by the high rents imposed on the tenants, and the conclusion was that all the land now by right ought to revert to the crown. Obviously the farmers would prefer the government to private proprietors.

The government was not willing to accept this radical suggestion. It strove, however, to help the farmers in other ways. By royal decrees of the 1680's, which consequently were included in the new Norwegian Law Book, a serious attempt was made to stabilize the land rent and other obligations of the tenants. At the same time, additional farms acquired by any farm owners were charged double taxes. When, after a new war, crown lands were again offered for sale, the burghers did not prove so anxious to acquire them, and the tenants were able to buy them.

At that moment the general economic conditions strongly favored the farmers. During the preceding two centuries, prices all over the world, particularly with regard to agricultural production, had been mounting and thus made it profitable for capital to acquire landed property. But from the closing decades of the seventeenth century prices tended to fall. That gave an opportunity to the farmers, and those of Norway now had the advantage of having maintained their freedom. They started in as buyers not only of crown land but also of private property. In the course of three quarters of a century, their position in relation to the farm land was completely reversed.

According to the registration of inhabitants and farms in the 1660's, the number of odal farmers in Norway was only a fourth of the total number of farmers—about 13,000–14,000 as contrasted with well above 40,000 tenants. At the middle of the eighteenth century, there were twice as many odal farmers as there were tenants—somewhere around 40,000–50,000 of the former group as against 20,000–25,000 of the latter. In fact, much more than half of the land had come into the possession of the farmers themselves.

Quite naturally, such a change immensely increased the farmers' self-consciousness and sense of independence. They began to feel like the masters of the country and the true upholders of the nation. Just at the middle of the eighteenth century a new edition of the sagas of ancient Norway became popular and was to be found on the shelves of the leading farmers in many parishes. Ancient traditions were recalled, and more than one farmer might reply to the pretensions of supercilious noblemen: "I, too, am a nobleman."

One particular aspect of the economic development really tended, at any rate in certain parts of the country, to create a kind of aristocracy within the farmer class. That was the strongly increasing number of agricultural laborers, settled on small parcels of farms. There had been such cotters for a long time, though they had not been very numerous. The cotter's position was regulated by old customs. Generally from spring to fall he worked at the main farm for board and a low wage, whenever he was needed there. He had for his own use a cottage with some few acres of land on the outskirts of the farm. The busy lumber industry that had sprung up since the sixteenth century gave a new stimulus to the demand for labor in the country districts. The felling and hauling of trees was essentially winter work, and so it was easily combined with the work on the farms. In fact, this was an arrangement profitable both to the farm owner and to the cotter. As a consequence, the establishment of cotters advanced rapidly, particularly in the large forest districts of eastern Norway. In the 1660's their number amounted to about 10,000, still no more than a seventh of the total farming class. During the next hundred years, it increased with such speed as to become almost a third of the whole class, embracing about 30,000 men.

Obviously, the cotters constituted a lower class in the farming society, and when the owner of the farm might have at his service some twelve or even twenty cotters, he truly could feel himself a kind of lord. Nevertheless, both parties regarded themselves as parts of the farmer class. Most of the cotters were safe in the enjoyment of their land for their lifetime and might even leave it to their children. Often the younger sons of the farmers might accept the cotter's position. The social cleavage was most clearly felt in eastern Norway, where the farms were large and the cotters more like a laboring class. In other parts of the country, the feeling of unity was more prevalent. Nowhere did the cotter lose his personal freedom.

Thus, on the whole, the eighteenth century saw a strong and free farmer class winning its place in Norwegian society, protected by the laws and conscious of its rights.

At this time local self-government, even in the country districts, began to be organized. The cities already had such autonomy in many respects and they won it in a new domain with the general establishment of grammar schools by royal decree in 1739. In the same year another decree ordered the organization of elementary schools in all country parishes, and, two years afterwards, the control of appropriations for local schools was put in the hands of the congregations themselves. In 1741 boards of relief for the poor were ordered elected in all municipalities. By both decrees the people were authorized to assess taxes for the objectives indicated, and so acquired financial powers in public matters.

When, in the 1720's, after the Northern War, the government sought cash to meet war debts by selling the churches, in many parishes the congregations themselves offered to buy them. In this way the particular part of the tithe that was destined for the repair of churches came under the care of the parishioners, who, here again, won a certain financial authority.

In all such ways, democracy began to shape itself into fixed forms.

RISING for FREEDOM

I

From 1720 to 1807, for almost a century, Norway enjoyed a period of unbroken peace. A war of three weeks in 1788 meant nothing to the country and was, besides, carried on outside the frontiers. Despite some years of bad crops and famine, this period proved the happiest age of progress in national history since the early Middle Ages.

In the fourteenth century great plagues had reduced the population of the kingdom by a third, or perhaps even a half, of its number. This terrible loss of population, affecting as it did the upper as well as the farming and laboring class, diminished the area of agriculture and consequently the national wealth. It cannot be doubted that it considerably weakened the national power of resistance against foreign intrusion.

During the following centuries, the rate of rebirth was so slow that the population probably did not reach its former height until, at the earliest, the end of the seventeenth century. At that time it numbered about half a million. The peaceful period of the eighteenth century powerfully accelerated the increase in population. At the close of the century it amounted to almost 900,000.

The unfortunate wars of the seventeenth century had deprived Norway of a couple of border provinces. That loss, however, was comparatively small in relation to the losses suffered by Denmark, which had to cede to Sweden vital parts of the country. As a consequence, the population of Denmark did not far surpass that of Norway. The two united kingdoms were thus on a more equal footing.

Increase of population in itself led to an increase of wealth because much more work could be done. Deserted land was brought under cultivation again, and new land was cleared. But the wealth of the country rose at a far quicker rate than the population, by virtue of the new industry and trade that were centered in the cities. The increasing importance of the cities can only partly be measured by the swift growth of their population. From having about 40,000 inhabitants at the beginning of the eighteenth century, they exceeded 100,000 at the end of it. Much of the lumber industry, however, was located outside the cities, although it was in the hands of city burghers and was the basis of many of the largest fortunes.

One of the most remarkable features of this economic development was the rise of an independent merchant marine. Until the end of the sixteenth century the exports of Norway were mainly carried in German ships. With the rise of the lumber industry, Dutch shipping stepped in and became dominant. Later, English ships, too, took an increasing part in the shipping of Norway. Norwegian shipping was as yet relatively trifling, although many Norwegian seamen served in the Dutch marine. After the destructive wars of 1700–20 the merchant marine of Norway numbered scarcely 200 ships, all of them rather small. By the middle of the century, however, the country had a merchant marine of approximately 600 ships, many of them really large, and in the course of another half century, the tonnage was more than doubled. Neutral Norway profited largely by the great European wars of the eighteenth century, and from this time on Norwegian ships began plying all the seven seas. Norway became a seafaring nation.

Among the old cities, Bergen and Christiania (Oslo) had the largest merchant marines, Bergen remaining the staple port of fish exports, Christiania growing into a center of lumber industry and exports. They were, however, at times surpassed by Arendal on the southern coast and Drammen in the east. Each one of these cities was wealthier than any Danish city except Copenhagen.

This whole development could not but strengthen Norwegian self-confidence and pride. In the great Northern War the people had earned high honors. They had fought bravely against the armies of Charles XII, and the hero king of Sweden found his death in vainly besieging the Norwegian border fortress of Halden. In particular, however, the hardy feats of the naval hero, Peter Wessel, fired the imagination of the people. He was a burgher's son of Trondheim who had made his way up to the position of admiral of the Dano-Norwegian navy, even being raised to the peerage with the name of Tordenskiold ("thunder shield"). The stories of his adventures, often seasoned with the salty humor of a reckless sailor, were retold everywhere. The whole nation participated in his glory.

The commerce of Norway went chiefly to Holland and England, and the connection with these two countries grew steadily more intimate. Wealthy burghers' sons were often sent to England to complete their education. The new ideas that burgeoned forth in English, Dutch, and French science and literature, liberating minds from the oppression of sterile orthodoxy and social prejudice, filtered into Norwegian intellectual life. It was not by mere chance that it was a Norwegian, Ludvig Holberg, who, after studies in England, Holland, France, and Italy, became the first champion of these ideas in Denmark as well as in Norway.

In the course of the eighteenth century the Norwegians, more particularly those of the burgher class and the intellectuals, became generally known as ardent Anglophiles or Anglomanes. One of their own poets poked fun at their national pride by insinuating that they presumed no human beings were born but in England and their native country. Indeed, they felt closely bound up with England and English ideas. But ideas meant more to them than attachment to the English people. During the American Revolution their sympathies were with the rebels, and we are told that they were very angry when, in 1779, the government in Copenhagen freed American prizes taken into the port of Bergen, an unfriendly act which prevented for decades the conclusion of a treaty of commerce with the United States.

The shipping and exporting interests that grew so dominant in Norway in this period made the burgher class extremely receptive to the program of the physiocratic economists, who, from the middle of the eighteenth century, started the theoretical attack on mercantilism in France. They based their attitude on what they conceived to be the natural laws determining production and human life. They proclaimed, along with the philosophers of the age, the right of every man to work for his own happiness and they declared liberty a necessary condition of his existence. Their conclusion as to economic life was the free exchange of goods and the abolition of indirect taxes.

The Norwegian merchants and shipowners found themselves hampered by mercantilistic legislation at home and abroad, and they became liberals. They smarted under the unifying efforts of mercantilism that tended to favor the capital of the united kingdoms—Copenhagen—as their economic and industrial center. They began to feel their economic interests as differing from those of Denmark and to revive the idea of Norwegian independence. Their first practical claim was a separate national bank.

Government circles in Copenhagen complained loudly about the hardy "Christiania reasoners." In truth, the burghers of Bergen were at least as liberal-minded. Men of similar disposition were to be found in every city.

The extinction of national nobility, the immigration of merchants from abroad, and the amalgamation of Danish and Norwegian civil service had made all higher intellectual life in Norway largely dependent on Denmark. Since the middle of the eighteenth century, an evident change began to take place. Newspapers and magazines appeared in one city after the other. A whole school of Norwegian authors came to the forefront. Dramatic companies were formed. A national Society of Sciences and Letters was founded in Trondheim. Historians began to study Norwegian history as separate from Danish. A Norwegian student in Copenhagen, Nordahl Brun, wrote the first national anthem (1772), proclaiming his compatriots' will to "break chains, ties, and coercion."

As a matter of course such activities were mainly carried on by men with a university education, members of the bureaucracy. They acted, however, in intimate association with the burgher class and were influenced by the same ideas. Together they raised the demand for a national university.

Physiocratic thinking drew more general attention to the conditions of the farmer, the primary producer. The government issued questionnaires about all kinds of matters relating to the life of the countryside. Rectors of parishes and other administrative officials published researches and descriptions of particular districts. The Norwegian odal farmer was presented to the world as a type of the free son of nature (the program of liberating the peasants in Denmark being also advanced thereby). He was hailed as the representative of ancient free Norway and regarded as the basis of a new national freedom.

Foreign authors ventured the theory that the idea of freedom had spread over Europe with the wanderings of Northern people, their cradle being found in the northernmost districts of Norway. It was in Norway that a city burgher christened his ship *The Norwegian Yeoman*, something that could scarcely occur in any other country.

The free farmer came to stand in the center of national traditions; his language, directly inherited from the Old Norse, became an object of interest, and poets of the upper classes even used his idiom for their poetry.

Thus, the idea of personal freedom joined hands with that of national independence.

II

The farmers themselves did not look on the upper classes as their liberators. On the contrary, they rather felt oppressed and driven to rebellion. The second half of the eighteenth century brought new trials to them. The economic expansion of the burgher class, accompanied by a general rise in prices, again became a danger to the economic independence of the farmer class. The merchants and the industrial capitalists started anew to buy up forests and farms, and the farmers often ran deeply into debt to them.

But this time the farmers could offer a far stronger resistance than ever before. They had a broader economic foundation, and they were more conscious of their social position. Their complaints of economic exploitation and of unjust extortions on the part of wealthy burghers as well as government officials found an expression in spiteful propaganda stories and songs that were spread throughout the country. In particular, the sheriff, the prosecutor of legal offenses and the collector of taxes and duties, was a never wearying subject of malicious jokes and stories which almost invariably paired him with the devil. The popular conception of official justice is drastically stated by a Norwegian proverb: "Virtue in the middle," said the devil as he sat down between a sheriff and a judge.

Still more remarkable is the fact that the farmers proved able to coöperate in uprisings and movements that embraced larger and larger districts. The first of such rebellions occurred in western Norway in 1765, as the poor farmers of the coast districts surrounding Bergen spontaneously rose against the merciless collection of extraordinary taxes. At one time, they even made themselves masters of the city of Bergen, maltreated officials and recovered their taxes. Their rebellion had ramifications both north and south along the coast.

Still more significant was the rebellion of 1786–87 in southern Norway, in many respects a parallel to the contemporary Shays' Rebellion in Massachusetts. It was a movement against the merchant creditors of the city of Arendal, the sheriffs and judges who assisted in their extortions, and the lawyers who exacted additional oppressive fees. The leader was a remarkable man, Christian J. Lofthuus, at once an agitator and an organizer. He represented himself as speaking on behalf of the whole nation, and he put forward a truly national program, tending to unite all the common people in order to "compel the public authorities to keep justice in the country so that the farmer might obtain his rights according to divine and royal law." He wanted the privileges of the burgher class restricted and the activities of public servants severely controlled. He gathered an army of several hundreds from both inland and coastal districts, and for a time there was a state of civil war.

Both uprisings were finally suppressed by arms and the leaders captured. But the cases were treated in quite another way than the local insurrections of earlier centuries. None of the rebels were executed, and the special commissions that were appointed to inquire into the complaints and the guilt of the people, made a point of getting to the bottom of the conditions that fostered such a rebellious spirit.

It is a curious coincidence that in each case the leading man of the investigation was a member of a family of officials, Danish by descent, who were to take a great part in the history of Norwegian freedom. In the case of the farmers of the western coast it was Christian Magnus Falsen, already plainly influenced by physiocratic ideas. He wrote in a private letter about "the poor farmer who, in fact, should be the strength of the country," and he was anxious to give a complete and sympathetic picture of the economic situation in the coastal districts. In the investigation of the Lofthuus's Rebellion, the active mind was Falsen's son, Envold Falsen, and he certainly was glad to record in the minutes of inquiry the declaration of the farmers that they represented "the most useful and industrious class of the country," working in the profession that ought to be "the foundation of national wealth." He himself, some years later, tried to justify the uprisings of the people as provoked by unjust extortions. He asserted that the people desired nothing but justice and were "electrified" by the idea of law.

Lofthuus had been kept in prison, loaded down with chains, as long as his case was pending in the court, and he died there before the final sentence was passed. He was remembered as a martyr of the people's cause, and his memory was often recalled as a stimulus in the fight for freedom and law. During the next years much unrest and more or less violent resistance to real or imagined oppression occurred. One remarkable fact is to be noted here, namely, a decreasing confidence in the king as the incarnate defender of law. There are accounts from many parts of the country of the people's venturing to oppose their duly acquired rights even to royal decrees, and it was said that the king might well be supreme in Denmark but in Norway the old laws had to be obeyed.

The first movement to create a definite unity of aspirations within the whole farmer class was a religious one. Though it had no sectarian character at all, it became a fighting movement because it collided with royal orders and public authorities. Just as the government, as a consequence of the rebellion of 1765, had issued a decree forbidding by sentence of death all gatherings of crowds, so it had, in 1742, in the interest of ecclesiastical discipline, forbidden all "conventicles," that is, assemblies, to listen to unauthorized sermons by laymen. This order became the stumbling block to the revival started by Hans Nielsen Hauge in 1796.

He liked to call himself a "modest farmer's son," a term implying not solely true humility but also a certain pride. He had no higher education than that obtained in the poor parish schools of those days, and he never succeeded in mastering the literary language. But he had a genius for grasping the longings of the common people with profound psychological insight. His speeches and personality made a powerful impact on simple minds and could even impress themselves on more educated people. Year after year he traversed the countryside from the farthest south to the farthest north, everywhere preaching the gospel and arousing people to a vivid acknowledgment of sin and grace.

Most of the clergy conceived this activity as an encroachment on their official domain, and, by virtue of the royal decree of 1742, public authorities endeavored to stop him. Repeatedly he was sentenced to terms of hard labor for his violation of law, and from 1804 he was even kept imprisoned for many years, awaiting a new sentence. By that time, however, his preaching had created a powerful popular movement, many "teachers" followed his example, and a dangerous question confronted the officials who tried to prevent their teaching: do the public authorities want to impede the advancement of Christian morals? A movement of such a character could not be suppressed.

Hauge was a practical genius, too. He was interested in setting afoot new industries, and he saw the need of a strong economic basis for the movement he roused. He had a kind of communistic conception of Christian brotherhood. In practice he settled the most prominent of his followers as printers and merchants and in-

dustrialists in different parts of the country with the idea of breaking down the monopoly of the upper classes. And everywhere he
established centers of revival that were in steady communication
with him and with each other. In these ways the movement acquired a truly national character.

However, it always remained essentially a farmers' movement,
and before long observers were speaking of the Haugeans as a
group of "Independents" who were only awaiting a Cromwell to
gain power in the country.

At the beginning of the nineteenth century, from many different
sides a revolution was fomenting in Norway. All classes of the
nation were demanding liberty.

The REVOLUTION of 1814

Through dark and hard centuries the Norwegian people had fought against all kinds of oppression—economic, social, political. And they had managed to rescue the fundamentals of their liberty.

For three centuries Norway had seemingly disappeared from the European society of nations. It was governed from a foreign country and by foreign masters. Yet it preserved its legal existence as a kingdom and, still more important, its national traditions, the proud consciousness of hereditary freedom and law. In fact the particular development of the country had made its social constitution the most democratic in existence in all of Europe, the only European country where practically no nobility, and certainly no serfs, were to be found.

The nineteenth century brought the restoration of national independence and the complete liberation of the people.

I

The Napoleonic Wars brought about the dissolution of the union of Norway and Denmark. The rash action of Canning in trying to force the hands of their government by arms drove the united kingdoms into the war in alliance with Napoleon (1807); and the Swedish Crown Prince Charles John, leading his army into the opposite camp, used the opportunity to have Norway ceded to the king of Sweden by the Treaty of Kiel (January 14, 1814).

During the six years of war, while the British blockade virtually broke the communications between the two united kingdoms, Norway was governed more or less as an independent kingdom. The Norwegian demands for a university and a national bank had to be fulfilled. A nation-wide organization of private efforts for the economic and intellectual progress of the country was created.

The REVOLUTION of 1814

The opposition between Norwegians and Danish interests was more intensely felt since the shipping and commerce of Norway had become increasingly tied up with the English market. In the same degree the Norwegians felt attached to English political ideas. Their hearts were not with Denmark.

When the news of the Treaty of Kiel arrived, it aroused a storm of anger throughout the whole nation—not on account of the separation from Denmark, but because the cession was felt as an indignity to a free nation. Everywhere was the indignant cry: We cannot submit to be disposed of like cattle—we do not want to be made Swedish subjects—no Norwegian will be a slave! (They must certainly have had in mind a line in the British national anthem: Britons never will be slaves.)

The Treaty of Kiel struck their minds as a violation of the ancient rights of the nation, of the duty of the king to defend her independence, of the modern ideas of popular sovereignty. The Norwegians were by now too conscious of their national life and traditions to allow themselves to be treated in such a high-handed way. They also felt a union with aristocratic Sweden to be dangerous to their own democratic society. Leaders arose to unite them for resistance, and acts of independence followed rapidly.

When Sweden, in the spring of 1813, had officially put forward her claim to Norway, the Danish king had hurriedly sent his heir-apparent, Prince Christian Frederick, up to Norway as governor, to lead the national defense. Of course, it was the prince's primary object to maintain the loyalty of the Norwegians to the crown and the dynasty. But the youthful idealism that filled his soul was carried along by the national enthusiasm he met in Norway. As he had not from birth been expected to become the heir to the throne, he had escaped the usual military education of kings, and his innately gentle character had not been hardened for warlike exploits. He was frightened by bloodshed and suffering. There was a natural humanity in his soul, which led him to abolish the cruel punishments in use in the army as well as all tortures in criminal cases, and he loved the people to whom he was sent. He preferred political solutions to war.

On the news from Kiel he summoned to him a number of representative men from Oslo and the surrounding districts (February 16), and laid before them the question of whether he should proclaim himself king of Norway. The man who took upon himself to answer on behalf of the Norwegian nation was one of the new university professors at Oslo, Georg Sverdrup. Frankly and clearly he stated the law of the case, which was the law of freedom —you might define it as the ancient law of the kingdom adjusted to modern ways of thinking: "After the king has abandoned the country, Your Royal Highness has no more right to the crown than I myself or any other Norwegian. Now the supreme power has reverted to the nation, and only the nation herself is entitled to elect the new king." He added that the nation would no doubt be happy to elect the prince her chief and king, and that it would be a greater honor to him to obtain that position by the free assent of the people than under the plea of royal sovereignty.

The prince was deeply moved by the argument and accepted it as the guide to his action. To the nation it was an asset to have him remaining at the head of the administration, for in that way the whole civil service as well as the military command might continue functioning smoothly without any kind of rupture; the legality of the administration was undisputed. Besides, the deep-rooted loyalty of the people to the king would be useful in uniting them around the natural symbol of independence.

Following the advice he had received, the prince immediately issued a call to the nation to meet in all the churches of the country and take a solemn oath to defend their independence and at the same time elect representatives for a constituent assembly. This was done, amid general enthusiasm, on February 25 and the following Sundays. There were no rules of voting. In fact, the congregations embodied the whole nation, like the *thing* assemblies of ancient times.

It was decided to have the national assembly meet at Eidsvoll, one of the most famous *thing* places of the past, some forty miles up in the country from Oslo. The mansion house standing there became the Independence Hall of Norway and is still preserved as such.

II

The assembly, the *Riksforsamling*, composed of 112 delegates, met on April 10, Easter Sunday. For six weeks they lived there almost like a great family, civil and military officers, even some few noblemen, united with merchants, farmers, and sailors. Daily they had their dinner together, and, as the country had been blockaded for almost seven years, the fare was rather plain and uniform; the veal which steadily returned on the menu was too often cut from mere baby calves, and the French red wine was very sour. Their lodgings in the farms around were in many cases poor; sometimes two or three of them even had to share a bed. But all such inconveniences were accepted in good spirits, and the close living together fostered a comradeship highly advantageous to their common task.

The delegates were unanimous about the adoption of a free constitution for the country, establishing national self-government and democracy. Everybody wanted to abolish absolutism and to make the existence of Norway as a separate kingdom a reality. The February action had combined both ideas into practical and theoretical unity, and they formed the basis of the task of the assembly.

Yet there was room for dissension in various respects. A minority, numbering about thirty members, thought it would be wise to keep the door open for a union with Sweden on a basis that would not impair the freedom of the nation. It was led by the only privileged nobleman living in Norway, Count Herman Wedel-Jarlsberg. He was a leader not by reason of his rank but by virtue of his abilities. He was a liberal, educated in England and there imbued with the ideas of constitutional rule. He had been the most prominent member of the independent government of Norway during the war and had been energetically active for the establishment of new national institutions. He had been the first man to form serious plans for a separation from Denmark, and he had, even then, secretly discussed with Swedish representatives a voluntary union with Sweden. In view of the European situation—the support given to Sweden by all the great Powers allied against France—he regarded the union with Sweden as both useful and inevitable.

The great majority of the assembly, however, wanted to establish unconditional independence. They were not so pessimistic about the European situation; they even imagined it might be possible to win British support. Their leader was Judge Christian Magnus Falsen, a man of commanding personality and brilliant political thinking. His grandfather, of the same name, and his father, Envold Falsen, had both shown their sympathy for the people's rights on the occasions of farmers' rebellions. The latter had even been, until his death when he was replaced by Count Wedel, the leading spirit in the war government of Norway. The son had inherited and further developed the conception of the farmer class as the bearer of Norwegian cultural and social traditions, and he dreamed of restoring the principles of ancient liberty and law. At his side stood Professor Georg Sverdrup and other able men, all of them more eloquent speakers than Count Wedel, and they carried the Assembly, which decided for nothing short of full independence, including the election of a national king.

Falsen was at the same time the leader in the work of shaping the constitution. Many drafts for a constitution were laid before the assembly; some of them were even published in advance and had been discussed in the press or in meetings. They were formed upon patterns from many countries—the general ideas of Montesquieu and Rousseau; the principles of English government, in particular as represented by the work of a Swiss author; the French constitution of 1791; the Spanish of 1812; the Swedish of 1809; the American of 1787, together with the constitutions of the individual states within the American union. The copy of the state constitutions, published in French in 1783 through the efforts of Benjamin Franklin and brought to Eidsvoll by a merchant representative of Bergen, is still preserved there. Falsen felt himself personally indebted to the example of the American Revolution: for example, he christened two sons after Washington and Franklin. In the Committee on the Constitution, of which he was president, his own preliminary sketch was made the basis of the discussion and the drafting of the articles of constitution. He is justly honored as "the Father of the Constitution." In less than five weeks the work was finished.

The constitution, as it was adopted, was the most democratic in the whole world. It was indeed democratic through and through, and in all its essentials it has been able to stand until today, proving an excellent framework for free development. In accordance with practical examples and general theory, the power in the state was divided between legislative, executive, and judicial authorities. But the line of division was not as sharply drawn as, for instance, in the American constitution. In fact, the sovereignty of the people, which just at that moment manifested itself in action, was maintained as the ultimately deciding power. The executive was to be under full control of the representatives of the people and was allowed only a suspensive veto in legislative matters.

The alternatives of a one-chamber or a two-chamber system were much discussed. Virtually, there was no social basis for an upper house, and it could be thought of only as a check on the popular will. The discussion led to a kind of compromise which, however, left the principle of popular sovereignty untouched. It was decided that the people should elect a general assembly of representatives without any distinction of electors or elected. But then, when the Assembly met, it would have to divide itself for legislative purposes into two chambers. One of them, just a fourth of the assembly, was intended to be a selection of "wise men" or "lawmen." Therefore this chamber was called *Lagthing* (that is, "Law *Thing*"), abridged from lawmen's *Thing*. The other chamber was called *Odelsthing*, considered as the representative of the odal men, the true people.

In practice, this division did not work out according to the theory. Very early the tendency prevailed to even out the difference between the two chambers so that the same views would dominate in both of them. And, by the constitution itself, it was provided that in cases of disagreement the laws would have to be voted in the full assembly. Further, it must be noted that the division into two chambers was valid only in regard to purely legislative matters. All other matters, including budget and taxation, were to be handled by the full general assembly. For this was adopted the newly coined name of *Storthing*, that is, the "Great *Thing*." (In modern Norwegian, Thing is pronounced Ting, and is now even spelled so.) By the use of such terms the constituent assembly tried to impress on the nation the notion that an ancient constitution was being restored.

It is not the intention here to give a complete outline of the constitution as adopted in 1814. The essential matter is the establishment of political democracy as the natural combined result of the preceding development and the general ideas of the Western World, in particular those which were expressed by the growth of parliamentary rule in England and by the American and the French Revolutions.

Parallel with democracy went the assertion of personal liberty. It is a significant fact that the most universal demand which followed the news that the Danish absolute monarch had renounced his hold on Norway was the cry for freedom of the press. The Eidsvoll assembly hastened to proclaim freedom of the press and freedom of religion as principles of the new constitution—the latter, to be sure, extending only to Christian denominations. At the same time it laid down the rule that no new limitations of freedom of trade might be introduced and that in the future no hereditary privileges might be granted to anybody. Equality of all citizens would have to be the reigning law.

In the drafting of the constitution, state officials and members of the burgher class were undisputed leaders. The farmer class had not the political education needed for such a work, and not a single farmer was put on the Committee of the Constitution. That does not mean, however, that they had no influence in the decisions of the assembly. The other classes understood very well the necessity of considering the interests and the wishes of the farmers.

This was already demonstrated by the rules governing the election of delegates. The prince had ordered that from every shire at least one farmer had to be chosen, and, in allotting representation to the Army and the Navy, he had stipulated that all officers should be accompanied by privates. The result was that the farmer class numbered a full third of the assembly. They represented the great mass of the population, the most important industry of the country, the chief element of the national defense, and the sum of national traditions. Plainly, they could not be left unconsidered; too much of the future depended on them.

They, too, met, with a program which, in its essentials, could not be included in the new constitution, but which, at any rate, pointed to a future development and left some important marks in the constitution that was adopted. They were in agreement with the demand for national independence; they hated the idea of the country's being put under Swedish rule, and, in particular, they feared the domination of the powerful Swedish nobility. They, too, were opposed to absolutism and wanted a system of popular representation. Their chief desire, however, was to become the sole proprietors of the soil of their country. They wanted to oust the burgher class from all landed property and to win for themselves all crown lands. Further, they demanded the abolition of all the economic and social privileges of the burgher class.

They were not able to carry out at once any part of their economic program. They succeeded only in preparing the sale of crown lands to their profit. And almost everybody agreed to the absolute maintenance of the odal rights. In regard to social privileges, however, they won one notable victory. After a vehement struggle it was finally voted that military conscription, which in the seventeenth century had been extended only to the farmer class, should in the future be general, embracing all classes of the nation. However, the practical realization of this principle was left to later Storthings.

With respect to political representation, a certain rivalry arose among the classes of the people. It is remarkable, and a sign of the prevailing influence of the state officials in the assembly, that no one made any objection to the extension of suffrage to all government officials; they were even given the first place in the total of voters. Similarly, all agreed to separate city constituencies completely from country districts, even granting quite small cities the right to elect their own representatives. In this way, the burghers secured a relatively much greater strength in the Storthing than the farmers possibly could. But in the end the farmers succeeded in fixing the rule that at least the cities should never acquire more than a third of the seats in the Storthing.

In all such questions the farmers of the assembly acted as a unit, and it is a remarkable testimony to their sentiment of unity that when it was proposed to limit the vote to holders of farms of a certain extent, this idea was rejected by the farmers themselves. On this occasion, a wealthy farmer in the assembly, virtually the only man of his class who made some claim to leadership, emphatically exclaimed: "It is the man, not the tax dollar, that shall vote." And the vote was given to all farmers and tenants without any distinction.

It is to be noted and stressed that the whole drafting and adoption of the new Norwegian constitution was accomplished by the national assembly alone. It was a product of unrestricted popular sovereignty and did not demand the assent of any other sovereign.

It bears the date of May 17, and this day has ever since been the national festival of Norway, her liberty day.

On the same day the assembly elected Prince Christian Frederick king of Norway, and after the election the president, at that moment Professor Sverdrup, in a brief address emphasized that what was now achieved was the restoration by an act of free men within the national boundaries, of the ancient royal throne once held by Hákons and Sverrirs.

III

A minority of the Eidsvoll assembly had opposed the election of a king at this time. They held to the opinion that it would be better to try peaceable negotiations with Sweden and eventually accept a union with that country.

Succeeding events may seem to have proved that such a policy was more realistic, since, in the end, it became necessary to agree to the union. There can be little doubt, however, that the uncompromising attitude of the majority gave a firmer ground for maintaining the fundamental demands of the nation and, in particular, made it possible to rescue for the people the formal sovereignty as to the constitution.

In foreign countries it was generally assumed that the resistance of Norway to the cession was nothing but an intrigue of the Danish prince, and after the victory over Napoleon the four Great Powers sent their representatives to Norway to impress on Christian Frederick the inevitability of his retirement. He understood that he would be unable to resist the pressure of the Great Powers, and he declared himself willing to retire. But he proved his devotion to the cause of Norway in laying down as an absolute condition that a national assembly must consent to the union with Sweden and that the free constitution adopted by the representatives of the people must be maintained.

The emissaries of the Powers were willing to accept this condition. The British government had inserted into their treaty with Sweden, when guaranteeing their assistance to the cession of Norway, a clause to the effect that the union of the two kingdoms had to be effected with all possible regard for the welfare and the liberty of the Norwegian people. And the emissary of the Russian czar was a man of liberal ideas. The two allied powers, those of Prussia and Austria, took less interest in the whole business.

The Swedish crown prince felt the need of having stronger guarantees of his possession of Norway than a simple promise that the question should be laid before a Norwegian assembly, and he began war. He could claim to have all of Europe behind him. The United States of America was the only power in the world who fought on the same side as Norway. Their diplomatic agent at Copenhagen reported the situation to Washington:

The Norwegians had been groaning for nearly two years under the most dreadful privations, bordering on absolute famine, they had very inconsiderable numbers of disciplined troops, their enemy was abundantly furnished with every article necessary to carry on war, had a numerous, well disciplined and well officered army, returning from Germany flushed with success, and had the cooperation of a very considerable naval force of their own besides that of England. Under such unequal circumstances the Norwegians had only to rely on the defensible nature of their country, the justice of their cause and their enthusiasm and union.

The Norwegian army fought well, with partial success, but had to retire on the main front. The decisive element, however, was that the leader of the Swedes did not want the risk of a prolonged war. After having succeeded in little more than a week in occupying the nearest boundary districts of Norway, he thought himself safe and offered to negotiate. By a convention with the Norwegian government of August 14, he accepted the compromise advanced by Christian Frederick.

After elections held according to the constitution, the Storthing met in the month of October. It assented to the demission of the king and, however reluctantly, in principle to the union with Sweden. But it jealously watched over its absolute control of the national constitution, and stubbornly refused to elect the Swedish king a king of Norway before the Storthing itself had voted the amendments to the constitution needed for the achievement of the union. Swedish emissaries pressed hard for the immediate acknowledgment of their king and for his participation in the drafting of the amendments. The Storthing, however, stood firmly on its constitutional rights.

Falsen had refused to assist in the union policies. Neither was Sverdrup present. Count Wedel was a member of the Storthing, but even now he was not the master of the situation. The leadership was taken by Judge Wilhelm Christie, a man of Scotch descent, strongly imbued with Norwegian traditions. He had been the perpetual secretary of the Eidsvoll assembly and, beside Falsen and Sverdrup, one of the most influential members of the independence party. Now he became the President of the Storthing. He was both a shrewd and a courageous politician, and he mastered all the niceties of the legal questions involved in the decisions to be made. His imposing personality and his firm grasp of matters impressed Swedes and Norwegians alike. Though steadily in contact with the Swedish emissaries, he carefully managed to have all amendments of the constitution adopted unilaterally by the Storthing so as to evade any question of royal sanction, and he prevented all amendments that exceeded the necessities of the union. Only after all such amendments had been incorporated in the constitution did the election of the new king, the king of Sweden, take place.

Thus the Norwegian nation maintained its free constitution and its complete self-government. Only foreign affairs were left to the king, which meant that in practice they were handled by him with the assistance of his Swedish foreign minister. And the king was allowed to appoint a royal governor to head the Norwegian government. Otherwise, nothing interfered with the laws and the liberty of Norway.

As a consequence, when, in 1823, President Monroe announced the policy of the United States opposing the extension of the "European system" to any portion of the Western Hemisphere, Norway stood outside that system. In Europe only Great Britain could be said to be in the same situation. Indeed, Norway was much more truly democratic than Great Britain and might rather be regarded as representing in Europe the American system, or perhaps one might better define it as the American spirit. She has continued to do so during all the times that have followed and has even at certain moments been in advance of democratic development in the United States.

Americans generally have had no cognizance of this fact. A sensitive observer like John Quincy Adams, however, was early able to discern the similarity of the positions of the two countries. Passing through Sweden in the spring of 1814 and noticing there "the lust of conquest corroding every heart for the acquisition of Norway," he rightly concluded that then there could be "no room left for any just or generous feeling in favor of America." He immediately felt that Norway and America were both fighting for the same ideas.

Norwegians have always been conscious of their fundamental

accord with the great democracy of the West and found themselves much more at home in the United States than in any other foreign country. At the same time their world-wide seafaring interests bound their destiny closely to that of the two great Anglo-Saxon empires. So, from the start, Norway has constituted a living link in what has nowadays been called the Atlantic system.

GROWTH of DEMOCRACY

I

What happened in Norway in 1814 was virtually a revolution. A small nation arose against the dictate of the Great Powers and snatched its national independence. By the same effort it passed from firmly vested absolutism to full-fledged democracy. The feat was the more remarkable since it happened at a moment when reaction seized power in all the rest of Europe.

It is still more remarkable that, during the period of reaction that followed, the same small nation managed not only to preserve the results of its courageous revolt but even to strengthen and enlarge its democracy. The vigor and vitality developed in Norway immediately after the strain of 1814 attests to a stock of energy accumulated in the people through centuries. Both in individuals and in society as a whole, creative forces were released that worked as well for national solidarity as for spiritual liberty. Politics and literature joined vigorously in furthering this progress.

Symbolic, indeed, was the final and legal abolishment of all kinds of noble privileges and titles. It meant rather a confirmation of actual conditions than the establishment of something new. Nevertheless, it did not pass without a hard struggle. The measure was voted by the very first regular Storthing, meeting in the years 1815–16. The king, however, refused his assent. The motive behind his opposition had a more general and therefore more dangerous bearing than the simple desire to maintain the remnants of nobility in Norway. His fundamental idea was the amalgamation of Norway as much as possible with Sweden. For that reason he wanted the power to create a new peerage in Norway and, on the whole, to increase the royal authority, so sadly crippled in his opinion by the Eidsvoll constitution. His plans to that end were backed by Swedish opinion, and, by virtue of this support, represented a real menace to Norwegian democracy. He even felt himself fortified by the sympathy of the Great Powers of Europe.

From this experience the Norwegians retained a profound impression that the maintenance of their democratic ideals was at bottom a struggle against Swedish supremacy. Thus, democratic progress became a matter of national independence, and they stiffened in their struggle. As to the law for abolishing nobility, they took their position on the power, secured to them by the constitution, of carrying it over the royal veto when it had been adopted by three consecutive Storthings separately elected. So it was voted again in 1818 and—in spite of hard pressure from the king, which even included his menace of military measures—it was voted for the third time in 1821. Then the king, forsaken by his mighty Allies who wanted no further disturbance of established arrangements, had nothing left but to sign.

That was the first time the Storthing enforced a democratic reform against the resistance of the king. It was not to be the last. The Storthing now realized fully its constitutional power, and even the mere threat to use it often proved effective. The king, too, grasped the meaning of his defeat. He replied immediately by putting before the Storthing a series of amendments to the constitution, tending to increase his powers, particularly by endowing him with an absolute veto in regard to decisions of the Storthing. These amendments, however, were unanimously rejected by all following Storthings. The sovereignty of the people as the basis of Norwegian political life was completely secured.

II

During the following decades democracy and self-government advanced steadily. The Storthing began to demand a certain control even of foreign affairs, and the Norwegian government obtained representation in the handling of such matters. Still more important was the establishment of complete local self-government. This was a question taken up for consideration by a parliamentary commission immediately after 1814, and it went through quite a number of drafts and proposals, even being delayed by a royal veto, before a law was finally adopted and signed in 1837. This law, creating elected municipal bodies in all cities and country parishes, ceded broad powers of managing their own affairs to the representatives of the people within the local boundaries and provided for their coöperation within whole shires. It was, in fact, the outspokenly democratic character of the law, setting aside the authority of royal officials, that motivated the king's first refusal of assent.

The final struggle and victory of the demand for municipal self-government was a link in the great movement for democracy in the 1830's, partly inspired by the July Revolution in France and the victorious Reform policies in England. The very law of local representative assemblies borrowed some of its patterns from English and Scotch legislation. In one important respect, however, the movement in Norway differed essentially from that of other European countries. Everywhere else it was a rising of the middle classes, of the bourgeoisie, against the privileges of nobility. In Norway, it was the farmer class that arose against the privileges of the burghers.

This fight had been continuous since the very first regular Storthing of 1815. Even in that first assembly, the burghers and their allies of the official class had managed to maintain the Lagthing as a kind of conservative upper chamber, and by a trick of parliamentary rule they had been able to defeat the farmers' demand that military conscription be extended to the other classes. In the next assembly, in 1818, however, the farmers, assisted by liberal public officials, succeeded in curtailing the burghers' monopoly in working lumber mills, thereby overriding even a royal veto. And though the farmers were not able to carry their program of bringing all the cultivated soil of the country under farmer ownership, they were at least successful in starting the sales of crown land in 1821 and later in making the rules of purchase ever more favorable to the land tenants. By that measure the farmer class steadily strengthened its economic and social position.

Within the burgher class, and still more within the class of public officials, there was always a large measure of liberalism, maintaining full freedom of press and speech and, in particular, favoring free commerce with foreign countries. The movement for free trade became active immediately after 1814. The first measures of this policy were carried under the impact of American enterprise. Soon it was still more strongly encouraged by the victorious advance of liberal principles in England. The progress of free trade gave new stimulus to Norwegian shipping and commerce; only now Norway grew to be one of the foremost seafaring nations of the world. The social and political power of the burgher class increased in ratio to its wealth, and liberalism became the law in economic matters.

The official class supported similar ideas. It is to be noted that by the protection given them by the constitution all civil service functionaries enjoyed and used the freedom to speak their personal opinion in all public matters, even to criticize the government, and they were often leaders of the opposition in the Storthing. But, just as the burghers clung to their social and economic privileges, so the public officials generally wanted to preserve as much as possible their ruling powers in their domain. They were the backbone of the intellectuals in the country and they thought themselves entitled to the political leadership of the nation. The farmers might find valuable allies inside this class; their fight for full equality, however, must direct itself against both of the privileged classes.

In 1830 a young farmer who had profited by the sale of crown lands started a systematic propaganda for transferring the political power of the country to the farmer class. His name was John Neergaard. Like the religious revivalist Hauge, he walked around from the one district to the other, talking to his class fellows and leaving with them a small pamphlet he had written. He asserted that the other classes used their power for their own interests, and his program was simply the election of as many farmers as possible to the Storthing. That was a program that appealed strongly to the awakened class consciousness of the farmers, and in the elections for the next Storthing, that of 1833, they gained about half of the seats.

GROWTH of DEMOCRACY

This was a political revolution. It meant that the frame of democracy, created by the constitution of 1814, now was filled with life, a democracy at work. The control of the country was no longer left to the upper classes. Beside them there arose what from that time was called the Farmers' Party.

Organized parties were still unknown and, in fact, generally decried in Norway. Neergaard, however, gathered around him a group of farmer representatives, a "secret committee," that discussed proposals in the interest of the common people and gave the signal to the mass of the farmers. It was mainly due to his initiative that some of the most democratic features got into the law of local government, in particular the provision which in a later time became so eminently important, allowing the municipal bodies to consider all kinds of questions relating to their own districts.

As a political leader, Neergaard very soon was outmatched by a younger man, Ole Gabriel Ueland, who for more than thirty years retained the leading position among the farmers in the Storthing. He was a man of larger ideas than any farmer politician before him, and he had a tenacity of purpose that made him persist in a task until it was achieved. At the same time he was a shrewd parliamentarian and a clever debater, the first of his class who was able to stand his ground against men of higher education. While Ibsen made a caricature of him in *The League of Youth*, Bjørnson sang his praise as the finest scion of the farmers' soil.

His basic program was the complete realization of the principles of the constitution of 1814. He spoke out of his personal feelings when he once said: "Religion and the constitution are the twin pets of the Norwegian people." In the Storthing he initiated and patiently furthered a long series of seemingly small measures each of which, however, transferred functions of government officials to popularly elected bodies. In many cases he had to carry them through against royal vetoes. By such action be wanted to demonstrate the necessity of having a government more responsive to the wishes of the people. The influence of the Hauge movement manifested itself in the abolition of the decree against "conventicles";

it had to be adopted by three consecutive Storthings until the king in 1842 was at last compelled to sign it.

By this latter measure religious preaching was set free, but still only inside the established church. It was the task of intellectual liberals to make the principle of full religious freedom as declared by the constitution a reality. That was achieved by the law regarding Christian dissidents in 1845, and further by the opening of the country to Jews in 1851. Men of the same classes incorporated modern humane views in the new criminal law of 1842.

In this connection the great young poet Henrik Wergeland cannot be forgotten, the most vigorous champion of all reforms, liberal as well as democratic. One might even say that he was more democratic than the farmers and more liberal than his fellow intellectuals. In all domains of social and political, religious and intellectual questions, he was the prophet of the times to come. In his person all of Young Norway was incarnated. But he died (1845) before he could succeed in binding together all the separate forces of advance.

More unity was introduced into the progressive movement after the middle of the nineteenth century, but at the same time the political and social fight assumed a far more vehement character than it had had before.

III

A new epoch was inaugurated by the labor movement of 1848. All democratic aspirations were powerfully encouraged by the February Revolution and other movements in Europe of that year. The Storthing of 1848 urged the cabinet to meet more willingly the demands of the parliamentary majority, and a pair of presumably liberal ministers were appointed. But for future political development it meant far more that in December of that year the young school teacher, Marcus M. Thrane, set about to organize the laboring classes of Norway.

The Industrial Revolution had not yet begun to transform Norwegian society. The laboring classes consisted chiefly of the workingmen in the lumber mills and the shipyards and, at some few places, the miners, also the artisans of the cities, and—more important than all the rest—the cotters working on the farms, the last amounting to more than a third of the whole farming population.

Thrane was—after Hauge and Neergaard—the third peripatetic agitator traveling the highways and byways and fjords, and he was the first man to think of arousing the laboring classes to political activity. In a couple of years he achieved the well-nigh miraculous feat of uniting this heterogeneous mass into an organization embracing more than two hundred associations with about 20,000 members. He frankly preached socialism to them. His actual program was certainly limited to practicable reforms: universal suffrage, old age pensions, abolition of the grain duties, reform of the cotter system.

What most alarmed the government and large elements of the ruling classes as well was the very organization of the working people and the effort to unite them into a political party. There was no other national party organized in the country, and the founding of a party, large numbers of which even had no vote, appeared as an unambiguously revolutionary act. Thrane seems to have had no knowledge of the Communist Manifesto with its doctrine of class conflict. He based his teaching upon the ideas of Louis Blanc and other French socialists. But he strove to arouse a true class consciousness in the working people, and he took an unprecedented initiative in summoning their representatives to national congresses (1850 and 1851) that almost competed with the Storthing.

Imprudent utterances in these congresses about the possibility of armed revolution offered the government a pretext to strike at the whole movement. All the leaders were arrested and indicted for sedition, the labor associations were put under control of the police and by that measure forced to dissolve. After a criminal suit of several years, Thrane and the other leaders were sentenced to terms of hard labor, although it was proved that they personally had opposed all ideas of armed revolt. It was manifestly a political conviction, a flagrant case of judicial misfeasance. But it reached its aim: the labor movement was crushed. Thrane himself, after having served his term, emigrated to America, where he came to play a part in the foundation of socialist parties in the 1860's and 1870's.

His defeat, however, did not mean that the movement he had led disappeared without leaving traces in the political life of Norway. On the contrary, it affected national politics in a remarkable way. He broke down the political wall between cities and country districts. He united in his labor organization the working people of the farms as well as of the factories. By his political program he split the old parties along new lines. On the one hand, the large farmers, particularly in the eastern districts, frightened by the new radicalism, were driven to ally themselves with the bulk of the burghers and official classes, in that way laying the foundation of a general conservative party. On the other hand, the most democratic elements of the cities joined the main group of the farmers' party, building up what was already from the start generally known as the Left Party and was gradually firmly organized.

The chief exponent of this new orientation was Johan Sverdrup, a lawyer by profession, who entered the Storthing in 1851, elected by a combination of artisans and workingmen in one of the small cities. He was to be the leader of the Left, thereby in fact the leader of political progress in Norway through a whole generation, no doubt the greatest statesman of modern Norway. He was so highly beloved by his followers that after a time they adopted as one of their election slogans: "Trust in Johan Sverdrup!"

Bjørnson, who became his friend and fellow fighter, said about him—with some exaggeration—that he was the man who elevated the Storthing from a local assembly to a European parliament. In a poem about him, Bjørnson again characterized him as "the salty ocean stream pouring into our sluggish waters." Sverdrup was indeed well steeped in Norwegian tradition; he had lived his youth among farmers, and he was a nephew of Professor Georg Sverdrup of Eidsvoll fame. But, at the same time, he was a thoroughbred European. As a young man he once jestingly exclaimed: "I am Young Europe," thus recalling the revolutionary organization and program of Mazzini. He studied English parliamentarianism and he was influenced by the political writings of the American Francis Lieber. In particular he was struck by the idea stressed by Lieber that all political advance must be anchored in institutions.

Sverdrup founded his policies upon broad principles, and he had a great gift for coining his ideas into telling phrases. He was the first really great orator in Norwegian politics, and his eloquence as well as his appearance gave the impression of something new, almost foreign, which, at the same time, had a magnetic power in it. His small, steel-spring figure with the black hair and beard made him look like a Frenchman; and his pointed, precise manner of speaking increased the impression of something French about him. He had studied the public manner of Chatham and of Lamartine. He conquered his audiences as no one had before him and he became the idol of the rural population. He never wanted to win a majority for his proposals by concealing their true bearing; he desired to have them understood in their full consequences. On the other hand, he could very well accept temporary compromises and he knew the art of keeping a party together.

He was the first man in Norway who devoted himself completely to politics. By abandoning his professional career he became a poor man, always pursued by creditors. But in no other way was he able to keep a strong political movement under his sway. By allying himself with Ueland, who had not been frightened by the labor movement, he established that union between liberalism and democracy which became the basis of the policies of the Left Party.

IV

During the 1850's, Ueland was still the undisputed leader of the democratic farmers' bloc, and in that decennium all the privileges of the burgher class were practically abolished. The cities lost their monopoly of commerce and trade; conscription was finally extended to all classes; the farmers were freed of their obligation to furnish horses to travelers, and much of their labor on the public roads was taken over by public authorities; the representation of the cities in the Storthing was more firmly restricted. By all such measures, Norwegian society was put on a basis of more complete equality.

At the same time, the farmers' class was strengthened and the differences within were gradually leveled. A state bank giving loans at a low rate on farm mortgages was founded, and the number of land tenants rapidly dwindled. As early as the middle of the 50's they were no more than a fifth of the farming class. The cotters had their conditions regulated by a special law, which, to be sure, in all essentials only confirmed existing usages but did prevent arbitrary treatment on the part of the farm owners. It was of more consequence that, for the first time, their number began to decrease. This was owing chiefly to the introduction of agricultural machines, which was vastly promoted by the show of superior American machinery at the international exhibition in London in 1851.

On the basis of this social and political development, the formal organization of a Farmers' Party was finally initiated in 1865. The founder was Søren Jaabæk, a clever agitator and perhaps the purest doctrinaire of liberty in Norwegian politics. He looked to England as the model country of liberty, and, self-taught as he was, he even tried his hands at a popular history of England. He had imbibed the Manchester liberal doctrine in its most absolute form. He insisted that the activities of the state ought to be restricted to a minimum. Therefore he was an enemy of the official class. He could evoke disgust at it by asking such questions as this: "Why does a certain official have a salary of three dollars a day while a workingman gets no more than a quarter?" and answering: "Because the former is useless." He was of course an enemy of all kinds of privilege. He wanted all men to be equal and equally free. Therefore he demanded universal suffrage. To further such a program he began to form associations which he called "The Farmers' Friends," a name borrowed from Denmark. In that way the first organized political party in Norway came into existence.

Jaabæk, however, felt the impact of the political genius of Sverdrup and placed his organization at the service of the latter. By the end of the 50's Sverdrup had begun to gather a solid political group in the Storthing, and in the 60's, while Ueland was still alive, Sverdrup became the acknowledged leader of all democratic and progressive policies. He pointed the way ahead.

Sverdrup had a decisive experience in the Storthing of 1859–60, which convinced him definitely that democracy and complete national self-government were closely interdependent. Against a minority of only two votes, the Storthing voted to strike out of the constitution the provision authorizing the king to appoint a royal governor in Norway. The king had actually promised his assent. But in Sweden a vehement opinion was aroused against such a measure, which was felt as a blow to the claim of Swedish concurrence in the Norwegian constitution. In particular, the Swedish House of Nobles took a threatening attitude. The king bowed to the pressure and refused his assent.

Some thirteen years later it proved possible to carry the Norwegian demand without any conflict with Sweden. But the experience of the first defeat left deep traces in the politics of Norway. Sverdrup argued that if the Norwegian cabinet had truly represented the nation, it would rather have resigned than allow a royal veto to be used at foreign command. His answer was parliamentary government. Though only a minority followed him in this conclusion, nevertheless he set out stubbornly to fight for it.

Two measures he deemed necessary for the purpose. The first would be to make the Storthing more of a permanent power in the political life of the nation by having it meet annually instead of only every third year. This idea won increasing ground after Sweden, in 1865, had changed her system of four estates into a Riksdag of two chambers, meeting annually. The reform was carried in Norway in 1869.

The second measure, according to Sverdrup, would be to open the Storthing to members of the cabinet. The Eidsvoll constitution had followed the American pattern in making the cabinet more like a council at the service of the executive, and, since the king, unlike the president of the United States, had no backing in public vote or opinion, his counselors were little more than high civil service officials. For that very reason the old Farmers' Party had looked with disfavor and suspicion on the idea of giving the royal counselors access to the discussions of the Storthing. They feared that this would mean a reinforcement of the group of officials there. Sverdrup, however, asserted that inevitably the members of the cabinet would come under the influence of the views prevailing in the Storthing, and the result would be a majority government. When his opponents objected that this would be the end of the principle of the balance of independent powers in the state, he answered by paraphrasing Lamartine: "The division of powers is nonsense." He wanted unity in the action of the nation and he proclaimed as his program: "All power gathered in this hall."

He gradually won the farmers' representatives over to his views, and in 1872 the measure was for the first time adopted by the Storthing. On the advice of the cabinet, the king refused his assent. Frightened by the consequences he foresaw, one of the members cried: "By the introduction of this rule, the position of royal counselor will become a political calling and no longer an office."

Then followed the most violent conflict in Norwegian political history. Every third year, after each new election, the Storthing repeated its vote with increasing majorities. Since the question dealt with an amendment to the constitution, a majority of two thirds was obligatory. But on each occasion the royal assent was refused.

No issue contributed so much to the political education of large masses of the people. Never before had the elections occasioned such general and such vehement campaigning, with meetings and speeches. The whole nation was split into two opposing parties, the Left and the Right, which organized themselves all over the country and fought each other with increasing bitterness.

The Storthing majority followed up its votes on the cabinet question with the adoption of other democratic measures, the most important of them being the extension of the suffrage to all who paid taxes on a fixed income. This new attempt to change the constitution was promptly vetoed. The cabinet was put under pressure by the Storthing's taking out of its hands the decision of one administrative matter after another and laying aside important royal proposals. It was open war between the two political bodies.

GROWTH of DEMOCRACY

The conflict became acute when, after three successive adoptions of the amendment to the constitution, the king and the cabinet still refused to acknowledge its legal validity, pretending—from theory, not from any special provision of the constitution—that on such amendments the veto of the king had an absolute character, not merely a suspensive one. After this claim the conflict became one of democracy pure and simple. The question concerned the sovereign power of the people to amend the national constitution.

In 1880 the Storthing proclaimed solemnly the amendment of the constitution to be legally valid. The elections of 1882 returned the Left Party in overwhelming majority, and the whole cabinet was impeached for having violated the constitution; the tribunal trying the case was the Lagthing supplemented by the Supreme Court. The judgment as rendered deprived the members of the cabinet of their offices, and, after some hesitation, the king was forced to charge Sverdrup with forming a new cabinet.

This occurred in the year 1884, and since then parliamentary government has ruled in Norway. The government has regularly been in the hands of the leader of the majority party, and the royal veto fell into desuetude, until, at last, it was formally abolished. The political victory of democracy was complete, and nobody has disputed it since.

During the Sverdrup government, important reforms for the consolidation of democracy were achieved. The suffrage was extended; the jury system for criminal cases was introduced, mostly according to the English pattern; the army was organized on a completely democratic basis; the public school system was highly improved and was left in the charge of popularly elected school boards.

Sverdrup had to experience the tragedy that younger generations carried his principles further than he himself dared to go and he came into conflict with his own party. His achievements, however, were so fundamental that, in reality, all later politics followed the lines he had drawn up. Suffrage was made universal in 1898 and was extended to women in 1907. At an even earlier date both reforms had been enacted for municipal elections.

V

The progress of democracy turned the attention of the people to questions of national independence, strengthening the demands for control of foreign affairs and separate foreign representation. The rise of democracy in Sweden made these questions still more urgent, because, as the Swedish Riksdag gained increasing control of such matters, their disregard of the Norwegian Storthing was more painfully felt. The world-wide shipping of Norway made the want of an independent consular service ever more acute. In foreign policy the Norwegians did not feel that their ideals of international justice and peace were being satisfactorily served.

After 1885 the Norwegian cabinet and Storthing repeatedly put forward proposals and claims for a settlement of these questions. The king, however, backed by Swedish opinion, frustrated all serious reforms. When, at last, in 1905, he was about to use his royal veto against measures for establishing a distinct Norwegian consular service, the cabinet resigned, refusing to countersign such a veto, and thus did what Sverdrup had wanted them to do in 1860. Neither side being willing to compromise, the Storthing cut the knot by unanimously declaring that the king had forfeited his crown and that, as a consequence, the union with Sweden was dissolved. The line of argument followed in this proclamation of the Storthing was not unlike that of the American Declaration of Independence.

The decision provoked much agitation in Sweden, where most people conceived of such unilateral action on the part of Norway as a breach of treaty. The Norwegian nation, however, unanimously insisted on its legal right to withdraw from a union that impaired the self-government guaranteed by its constitution. Sweden finally acknowledged the *fait accompli*. The complete liberty of Norway was restored.

GROWTH of DEMOCRACY

The dissolution of the union led to no changes in the Norwegian constitution except the removal of the amendments occasioned by its creation in 1814. A large majority of the people voted to maintain the monarchical form of government. This was done not from love of monarchy but precisely because the monarchy at that time had become nothing more than a form and a symbol of tradition. After 1905 the government of Norway only became more completely democratic than before. The Danish prince who was elected king and who as Haakon VII assumed the name of his predecessors in ancient times, proved himself to be a faithful guardian of democracy and popular liberty. In no country in the world can the will of the nation be more certain of reigning than in Norway, provided that no foreign tyranny intrudes itself by sheer force. When, in 1940, German armies invaded and occupied the country and attempted to suppress all ideas of liberty in the people, the king became a useful and inspiring symbol of national will and unity in the fight for freedom. He was the living embodiment of a free nation.

The parliamentary system had its obvious weaknesses. As a heritage from the times when the scope of national activities was extremely limited, the Storthing often continued to occupy itself with administrative details, and this habit had even been strengthened in the times of political conflict. After the cabinet had become the direct representative of a majority and ordinarily enjoyed the confidence of the Storthing, it proved difficult to change the old habits. To a certain extent this inhibited promptness of action on the part of the cabinet. On the whole, however, the government of Norway has proved remarkably efficient and it has not been exposed to the frequent changes that are the consequence of parliamentary intrigues. In fact, there has been an almost surprising stability of government. During the period since 1905, it even happened twice that a cabinet was in power for a length of seven years.

The reason is that the parliament never became an institution living, as it were, its separate life. The Storthing was always in close contact with the people, and the people never lost their hold on the politics of the country. All classes took a vivid part in politics through frank discussions in meetings and in the press, because the whole people had a true political education. Democracy in Norway was not a mere form but an active reality.

A hundred years ago, in 1845, the diplomatic representative of the United States at the court of Norway and Sweden sent a glowing report to his government of the magnificent progress of Norway under its free constitution. He stressed the "general diffusion of correct political information" in the Norwegian nation in contrast to that of other European nations, and their "clearer perception of the true interests of their country." For that reason he found in Norway a stronger unity of national efforts than in other countries. At that time, too, Norway was ahead of all nations in Europe by virtue of the constitution of 1814, and the American observer admired the political maturity of the people.

A hundred years later he might have used no weaker words, and they would have had still more truth. The spirit of democracy continues to live in full force in the Norwegian nation.

VI

As democracy advanced, the minorities which represented the ideas formerly in power began to fear the establishment of a tyranny of the majority. Full democracy meant the political liberation of all classes of people. But who could prevent them from adopting laws that implied the subservience of minorities?

In a democracy, law, as defined by Rousseau, is the expression of the social will. Medieval society did not foresee any fundamental difficulty in defining the social will; everybody was presumed to be imbued with it and to agree to it. The differentiation of individuals and the appreciation of personal self-assertion led modern democracy to institute the system of voting and counting the votes so that the majority would decide—a system that cannot work well unless, as in Norway, it is combined with universal political education. In order, however, to avert the possible danger of abuses, several methods have been invented as checks on the majority.

In Norway all amendments to the constitution of 1814 must be adopted by a two-thirds majority, and in no case may they conflict with the spirit and the fundamental principles of the constitution. If there is a disagreement between the Odelsthing and the Lagthing, new laws cannot pass the complete Storthing except by the same majority of two thirds. Furthermore, in order to make certain that the majority of representatives shall have behind them a corresponding majority of the nation, the system of proportional representation was introduced in municipal elections in 1896 and in parliamentary elections in 1919.

The essential matter in the protection of minorities, however, is the existence and maintenance of the fundamental freedoms: freedom of speech, freedom of the press, freedom of assembly, freedom of association, freedom of vote, and freedom of religion. These freedoms, together with equality before the law, are guaranteed by the Norwegian constitution and, what is still more important, they are living elements in the mind of the nation. They cannot be destroyed by any majority nor by any temporary dictatorship supported by foreign armies.

ECONOMIC and SOCIAL POLICIES

I

After the wars of 1807–14, Norway had another long period of peace, lasting for a century and a quarter, until 1940. This new period of peace was again an age of conspicuous progress, both material and spiritual, even more notable than that of the eighteenth century. Indeed, in economic activities, as well as in the domains of literature, arts, and sciences, it gave to little Norway a prominent place in the world's life. It was a display of vitality and energy that could occur only in a healthy people, striving and advancing in full freedom and using all its forces in national solidarity.

This is not the place to depict even in the briefest sketch the intellectual and artistic activities that had such a remarkable flowering in Norway during the nineteenth and twentieth centuries. It may suffice to recall simply some names of men who won world fame by their deeds or their production—in mathematics, Niels Henrik Abel and Sophus Lie; in meteorology, Vilhelm Bjerknes; in literature, Henrik Ibsen, Bjørnstjerne Bjørnson, and Sigrid Undset; in music, Edvard Grieg; in painting, J. C. Dahl and Edvard Munch; in philology, Sophus Bugge; in geographical exploration, Fridtjof Nansen and Roald Amundsen. Alongside these men, in the same fields or in other fields such as history and sociology, biology, physics, and chemistry, there were others who by talents and achievements might be put on a level with those mentioned or even higher, but whose activities and fame for several reasons remained limited to their own country or to the Scandinavian orbit. Manifestly, the Norway that emerged from the sudden rising of 1814 produced and conveyed to the world a spiritual wealth and strength far above her numerical forces.

[91]

ECONOMIC and SOCIAL POLICIES

In this period the population of the country increased from less than a million to close to three millions, at the same time that more than three quarters of a million people went as immigrants to the United States of America, where they helped most actively in building up the West. But while the population of the nation was trebled, her material wealth was multiplied a hundred times or more. While agricultural production was effectively enhanced, industry, after the middle of the nineteenth century, passed through a striking development, conquering many new fields and growing at an increasing pace from one decade to the other.

Norway ceased being an essentially farming country. The census of 1890 was the last to show more than half the people living by agriculture and forestry. At the end of the period scarcely a third of the population gained its livelihood from these old national occupations. Another third was busy in manufactures of many different kinds. Then there was the merchant marine that grew up to take fourth or even third place in the world's shipping. Later came the whaling fleet, the foremost in the world. Foreign commerce and all the new public utilities took an increasing number of people in their service. The social composition of the nation was thoroughly revolutionized.

It is a remarkable feature of this development that, although agriculture lost its dominating part in national economy, the cities did not become so overwhelmingly important as in many other industrial countries. At the end of this period, not over 30 percent of the population lived in cities. And most of the cities were quite small, only two of them—Oslo and Bergen—having more than 100,000 inhabitants.

The reason was that so much of the new industry, like the older one, grew up by the waterfalls of the country. The textile factories of the 1850's, as well as the wood pulp and paper mills of the 1860's and 70's, made use of the abundant and cheap water power of the rivers, and so did the colossal electrical plants of the twentieth century. New cities rarely arose. The workingmen had the same ideals as their farmer ancestors: every man his house! They loved to have a garden of their own and a piece of land to cultivate.

Thus they came to settle in groups of houses more like villages and garden towns than real cities.

This does not mean that Norway failed to experience the evils accompanying capitalistic industry in other countries. In the cities the working people often lived in crowded and unsanitary tenement houses, rather like slums. Everywhere they might be mercilessly exploited by long hours and low wages, and even their children might have to work in the factories.

The workingmen out in the country were slow to feel their solidarity with those in the cities, and slow to organize. On the other hand, they had higher aspirations as to ways of living, and, when their ideals conflicted with a capitalistic society, the result might be social radicalism of an outspoken revolutionary character. The ties that bound the workers to agricultural society were never completely severed, and that may help to explain the alliance between labor and farmers which on several occasions has had a decisive influence on Norwegian politics. It is a noteworthy fact that universal suffrage was introduced in 1898 by a majority chiefly composed of farmers. And the Labor government that came into power in 1935 relied from the start on the support of the new Farmers' Party which had formed itself out of elements from both Left and Right.

II

As a matter of course, the industrial development profoundly affected the conditions of agriculture, and certainly not altogether to its profit. Industry steadily drained labor away from the farms; competition in wages and prices was often ruinous to the farmers, and it was mainly the agricultural population that sought an outlet for its economic difficulties in emigration. One of the consequences was the almost complete disappearance of cotters and tenants, so that, at the end of the period, 94 percent of the farms were owned by the farmers themselves. At the same time, the number of farms was increasing steadily, and their average size was just as steadily decreasing, until more than 90 percent of them were embracing less than ten acres.

As a matter of fact, the great mass of the farmers always lived approximately on the level of the working people. What now distinguished them from their ancestors was that well-nigh all of them had become the owners of the land they cultivated. In the eastern districts, not a few large farms were still in existence; mostly, however, the farmers worked exclusively for themselves and employed very few assistant hands.

In one way it might be said that they were not economically independent. Almost all of them had mortgaged their land to some bank. The banks, however, were in most cases either state banks or coöperative credit institutions, and thus, from another point of view, the farmers were their own creditors.

Two things had come to the rescue of agricultural activities: one was their industrialization, another was coöperation. All farmers used machines for the cultivation of their land, and they produced more for selling than for their own consumption. Both for buying and for selling they established a wide-branched coöperation. They had coöperative societies for the purchase of machines and, still oftener, for that of seeds and fodder. Most important, however, was their coöperation for marketing purposes.

The coöperative movement had begun in the 1870's, with small dairies for limited districts. But by degrees it was extended to embrace ever larger areas. Then municipal or coöperative slaughter-houses were established, and later, special associations for selling eggs, honey, or other products. The growth of all such activities led to the founding of a few centrals that took over the control of distributing and selling nearly the whole production of milk and butter, eggs, meat, fruits, silver fox furs, etc. The last step in this development was the recognition of the most important centrals as public institutions, working together with state authorities for the regulation of prices in the interest of both consumers and producers.

The progress in this field, the combination of private initiative and association with state regulation, is characteristic of the whole social and economic development in Norway during the last two generations. It has close parallels in the other Scandinavian countries. But in certain respects the social organization of economic activities had gone further in Norway than in the other countries before the Nazi invaders came and crushed it.

III

Increasing industrialization created the usual problems of capital and labor, beginning with tensions and conflicts between these two interdependent forces of production. Out in the country districts, to be sure, some factories were established on an almost patriarchal basis, the owner and manager living together with the workingmen, presiding at their common meals and taking personal charge of the welfare of his people. There are even some early instances of profit-sharing by the workingmen. To an ever greater extent, however, factories were organized exclusively as enterprises of private capitalism, looking essentially to the profit of the owners, exploiting the workingmen to the limit. Here arose the conflicts.

Trade unions were formed. In some trades they began to unite on a nation-wide basis in the 1870's. The really important labor movement dates from the 1880's. At the end of that decade the first serious strikes occurred. The workingmen's associations began to take up general social questions for discussion. In 1887 a Labor Party was established, and two years later it adopted a socialistic program. In the 1890's, after the introduction of proportional elections for municipal bodies, labor began to gain a place in local politics. In 1899 the National Federation of Trade Unions was founded. In the twentieth century a period of severe labor conflicts accompanied labor's rise to power in national politics.

The most conspicuous aspect of this development is the element of opposition and conflict. As a matter of fact the whole period since the 1870's has been one of struggle and conflict in political as well as in economic life. But it is important to stress that this period has also been one of organization and construction. The relations of trade unions and employers have not only been those of enemies fighting each other. Some time did pass before the employers would recognize the trade unions as representatives of their work-men. But they were finally made to realize that they could gain greater stability by negotiating with the unions than with the in-dividual laborers. In 1900 the employers founded their own na-tional organization, and the general agreements regarding wages and other labor conditions which gradually replaced the individual contracts were even more characteristic of the tendencies of the new age than all the strikes and lockouts taken together.

Not until 1903 did the Labor Party succeed in winning its first seats in the Storthing. From this time on its influence began to be felt in the formulation of state policy on labor and other social questions. By the end of the 20's it had become the largest political party, but was still not a majority. Meanwhile, radical laws and measures inspired by socialistic ideas were being increasingly adopted by the Storthing, and possibly the most remarkable fact about them was that most of them were passed unanimously. Much bitter dispute might precede them; but when, at last, they had gone through this ordeal and special commissions had agreed upon practical compromises, the result appeared acceptable to all parties.

I think there can be no doubt that the feeling of social respon-sibility and solidarity which proved so strong in labor legislation and social reforms was largely strengthened by the strong national consciousness that prevailed in Norway as a consequence of the constant struggle for independence and national self-assertion. The nation felt firmly united in spite of all class differences and con-flicts; it was a fact that those differences were considerably less prominent there than in most other countries. The national idea was always intimately bound up with that of democracy, conceiv-ing all citizens as equals.

It is a significant fact that national elections always aroused a far livelier and more general interest than merely local elections. After the establishment of local self-government, the number of voters who went to the polls for municipal elections was for many years amazingly small compared with that of votes for members of parliament. Only after the social questions began looming up in the life of the nation and demanded action even of local powers did participation in municipal elections grow really considerable. Even then national politics remained in the center of public interest and discussion, and the votes cast in national elections usually amounted to between 80 and 90 percent of the electorate. There were constituencies where the percentage ran as high as 99.

People in Norway were more inclined than most other peoples to conceive of the state as their natural common instrument. In all countries the liberals of the nineteenth century, rebels against despotism, had felt the urgent need of warning and protecting the individual against the interference or, as they would say, the tyranny of the state. True democracy must put an end to such a conception. A genuinely democratic state could not be felt as an enemy of freedom but rather as a citizens' association, and would therefore not be feared but would be employed for their common benefit. In Norway democracy was established earlier than in other countries and, as a consequence, this conception early won a firm foothold.

Even in the period of economic liberalism, in the 1850's and the following decades, the primitive stage of Norwegian capitalism had made it almost a necessity for the state to undertake the establishment of the new public utilities made possible by new inventions, the construction of railroads and telegraph lines. Such enterprises always remained in the hands of the state. Nobody thought of taking them away, and others of similar character joined them, the telephone, for example. More purely local utilities were generally taken in hand by municipal bodies—street cars, gas works, and electrical plants falling into this class. People were accustomed to having recourse to the public authorities for such common enterprises.

This explains to a great extent why all parties in Norway so readily agreed to state leadership in the new social and economic problems created by industrial development, and why the following statement by an American author may be true: "It would be difficult to find a society where there is more protection of community interest and more coöperation for social amelioration than prevails in Norway."[1]

IV

The Conservative Party made the first proposals of labor legislation in the 1870's, aiming at the restriction of child labor in factories. These proposals, however, were drowned in the violent political conflict of those days. Then the first government of the Left Party appointed, in 1885, a great commission, composed of members of all parties, to consider a wide range of labor questions, and it is worth while to notice that even the dogmatic enemy of state interference, Jaabæk, agreed to the proposal that maximum working hours should be fixed by law.

The first practical result of the discussions was the factory control law, adopted by the Storthing in 1892, which established state control of all factories, prohibited the employment of children, regulated night work and holiday work, and so forth. Two years later came the passage of the first social security legislation, the establishment of state insurance against disabilities caused by accidents in factories. In the 1890's also the first law regulating working hours was adopted, limited for the time being to bakeries, where the sanitary conditions seemed to make it most urgent.

The great age of social legislation came with the twentieth century. In several respects it was prepared by municipal reform measures, particularly in the city of Oslo. Here was initiated, in 1896, public housing for working people and, at the same time, free meals for school children—who has not heard of the "Oslo breakfast," planned by nutrition specialists and given free to all children (not only the "underprivileged")? Municipal authorities in several cities began to organize and control labor exchánges. They appointed dentists to care for the school children, and, in municipalities where the Labor Party won power, all medical treatment was given free of charge by salaried physicians. Later, in the 1920's, many municipalities established old age pensions. And

[1] J. E. Nordskog, *Social Reform in Norway* (Los Angeles, 1935).

a highly illuminating evidence of their conception of the municipality as an organ of common interests is the fact that nearly everywhere the cinemas were municipal enterprises.

The twentieth century also witnessed the mighty advance of private economic coöperation. The National Coöperative was organized in 1906, and it grew to embrace more than six hundred local associations, while about four hundred others were still outside the national organization. Their membership grew to some 170,000 families, which meant about a fourth of the entire population of the country. The National Coöperative did not limit itself to the distribution of purchases; it went into the domain of production as well, and established a number of factories in different lines. Viewing these matters in connection with the farmers' coöperative enterprises, it may fairly be stated that Norway was in the vanguard of the coöperative movement throughout the world.

All such activities supply a background for the social policies prevailing in Norway in the same period. There was in all quarters a deepening comprehension of common social responsibility, demonstrating itself in all fields of legislation and administration, not least remarkable in the new criminal law that was finally adopted in 1902. The large-minded humanity of this law, so carefully considering the social causes of crime and the educational aims of punishment, made it a pioneer work that was studied and imitated by foreign legislators. It was supplemented by particular laws for the moral protection of unfortunate children, one of them giving full legal status to children born out of wedlock.

The issue that really roused discussion and struggle between the political parties was the question of state control over the exploitation of waterfalls made possible by new inventions. As foreign capitalists immediately turned up to harness the waterfalls for their private interests, the problem quickly took on a decidedly national aspect. The coalition government of Left and Right that had led the nation in the fight for full independence in 1905 also took the initiative in temporary legislation establishing a system of licensing for the acquisition and the exploitation by foreigners of the most vital national fundamentals of industry, namely waterfalls, mines, and forests. Soon, however, the problem grew to be one of capitalism generally. The farmers were profoundly agitated by the prospect of great capitalists dominating the treasures of nature which suddenly had sprung to such unexpected values and which, in many cases, had been bought from themselves at ridiculously low prices. The anti-capitalism of Norwegian farmers was strikingly parallel to movements in the American Middle West.

Labor supported all measures for curbing capitalism, and finally, in 1917, a system of licensing was extended to all buyers of these properties. The licensees were obliged to pay fees to the state as well as to the municipalities concerned and to cede for local benefit a part of the power acquired. More remarkable still was the limitation of the licenses so that, after a certain term of years, the whole property would "revert"—such was the term employed, although the question was chiefly with what had been private property—to the state without any kind of repayment to the licensees. Opponents asserted that the right of "reversion" without any further compensation was at variance with the principles of the constitution, and the matter was brought before the Supreme Court, which, however, by four votes to three, upheld the legality of the measure. Curiously enough, this was exactly the principle advocated by the farmers with regard to land in the 1670's.

There came a time—rather, I should say, an intermediate period —when the farmers, or at least a section of them, abhorred socialistic doctrines and looked at labor as an enemy. Still, however, they were interested in maintaining the ties that bound both classes together. Therefore they persuaded the Storthing to vote in 1903 a counterpart to the state bank of farm mortgages, the establishment of a special bank for workingmen's landholding and housing, later transformed into a bank for small holding and housing in general. This bank helped much to further the growth of small holdings that was so characteristic of recent social development in Norway. It obviously influenced the political development, too. A great many of the small holders, even if they lived completely from their land, turned socialists and joined the Labor Party. In this way labor struck still deeper roots in the agricultural life of the country.

Meanwhile labor legislation was primarily engaged in extending social security. Unemployment insurance was established as early as 1906, but at that time in a very imperfect form. State contributions to the unemployment funds of trade unions were granted in so far as certain conditions were accepted. The trade unions, however, were mostly interested in using their unemployment funds as weapons in strikes and lockouts, so that very few of them were ready to comply with the conditions of the state. The law of 1906, therefore, remained rather ineffective. A thorough state assistance in this field had to wait until labor won more direct political power.

It was different with other social securities: the public disabilities insurance laws were extended to fishermen in 1908 and to seamen in 1911; health insurance was adopted in 1909, originally applying only to workingmen but gradually extended to ever wider circles. According to the rules of all these types of insurance, the state and the municipalities were to carry an essential part of the expenses, so that in fact the whole nation was a party to them.

During the same years, the factory control law was repeatedly amended in order to embrace all domains of industry and to improve the conditions of the workingman. In 1915 the principle of maximum hours even for day work was finally included, establishing a regular maximum week of fifty-four hours, cut down in 1919 to forty-eight hours. A law in 1919 even regulated the working hours in the merchant marine. Except in the case of the sailors the law really only sanctioned what the workingmen had already won through their own organizations.

At the same time all the political parties were hotly discussing the interference of public authorities in labor conflicts. There was a general feeling that strikes and lockouts could not be regarded as matters which concerned only the conflicting parties; they struck a blow at the whole nation and ought to be treated as general social affairs. In 1915 a law was adopted which established a labor court to judge in all disputes regarding the interpretation of labor agreements and other matters of a legal character. In cases of conflicts of interest, particularly regarding wages, the same law instituted public mediation as obligatory in advance of stoppage of work.

The adoption of compulsory arbitration in conflicts of large social importance had been widely mooted and even formally proposed. But as long as labor felt itself to be the weaker party in national life and unable to reconstruct society along its own lines, it could not accept measures that might obstruct its economic and social progress. So arbitration courts were not included in the law of 1915. The violent economic changes and conflicts that followed in the wake of the First World War led, however, to the adoption of temporary arbitration laws, and the fact that the decisions of the courts were mainly in favor of the workingmen made them look at the new institution with less hostility. Their increasing political power, which offered them more and more influence on social development in general, put the whole question in a different position, and, after a labor government was formed in 1935, it more than once committed labor conflicts to arbitration courts.

V

Labor legislation in Norway was substantially accomplished in the period 1906–19. The 1920's were a period of social and political unrest. The full consequences of the transformation of economic life began to assert themselves. There was an increasing movement to change the whole social structure of the nation. One economic conflict followed another. Financial and industrial crises harassed the country. Unemployment mounted to unimagined heights. Fiery demands for reforms or revolution arose on all sides. The old political parties crumbled and disintegrated. No single party was again able to win the majority of the people or the Storthing. Governments changed more frequently than before, mostly every second year.

Two lines of progress, however, were clearly evident. One was the increasing organization of the farming class both economically and politically. The other was the advancing strength of the Labor Party, parallel with the trade unions.

The elections of 1927 suddenly made the Labor Party the strongest single party in the Storthing. The attempt, in January, 1928, to form a Labor government was wrecked by a temporary coalition of the other parties. The Storthing, however, proved able to carry two measures, both of which were inspired by the new social ideas.

One was the final establishment of the state grain monopoly that had been set up temporarily during the World War. It took in hand all importation of grains, and it bought up the home production at prices that made agriculture more profitable than before. At the same time it was obliged to keep the same selling prices all over the country. Thus it served the interests of both consumers and producers. By virtue of this solidarity of interest it helped to allay former class oppositions, often of very bitter character, and in itself it meant an important advance in social organization.

The other notable measure adopted by the Storthing of 1928 was a law providing for obligatory cession of land in the interest of soil cultivation. It was thought intolerable that big landowners should leave cultivable soil unused, and, at the same time, it appeared natural to give to all cotters the right to become proprietors of the land they cultivated. All such cessions were hedged in by so many guarantees to the original proprietor that they could not easily be achieved. The very adoption of the principle was, however, almost revolutionary, and the application of it would be highly dependent on the spirit of the administration by which it eventually was executed. It acquired its practical importance only after a Labor government was firmly in power.

The disastrous crisis that upset the whole world about 1930 awakened everywhere a growing consciousness of social responsibility and a demand for effective action by national authorities to fight economic collapse. The same conditions decided the American elections of 1932 and, likewise, the Norwegian elections of 1933, when the Labor Party gained almost half of the seats of the

Storthing (69 out of a total of 150). The other parties were too divided to keep labor out of power. With the support of the Farmers' Party, a Labor government was formed in 1935. Later, on several occasions, the Left or Liberal Party actively helped to keep it in power.

The result was that new energy was put into the work of social reconstruction. The other parties mostly followed the lead thus given, and, despite many dissensions regarding details, the reforms adopted were generally backed by a united nation. The elections of 1936 attested the will of the people to see the labor policies continued.

The field of social security was notably enlarged by the establishment of old age pensions (1936) chiefly by state allowances. Next year, a new unemployment insurance law made this reform a practical reality.

The factory control law was again revised and modernized. Perhaps the most significant novelty now introduced was the setting up of workingmen's delegations in all factories for the protection of labor's rights. By this arrangement a closer collaboration between employers and employees was instituted, and mutual vexations due to political or other divergences were largely prevented. Another remarkable reform was the provision for holidays with full pay fixed by law at nine days. As a matter of fact, most of the trade unions had already got agreements providing for holidays of two weeks. Thus the law was only following established practice.

Still more important, and in some degree more hotly disputed, were the public economic activities started by the Labor government. In this field, too, it could base itself on earlier efforts, but it carried them further than former governments had ventured. The Labor Party had put forward as its program the abolition of unemployment, and it intended to use the whole economic power of the state for this purpose.

Consequently, it increased in successive years the state credits for public works as well as for the support of municipal and private enterprises, all of them intended to further national consolidation and strengthen the forces of production. The construction of highways and railroads likely to tie the separate parts of the country more closely together was vigorously speeded up, and many outlying districts were brought inside the orbit of national economic life so as to make them fit for profitable cultivation. The clearing of new soil was advanced by all means, through state loans for acquiring uncultivated ground, for equipment and machines, for building of houses and barns, and through a more energetic use of the expropriation law of 1928. As a result, the establishment of new farms rose from 500 to about 2,000 annually. By similar means the fishermen were assisted in acquiring motor sloops and other more modern tools for their industry. A National Industrial Bank was founded for the promotion of new industry, and a special state commission was appointed to plan new industrial enterprises by exploiting more effectively the water power, the ores, and the forests. One of the results was the establishment of rayon manufacture, using the abundant wood-pulp production. Many unused waterfalls were harnessed in order to bring electrical power to new districts.

Possibly the most revolutionary measures were those inaugurated to organize the primary producers as the real masters of their production. Through many years of struggle the farmers had already succeeded in organizing themselves to handle their particular products. At least four fifths of all the farmers in the country were members of the different sales organizations, and by the assistance of the state these organizations were finally united in a national board for adjusting prices and profits. In this board even the consumers were represented by delegates from the coöperative societies and the merchants' association.

The Labor government tried to organize the fishermen in a similar way. That was a more difficult task because the fisheries were based essentially on exportation to foreign countries, and the attempts of the fishermen themselves to establish sales organizations for smaller or larger districts had been only partially successful. The government managed for the first time to found a national organization for the herring fisheries for which the marketing opportunities were least complicated; this organization was granted virtually a monopoly on the export of herring. Then the government tried its hands at the cod fisheries, starting with the fixing of minimum prices to be paid to the fishermen by the exporters. They passed on to creating an organization of the cod fisheries that would be able to manage even the export trade. The work on this undertaking was in progress when it was stopped by the new World War.

All such measures were permeated by one fundamental idea. That was the social solidarity of the whole nation. In this survey of social politics of Norway during the last half century, it has not been possible to include all the single reforms sprung from that idea. I have tried to present simply the most significant ones which clearly show the trend of the whole movement. I only want to add one more, initiated in recent years, because it offers a new aspect of the same idea. That was the measure adopted to equalize the municipal taxes.

In a country so varied as Norway there are all imaginable types of municipalities, many wealthy and many very poor. They were very unequally equipped to meet the tasks of modern development, and in a number of them the local taxation exceeded the economic power of the residents. Finally, the government found a means to make the wealthy municipalities come to the assistance of the poor ones. It instituted a general scale of taxing for all bank deposits and distributed the income from this tax so as to favor the poor municipalities. Thus was practiced in a new way the old principle of taxing formulated by the decrees of absolute governments in the rule: the wealthy help the poor! Those governments were more interested in cashing the money than in the mode of collecting it. Democracy had in view the social aspect of taxation and based itself on the principle that the economically advantaged should assume necessary social burdens that cannot be carried by the economically disadvantaged. For that reason all income taxes were made progressive, increasing even by percentage for higher incomes, and the same idea decided the measure of directing a part of municipal wealth to the benefit of the most needy communities.

Further, I think it important to mention, without details, the manifold efforts by legislation and national credits to develop public instruction in all possible fields and to make all kinds of education available to all classes of the people. In Norway the elementary public school has really been made the common school for all children, while higher schools are almost exclusively in the care of the state and the municipalities. The latter were being profusely helped by state allowances for all educational enterprises, libraries and public lectures as well as schools. In 1933 the state took over the National Broadcasting System, chiefly in order to make it another instrument of public instruction. In this whole field, too, national solidarity manifests itself, perhaps in the finest spirit and in the most creative way.

VI

The Labor government frankly professed itself to be socialistic. Seen in the light of history, it appears as the logical continuation of a movement based on national tradition. Its actions obviously were determined much more by the necessities of the situation than by any kind of doctrine. Furthermore, it is evident that, though all the single acts were inspired by the same fundamental way of thinking, they led to social results of highly different types. In fact they furthered private enterprise just as much as national coöperation, and this national coöperation was placed under private leadership as well as under the state. That means that socialism did not necessarily imply economic uniformity or state dictatorship. It proved, in fact, thoroughly compatible with differentiation and freedom. Indeed, only in such a many-sided development is it able to satisfy all the spiritual aspirations of the people along with its material needs.

The essence of socialism is the effort to create law in domains of life that formerly were left more or less to arbitrary forces, and create it by the orderly coöperation of men and institutions. Coöperation is not identical with, but directly opposed to, slavery. It means human brotherhood's shaping itself in institutions. Its fundamental idea is the organization of free men, able to act from personal conviction but with a profound understanding of social solidarity.

Whether such efforts termed themselves socialistic or not, they proved in Norway highly effective in improving the material conditions of the people while at the same time shaping and fixing their social ideas.

Just before the outbreak of the present World War a serious attempt was made to define on a comparative basis the average incomes of the individuals belonging to different nations, considering not only the nominal money sums available to the population but also their real value in buying power. As one would expect, the United States of America appeared at the top of the countries examined, while Norway was to be found in a group of nations almost at the bottom of the list, with an average individual income of no more than a fourth of the sum available to each American. It would, however, be a completely false conclusion to transfer this picture of national wealth to the conception of the average standard of living within the two nations. Every observer will readily admit that, although the United States is a much wealthier country than Norway, the standard of living does not present such a glaring difference as is indicated by the bare figures for average income. The obvious reason is that in Norway the incomes are considerably more evenly distributed than in America. That holds true as to all the Scandinavian countries where, certainly, on an average the standard of living is higher than in most other European countries. If, in this group, Denmark may hold first place, Norway certainly comes in as a good second. That is a result of natural and historical conditions as well as of modern efforts, public and private. Together they have made Norwegian society more truly democratic than perhaps any other on earth by lifting the economic standards of the working classes to a level approaching that of other classes.

Still more uniform and elevated are the intellectual standards. Norway is inhabited by a highly enlightened people, reading comparatively more books and newspapers than perhaps any other nation, with the possible exception of Iceland. The most remarkable feature is the level of social morals, the spirit of freedom, and the consciousness of national solidarity that permeate the whole nation. That is at once the reason for and the result of the social policies that have distinguished the later decades of Norwegian history.

That is, also, what has given the nation her deep-rooted and invincible strength to resist the Nazi oppression which since the spring of 1940 has made all possible efforts to curb the spirit of the people. Friends of Norway, and the Norwegians themselves, may today regret that they held their budget for military defense so low as to weaken their ability to fight the invaders. But in using their economic means for the social consolidation and education of the nation, they laid the foundation of the spiritual defense that alone can carry them victoriously through their present sufferings.

The Norwegians were far from being satisfied with the social organization and the material improvements they had achieved. They were still cheerfully straining all their forces to build up a society corresponding to their ideals of freedom and law and offering conditions of life worthy of a nation of brothers, when suddenly a brutal invasion of foreign barbarians who understood nothing of these Nordic ideals disrupted the work and broke down all private and public institutions serving the progressive movement.

But in spite of all destructive efforts, the invaders have not been able to break the spirit and the ideals of the people. When the Norwegians are again masters in their own house, they will put all their energy into the rebuilding of their society and the realization of their ideas. They still firmly believe that they were marching toward the future of all civilized nations. Experience has proved to them that law, social organization of a broad scope, is not the enemy of freedom, but the shield without which freedom cannot be maintained.

For INTERNATIONAL JUSTICE

Sigrid Undset recently said that one of the most deep-seated traits in the Norwegian character was a passion for justice. History seems to prove the truth of her words. The Norwegians have never wearied of insisting on the ideal of justice. And the justice they wanted for and among themselves they would grant to others as well. Their own national development led them to dream of a realm of justice for the whole world. They looked forward to eternal universal peace founded on international justice.

To a large extent they were prepared for such an idea by the fact, otherwise a sad experience for them, that their country for many centuries played no independent part in foreign politics. They did not acquire the habit of thinking in terms of power policies and international alliances. Their minds were therefore open to the alluring pictures of common brotherhood presented by the French utopians of the eighteenth century as well as to the more practical peace proposals of the great German philosopher, Kant. With enthusiasm they listened to the preachings of the Saint-Simonists of the nineteenth century and to the international propaganda of the American blacksmith Elihu Burritt.

In their own country they felt able to reconcile and even combine the two ideas of national coöperation and personal freedom. They could see no inherent opposition between their claim of national independence and the ideal of an international organization that should make war impossible. Their most prominent champions of national self-assertion, the poets and prophets, Henrik Wergeland and Bjørnstjerne Bjørnson, were most ready to proclaim international brotherhood and justice. In fact, one of the reasons why they claimed Norway's right to control her own foreign affairs was that the Swedish government was not ready to participate in the organization of international peace.

For INTERNATIONAL JUSTICE

In 1890, as the first of all the world's parliaments, the Norwegian Storthing adopted by a great majority a resolution charging the government with the task of preparing for general arbitration treaties. Sweden temporarily blocked the attempt. It was just at this time that the movement for international peace began to gather force and advance more swiftly. In the same year, the first universal Interparliamentary Conference met in London, and the Storthing, alone among parliaments, sent delegates at public expense.

The 1890's in Norway were filled with the peace propaganda of Bjørnson. It was the period of conflict about the union with Sweden. And the voice of Bjørnson rang vigorously out on both questions—in speeches, articles, and poems. He was by nature a fighter and a reconciler at the same time, in meeting resistance with red hot indignation, but quickly ready to understand and to forgive. Conscious of his own superior strength, he was a loving defender of the weak, the suffering, and the submerged. Having lived in many foreign countries, in Denmark and Sweden, in Italy, France, Germany, and the United States, and being inspired by the ideals of Victor Hugo and Gambetta, he felt himself drawn to all nations. He hated wars between nations, and he fought passionately against all policies of conquest and domination and for the freedom of the small nations. He often appealed very definitely to the women on behalf of the cause of universal brotherhood and friendship. He became more than a merely Norwegian advocate of freedom and peace; often the whole world listened to his moving and courageous words.

Bjørnson wanted to draw both Sweden and Norway away from all kinds of power politics, and for that reason he proclaimed that an independent Norway should have no foreign policies at all. He would have his country acting within the family of nations exclusively in the spirit of peace and neutrality. In this plan the nation followed him. In 1897, after the Russian czar had announced his intention of summoning a general peace conference, the Storthing, this time unanimously, repeated its vote in favor of international arbitration treaties. Some years later it formulated the wish to see the neutrality of Norway permanently acknowledged.

For INTERNATIONAL JUSTICE

The realization of Norwegian independence was to Bjørnson a matter of course. He wanted, however, to have it achieved without the loss of Swedish friendship, and even while the conflict was hottest he went so far as to propose that the whole dispute be given over to international arbitration. This suggestion did not find much favor on either side, and very naturally so as the dispute was rather a matter of different ideologies than one of legal claims. The question was finally settled by the peaceful dissolution of the union of the two countries in 1905. Both nations shared the honor of this outcome of the conflict—Sweden because of her increased comprehension of the rights of freedom and democracy; Norway because of her sober-minded willingness to compromise on legalities.

The stand of the Storthing for peace policies and the championship of Bjørnson for peace ideas moved the large-minded Swedish industrialist Alfred Nobel, when he made his will in 1895 and dedicated his fortune to awards for the great benefactors of mankind, to leave the awarding of the peace prize to a committee appointed by the Norwegian parliament. This committee entered upon its duties in 1901. The task was a very delicate one, and it could not be carried on without mistakes being made. Still it had the effect of keeping Norway before the eyes of the world as a nation intimately allied with the cause of international peace. It also strengthened the feeling of the Norwegians themselves that they were in duty bound to continue their efforts for this idea.

Incidentally, it brought forward a man who was to devote his whole life to the work of international organizations, the only Norwegian of whom this can be said. The man was Dr. Christian L. Lange, the first secretary of the Norwegian Nobel Committee. He was one of the Norwegian delegates to the second Peace Conference at the Hague (1907), and for twenty-five years (1909–34) he served as secretary-general of the Interparliamentary Union. After the founding of the League of Nations he was one of the Norwegian delegates to all its assemblies until his death in 1938. As a historian of wide outlook he wrote a fundamental work on the history of internationalism. As interparliamentary secretary he traveled over the whole world, became intimately acquainted

For INTERNATIONAL JUSTICE

with personalities and institutions in all countries and he knew
better than anybody else all the technicalities, the difficulties, and
the means of international coöperation. The outbreak of the First
World War fell upon him like a lightning stroke threatening his
life work, but with undaunted courage he set about to restore the
international institutions that had been smashed and he took a leading part in the efforts to form a program and a public opinion for
the foundation of institutions that might prevent a new catastrophe. His clear, matter-of-fact thinking, combined with a highly
objective mind and the noblest character, made him the best adviser in all international matters. Quietly, unostentatiously, he
represented the ideals of international justice which were those of
Norway.

Norway gave to the world a still greater leader in the heroic
figure of Dr. Fridtjof Nansen. He was a character of the greatest
breadth, a distinguished man of science as well as a strenuous man
of action. He first won world fame as a hardy explorer, being the
first to cross the Greenland ice cap (1888), and on his *Fram* expedition approaching nearer to the North Pole than anyone before
him (1895). He became the ideal of Norwegian youth, admired
for his sportsmanship as for his wisdom in preparing for a goal and
his tenacity in seeking it. Norwegians felt him to be a representative of their very finest qualities. Without holding or accepting
any official position, he made himself their cherished leader in the
decisive fight for national independence in 1905, and his influence
on world opinion, particularly in Great Britain, was an important
factor in the successful outcome.

Nansen loved the struggle that came in solving fundamental
scientific problems, and he wanted to continue his explorations.
But his nation and the world summoned him to help in matters of
vital need in the life of the peoples. He was fully conscious of his
superior powers in carrying great responsibility, and just this consciousness made it difficult for him to refuse. He keenly felt the
urgent duty of devoting himself to the tasks that were required of
him and which nobody else appeared able to accomplish. Still
more, there was in his soul a deep pity for suffering and a strong

desire to help. "No appeal was ever made in vain to his active love of humanity," said a report adopted by the League of Nations after his death. And he translated every such appeal into an appeal to all others to assist him.

During the First World War he went to the United States as Norway's delegate to obtain supplies for his blockaded country and he did not shun the responsibility of signing urgent agreements before having received the authorization of his government. Immediately after the Armistice he began championing President Wilson's proposal for a League of Nations, and after the League was founded he became the greatest worker for its ideas. The last decade of his life (1920–30) was almost completely given to healing the wounds of those stricken by the war and to heartening the forces that might prevent another.

What he achieved for the various immense tasks which were entrusted to him by the League of Nations or which he took upon himself personally because the League refused to lend its authority, seems almost superhuman: the repatriation of half a million war prisoners from Russia and Siberia; the domiciling of a million and a half Russian political refugees, and later other refugees; the relief work that rescued millions of lives during the famine in Russia; the exchange of two million inhabitants between Greece and Turkey; the efforts for the settlement of the homeless Armenians. In all these undertakings he proved an organizer and administrator of extraordinary skill, and it is quite certain that these great tasks could not have been accomplished but for the personal authority and tenacity of Nansen.

Personally he was most profoundly moved by the sufferings of the starving children in Russia and of the straggling Armenians who seemed forsaken by God and man. Yet for all these he did not succeed in obtaining the support of the League of Nations. To him all sufferers had the same claim to pity and help, without distinction of creed or politics or nationality. He spent all his persuasive powers, his eloquence and his compassion, even his indignation, to arouse political authorities and public audiences to the necessity of action. After defeats his heart was sad and bleeding, but he could not abandon what he felt to be a duty. His voice was that of the world's conscience, and it reverberated through the world even after his death.

Most of all Nansen feared that the callousness of heart, the lack of brotherly spirit, and the failure to comprehend dangers might lead the world into a new war. He saw it coming and he warned that another war would mean the wiping out of human civilization. To prevent such a catastrophe he wanted to make the League of Nations as strong as possible. During all these years he was the delegate of Norway to its assemblies and at Geneva he was always the champion of energetic action for peace. He represented a small nation but he always had the courage to speak straight out on all questions and he was listened to as being a Great Power by himself. He worked hard to bring into the League the great European powers that were still outside (Germany and Russia), and on behalf of Norway he made the first proposal for the general arbitration agreement that was adopted in 1928. He hoped to build a durable bulwark against the evil forces of dissension, enmity, and war.

In all questions of this order, all the Scandinavian nations coöperated closely. Ever since the 1880's their separate peace associations have come together in more or less regular Scandinavian congresses. In the twentieth century the peace groups in their parliaments met, with increasing regularity, for the common discussion of international problems. At the founding of the League of Nations and later in the work of the League, the Scandinavian governments constantly consulted each other and agreed upon their attitude. An American author recently defined their role in Geneva by saying: "Throughout the League's history no members have been more active and determined in their loyalty to the Assembly than the Scandinavian States." [1] The great Swedish statesman Hjalmar Branting was one of its leading men until his too early death (1925).

I do not pretend that the Norwegian nation and its governing bodies were always on a level with leaders like Nansen and his as-

[1] S. Shepard Jones, *The Scandinavian States and the League of Nations* (New York, 1939), p. 96.

sociates. But the work of such men was a living heritage to Norway as well as to the whole world, and Norwegian statesmen strove honestly to uphold the ideals of international justice and peace. Not many nations have such a consistent history of effort for the organization of peace as Norway has.

Notwithstanding all efforts, the catastrophe came, and Norway was hurled into it. The German aggressors, disregarding all considerations of rights and humanity, after having devoured Austria, Czechoslovakia, and Poland, invaded and occupied Norway, too. Her king and government were forced to continue in exile their fight for liberty.

The terrible experience of foreign conquest and tyranny has not destroyed the Norwegian ideals of law and freedom. On the contrary, the nation is more determined than ever to carry these ideals to victory. No less than in the past Norway will in the future support international organization under law. In this she sees the only hope for her freedom and that of all other nations.

Part II

LIFE UNFOLDS In
LITERATURE

PROLOGUE

A modern Norwegian poet once gave utterance to some pessimistic thoughts about the study of the "national character" of his people. He has pondered much over the problem, he says, without ever being able to point out anything like a general type. He knows men from one region of Norway who could be mistaken for Danes, others who remind him of typical Frenchmen, others who have the chief mental traits of German Jews; and at the same time all of them are deeply and genuinely Norwegian. We had better accept the fact that nationality is and remains a "father's house of many mansions," a prism with a thousand facets.

A student of Norwegian literature will easily subscribe to this statement, at least at the outset. Few nations have lived under more diversified natural conditions and have been able to develop their local and personal individualism more freely throughout history than have the Norwegians. And the literature of the nation is as motley as the life behind it. If there is any striking common trait, it is the rich variety of human expression, amazing in a people which has never equaled in size the populations of the large continental cities.

When the puzzle is regarded at a distance, it settles into a pattern. Most national literatures gradually develop lives of their own, standards of thinking and emotion, predominance of certain problems, tendencies in the choice of themes and the means of expression, which distinguish them from one another. The peculiarities merge into a kind of common heritage, which meets each generation at the cradle. We do not know in detail how the different historical factors work together in building up a "national literature." But the thing itself is there, in Norway as in other lands.

For the study of such traditions the freedom-law antithesis may prove to be fruitful. It would be senseless to apply it as a dogma—

there is no master key to historical problems; but it offers an important angle of view. The choice involved in these two words presents itself to man in all periods of history; and in the solution he reveals his mental structure. His life as a political and social being, his struggle for the organization of a joint existence, proceeds through incessant clashes and compromises of these principles. The antithesis is predominant in his deeper personal life as well, in the development of his intellectual and moral personality, in his attempts to fit his individual existence into the general system of duties and responsibilities under the eye of eternity. In literature, as a picture of life, this interplay has always and necessarily been one of the main themes. And literary art itself is penetrated by the contrast of the same eternal forces, the formless emotional subjectivism and the counterpoise of rational balance.

If we follow Norwegian literature in its long struggle with these problems, some general lines unforcedly reveal themselves. Many of the features can be found in other nations, especially those of the North. But in their entirety they are Norwegian, or become so, an attitude of mind which has a thousand varieties of growth, but keeps and develops its fundamental traits. It takes shape in free literary creation. It is borne out in the dauntless assimilation or repudiation of foreign values; and it is predominant in that general moral atmosphere in which a tradition alone can thrive. In the very importance of these problems to Norwegians through a period of more than a millennium a historic current reveals itself, which carries the living heritage of the nation.

VOICE of ELD: The EDDA

The dawn of Norse literature is the Edda.

This collection of old songs was found in a torn and battered Icelandic manuscript three centuries ago. Ever since their origin has been at issue; and much will probably remain obscure. Several of them may have been written in the remote outposts of Norwegian colonization, from Greenland and Iceland to the settlements in the British Isles; and not all are as old as they appear. But the bulk seem to have originated in Norway itself, some of them as early as the ninth century or before, the outgrowth of a literary development of unknown ages. And in their attitude toward life, their feeling and thought, they picture the primeval times of the nation, the beginnings of everything, when the mists of prehistory slowly roll away and the features of the tribe emerge from the darkness.

There really is an air of morning over these poems—of great migrations across virgin plains in the dewy freshness of dawn. And the first impression they make on a modern reader, trussed up in his world of income tax and ration card, is an almost indescribable feeling of freedom.

In the heroic songs of the Edda, society hardly seems to have been invented yet. We hear little of the state, practically nothing of the nation, hardly anything of the prosaic necessities of life; we move on the level of a fictitious international heroship, among "the freeborn, the highborn, the noblest of men." They play in the sunlight, while the masses disappear as a shadowy background; history making clashes of nations are concentrated into gigantic combats of individual heroes. And the will of these sovereign minds seems to be checked by few of the moral restrictions which hamper the modern Westerner. It is a poetry of passion, of grand

and somber impulses, dramatic and tempestuous in their wild
pathos.

From his birth the hero is designed and chosen for a life of his
own: "blond is his hair and bright his cheek, grim as a snake's his
glowing eyes." His is the freedom from want and fear; he knows
no dull work, has hardly any social function. His task is war, as an
end in itself, unchanging and interminable, "sword-throng, helm-
throng, the host of the king," not a combat for wealth or ideas, but
an opportunity to display fierceness of courage and grandeur of
mind. The climax of life is death, the wilder the better. The heart
is cut out of the captured warrior, and it does not tremble; "still
less did it tremble when it lay in his breast."

All feelings are equally tense and overmastering, whether in
woman or in man; friends kill friends impelled by their hateful
wives, mothers murder their children in revenge against the father.
In combat the hero meets his bride elect, a battle maid who rides
air and sea, a Valkyrie sleeping behind leaping flames, a swan
maiden bathing in the forest tarn; and their love is a sudden and
tragic passion, irresistible through life and put to triumphant test
by death. Alone young Sigrun goes to see her dead husband Helgi
in the barrow, to caress his frosty hair, "damp with the dew of
death," to give him her love as before, and stay with him till again
he has to ride "the reddened ways" under the glow of the morn.

The hereafter itself is a reflection of the heroic life. The gods are
no dull moralists, but unrestrained aristocrats like the heroes themselves. Gold-bright Valhall stands with rafters of spears and roofed
with shields, home of the warriors killed in noble action. There
they daily fight and slay each other, and wake up again in the night
to eternal talks about "weapons and might in war," till once the
battle horn shall call them for the final struggle of heaven and
earth.

There is over these Old Norse songs an atmosphere of primitive
antiquity which has always made them grip the human heart, an
air of "olden days when eagles screamed and holy streams from
heaven's crags fell," and an air of spiritual grandeur, an almost unbelievable exaltation of one group of human qualities. Again and

again this attitude has proved to be a lasting force in Norwegian life and poetry: an indomitable craving for liberty, for ruthless self-assertion and self-expansion, a feeling of the magnificence of the free individual. It is phrased with the splendor of love in Sigrun's words about her dead husband, rising above all heroes

> Like the noble stag with dew besprinkled,
> Bearing his head above all beasts,
> Horns gleaming bright to heaven itself.

Everywhere these heroes act and die against an unmistakable setting of Norse landscape, of craggy mountains and barren shores that echo the icy roar of the ocean. This landscape seems to breathe the same wildness of mind, and hardly by mere chance. One feature of the Norwegian attitude toward life is here made to live forever.

These men and women of the Edda, however, in their chilling solitude of heroism, are not as lonely as they look at first glance. They move and make decisions as lawless individuals. But in their minds they belong to a group and act "under the law," far more socially bound than the modern metropolite in his apartment house.

What they obey is no extrinsic obligation, but a moral law, a community of ethical standards, "the honor," shared by the family, the brothers-in-arms, by all great minds. To us this ideal of wild courage and merciless revenge must seem narrow and limited, hardly ethical at all. But it also has brighter traits, of generosity and faithfulness, of wrath without cruelty; and it is conceived with a deep earnestness, an almost somber feeling of responsibility. Honor is categorical and knows no exception; the hero fights and dies that the ideal may survive. Deep in his soul is the conviction that this law is more than human, that all action has its consequence, that moral guilt is followed by inescapable Nemesis. He calls it "fate."

It is not an invention of the gods; they are themselves under the doom. It is the hidden knowledge of things to come which lends somber seriousness to the Norns of destiny and surrounds Odin with his air of mysterious horror. This feeling of subjection to superhuman forces gives the heroic mind a trait of deep tragedy in the midst of the most colorful adventures: "Ever with grief and all too long are men and women born into the world." The conviction that life is deadly earnest, that there is an inescapable difference between good and evil, that the choice is ours and decisive for our whole existence, before and after death, is general in the heroic Edda; the singers sometimes change the tales of foreign origin in order to bring out this thought more strikingly. It is as if the ruthless fierceness of mind were itself creating its counterpoise, striving already toward a balance of its violent forces.

This master race idealized in the heroic songs represented only a part of real Old Norse life and its ideals. In one of the most amusing of the Eddic poems the god Rig walks through the homes of the country, describing the kind of people he finds. He begins in the anonymous underworld of society, the wrinkled and bow-legged thralls, and ends his journey with the chieftains, the care-free warriors, those "with the bright brow." But the center of his picture is occupied by those who were the center of real life: "the yeoman race," the independent farmers. Their representative is called Karl, which means "free man." He is pictured with his wife in the natural dignity of their modest wealth; and their heroism is that of everyday work: "Oxen he ruled and plows made ready, houses he built and barns he fashioned, carts he made and the plow he managed . . . they built a home."

These people also had their ideals of life, and were able to express them in poetry, in the group of didactic poems called *Songs of the High One*. Here, after the chilling heights of heroism, we suddenly breathe the atmosphere of homelike human dwellings. Many kinds of advice are thrown together in this mottled poem; and sometimes we still hear the shrill cries of the heroic eagles. All life was still close to war, on the farm as in the castle, and law an uncertain thing, in man and around him. The advice shows it: never take a walk unarmed, look carefully around before you enter a house, rise early if you would take the blood or the goods of another! To these yeomen, as much as to the professional warriors, ruthless independence was an ideal, and heroic life a part of their daydreams. But for all that, their own existence was different. They, too, had their fate to follow; but the level was not the same. What they needed, was less a gesture for death than a courage for life—real life, which had to be lived by many common men, in the companionship of necessity, under the grim conditions of barren, wintry Norway, where spring is late and the frosty nights come early. Here the romantic dreams are tempered, and new ideals grow.

We are no longer in the world of majestic passions. Again we are "under the law," not that of hero's honor, but of quiet and deliberate common sense, the wisdom of the many and for the many. The speaker throughout the poem, "the High One," is supposed to be Odin himself. But the voice we hear is that of the village sage, who knows how things have always been and always should be and speaks slowly and forcefully with the weight of common experience. His advice is varied, and touches most fields of life. But the burden is always the same: cautious moderation, sound realism, practical discretion in finding the middle way, which alone makes life livable. Be neither loquacious nor too reticent, shun quarrels, don't wear yourself out by worries, be moderately economical, reserve your judgment till you know all circumstances!

Sometimes this commonplace wisdom is slightly ridiculous: it is wise to eat something before going to a party and still wiser to leave early and go to bed! But even the tritest prose fits into a human ideal, which has its dignity and its beauty: the thoughtful and enterprising farmer, who is up early in the morning and eager to learn, courteous and sociable, balanced and self-respecting, and in all things "holds the mastery of his mind." It is brought out more clearly by frequent reference to his counterpart, the witless and unbalanced fool, who knows no moderation either in eating or in thought. It is a Norse ideal, marked by the seriousness of grim nature, which must be fought in earnest and does not tolerate any dallying. It is the same attitude of mind that made the common man leave Odin to the intellectuals and make Thor his real god and helper—the red-bearded Thor, the trusty and simple-minded toiler, always busy slaying the trolls and the giants and making life on earth tolerable.

The ceiling is often low in these poems. There is no psychological piquancy, no enthralling grandeur of feeling. The moral law is shallow. It is anchored in common judgment, not in personal conviction; it lacks active appeal, it expresses a flat utilitarianism, hardly applicable outside the circle of family, friends, and neighborhood, limited by the principle of like for like, even toward the gods. There is much of suspicion and hidden distrust in this picture of rural community life, much of vulgar egoism and blunt brutality.

But there are also everyday virtues, which can grow only in common association, and which are the first signs of a richer humanity. There is a fellowship and a solidarity different from a brotherhood-in-arms, and with its own ethics. There is nothing in the Edda about the building up of local law in Norway. But the beginning of organized society is discernible in the song of Rig; and the spirit which made organization possible, speaks through the High One. Honesty is needful if joint life shall be bearable. Hospitality is a law in the lands of the North:

> Fire he needs, who with frozen knees
> Has come from the cold without.
> Food and clothes must the farer have,
> The man from the mountains come.

And friendship is indispensable if the heart is not to chill in death, not the stern fellowship of warriors, but the solidarity of hearts which makes it possible to "mingle minds." When the High One speaks of friendship, his voice grows vibrant with feelings which have their eternal background in the circumstances of the country itself: "Care eats the heart if you cannot speak to another all your thought. Rich did I feel when a comrade I found, man is man's delight." Again and again his words here take color from the landscape: see your friend often, for "brambles grow and waving grass on the rarely trodden road!" The climax of this feeling is reached in a deep-felt verse, which seems to be a silent counterpart to the lofty ideals of the heroic Edda and a symbol of the forces growing under them:

> On the hillside drear the fir tree dies,
> All bootless its needles and bark.
> It is like a man whom no man loves,
> Why should his life be long?

"The mingling of thoughts" would not be safe except on a common ground of ideas. This sense of safety relieves the pressure and opens the mind. There is much knowledge of human nature in this poem, not mere cynical cunning for practical purposes, but real insight into the diversity of souls. It urges a cautious and deliberate judgment: "None so good is found that faults he has not, nor so wicked that he naught is worth." It makes inner values count for more than wealth or luck (at least in theory): "One man is wealthy and one is poor, yet scorn for him none should know." And it points to sober self-knowledge, far from the blind self-assertion of the hero: "You find when among the brave you fare that you may not be the boldest."

At the bottom of this attitude there is again a sound resignation in the face of the unalterable laws of the mind and of the world, not basically different from the attitude of the hero, but reduced to human proportions. Even aspects which to us seem prosaic and poor, have this deeper background. Don't stay for weeks even with your best friend; "love becomes loathing if long one sits by the hearth." Never forget to gladden him with arms and garments; "gift-givers' friendships are longest found." This is not cynicism, the human mind is like that; you cannot expect much more than you give. And life itself has the same nature: complaints are futile. He is happy who takes things as they are. Even of wisdom you need a moderate measure, which does not destroy your peace of mind. Don't try to "see your fate before you!" Quietly enjoy what is given in the moment. Everyone has something to enjoy: "The lame rides a horse, the handless is herdsman, the deaf in battle is bold"; everything is better than being dead.

This classical attitude of mind with its austere serenity is not only a refuge in grief. It is also the basis for a sound joy in life, a feeling of acquiescence within the eternal boundaries of fate: "Bravely and gladly a man shall go till the day of his death is come." Within its confined limits it gives a real sense of inner freedom, different from the heroic attitude, but hardly less sturdy, and the same feeling of personal independence, only closer to the life of the common man:

> Better a house though a hut it be,
>   A man is master at home.
> A pair of goats and a patched-up roof
>   Are better far than begging.

Even within this narrow group life has its ethical grandeur, if it is lived according to the standards of good men:

> Cattle die and kinsmen die,
>   And so dies one's self.
> One thing I know that never dies:
>   The fame of a dead man's deeds.

The "Songs of the High One" express the ideals of the Old Norse middle class; other poems of the Edda move on the heights of society. But if we fix our mind not so much on the heroes themselves as on the poets who wrote about them, we shall find even in the heroic songs many of the same traits. There is no homogeneous "Eddic" style. The authors are different in time, background, and intentions and do not speak in the same voice. But the main features of their mind are common, and so are those of their art.

There is much of wild romance in the Edda. The poet who conceived the splendor of Helgi, the pathos of Sigrun, and the somber hatred of Volund was no prosy village sage. Much he has to say is deep and difficult and cannot be told in everyday language. More than once the form is broken by waves of violence, exuberant, mysterious, and troll-like; the diction is restless and jerky, the lines entangled and distorted by passion as in the archaic ornamental style. But this is not the main impression. What the poet tries to do —even if he does not always succeed—is to master the unruly forces, bring things into form, tell them in an understandable way. In his very approach there is a soberness and closeness to life, a will to objectivity and direct, natural communication.

The Eddic poet is not singing to please himself alone. The hero may be an apotheosis of subjectivism; the poet never forgets those who listen to him. His anonymity is significant: to him as to the High One the subject is not the peculiarities of his own soul, but the great common things of life. This creates a distance between him and his work, a reserve: many are to see through his eyes and judge through his art. The hero may be whirled away by the storms of passion; the poet never is. He does not himself talk; all his emotion is in the tale, and even if his heart throbs, he views with a cool eye. That sense of "decency" that is so strong in the farm society of the common man, is here again at work in the highest poetic creation. It appears in a shyness about sexual life and all kinds of mental perversion, in a general restraint of the imagination, a striving toward reasonable explanation and motive, an ever-present feeling of moral standards, a sense of justice toward people, a love of truth woven into the very detail of fiction. Even in moments of the utmost excitement the wording usually remains concise and weighty, plain and unadorned, with the powerful expressiveness of things not spoken.

The poet has leisure to observe. The mark of his vision is not a dim, Wagnerian haze, but the striking detail of reality with all it may reveal, "a style of things, not words." This intense concentration of the view accounts for the unevenness in many of the poems. The description moves by leaps, in great flashing glimpses, always focused on the main points of emphasis, as is the rhythm of the verse; and the connection may be loose, with a chasm of mystery between. But each image grips the reader as it did the listener with an intensity at one stroke: so white were the arms of Gerd that "from their gleam shone all the sea and sky."

What interests the poet most deeply everywhere, is the soul. In these poems of combat and death there is surprisingly little of battle descriptions. What matters is not the gigantic dimensions of the deeds (as in the Irish epics), but the mind of the heroes and heroines; and the poet reveals their secrets in the sublime calm of understanding. Many of the lyrical outbursts in the Edda are virtually psychological studies of amazing penetration: the quivering cry of impatience of the loving Frey, the hateful quern song of the imprisoned giantesses grinding death and destruction for their unsuspecting master. But most often the observation creates drama; a half or more of the Eddic texts are dialogues, actually short plays. Again, the scenes may be incoherent and much is left to be filled out by the imagination. But wherever the eye is brought to rest, things and minds are visualized with almost sculptural power, in a mastery of contrast which may recall the sudden shifts of Norse climate.

The author's art in evoking a situation is matchless in old literature. Peacefully Rig wanders through the dwellings of man; and in a few stanzas the basic forms of human life are staged in full before our eyes with their material background and intellectual horizon, their powers and limitations, from the thrall couple "with flat nose and big heels" who devour their coarse bread and "whispering make their bed ready" to the earl's wife with the snow-white neck who "looks at her arms and smooths the cloth." With the same sureness the poet penetrates into the moments of extreme tension; and almost always the conflict is moral: a clash not so much of law against freedom as of law against other law. He is a part of the ethical conflict as much as his heroes, and fully shares their struggle. The more impressive is his imperturbable impartiality and the cool consistency of his analysis. This hidden complexity accounts for the terrible intensity of some of these laconic scenes, which can only be compared to Greek tragedy. Brynhild pursues Sigurd with implacable hatred because he has loved her and left her, and because she still loves him; she breaks all divine and human laws in order to reach her aim. Not with a word does the author reproach her; mercilessly one act creates the other. In one scene he has concentrated and released the almost unbearable tension, her horror and his own: Brynhild's terrific outburst of shrill laughter when she finally is told that Sigurd has been killed, a flashing glimpse of boundless misery, where aversion and disgust curiously mingle with compassion and awe before the greatness of the human soul.

There is breathing space in this art, not only for observation and analysis, but for sympathy and human feeling. Inexorably life has its will; but to understand is also to pity. The atmosphere is mostly harsh and virile; but toward the victims of fate there is a delicacy of feeling which betrays a new mental climate. Volund (the English Wayland) is captured and mutilated by a cruel king, and imprisoned on a lonely island to forge jewelry for his tormentor. In order to revenge himself he entices the king's two small sons and his young daughter Bodvild, almost a child, to visit him in the smithy, kills the boys and violates the girl; triumphantly he flies over the king's palace on wings which he has secretly forged, tells his enemy what he has done to him, and disappears. From the beginning all our interest is centered on Volund, his long years of suffering and the final triumph of just retaliation; the author never for a moment calls in question the righteousness of Volund's deed. But almost despite himself he makes the innocent victims of the revenge come to life before our eyes as well: the boys entering the forge in childish curiosity, Bodvild seeking Volund's help for her broken ring with the unsuspicious trustfulness of the unroused teens: "I dare not say it save to thee." Not with a word does the author betray any compassion. But curiously *our* feelings are divided between rejoicing and pity; and it is Bodvild's almost inaudible confession, her helpless perplexity in the face of the sudden brutality of life, which rings in our ears as the sound of Volund's wings dies away.

There is leisure for humor as well. There is much healthy laughter in the Edda, especially in the poems of the gods. Most of them were probably written in a period when the old religion was already losing its grip on men's minds. There is little of awe, still less of speculative depth: after the heroic tension of nerves the author relaxes into disrespectful drollery.

Some of these poems are masterpieces of dramatic characterization, broad and colorful in spite of their sketchy swiftness. The glib, mephistophelic Loki comes alone to the party of the gods. He holds forth only a few short minutes before the angry Thor reaches around to silence him with his hammer; but in these moments he has hit all of the divine highnesses in their tenderest and most human spots, has stripped and reduced them, and leaves gods and men in a confusion of indignation and giggle. The joke is often burlesque, and the poet is not afraid of using natural words about natural things; but almost always the witticism has a psychological point. The chef-d'oeuvre among these poems is the description of how Thor, the good-natured and naïve giant killer, had to regain his stolen hammer by going as a bride to the king of the giants disguised as the beautiful goddess of love, foaming with fury and degradation, with a veil over his rolling eyes, "with gems full broad upon his breast and a pretty cap to crown his head." It is a poem where the tight and laconic form vibrates with restrained laughter. Here is nothing of religiosity, and much of free humor, the kind which is not easily found in the thrall nor in the hero, but which is the unmistakable sign of sound superiority, of balance between the world and the spirit.

This is not the sunny harmony of the Homeric songs, where thought and expression meet and life seems to obey its own laws almost playfully. Its style reflects a struggle, between the lawless ferocity and the will to clarity and order, a tension inherent even in Norse landscape with its brooding winter mists, the coolness of summer, and the vitreous lucidity of fall. And there is no definite equipoise, any more than in life itelf. But it is a tension of abundance, not of poverty, and is fertile in promises.

These promises are complex and point in many directions. Problems which to us are a matter of course were then hardly

broached. There were many sleeping forces, open questions and
unsettled contrasts, much of freedom without law and still more of
law without real freedom.

But the issues were soon to be deepened and clarified under the
impact of foreign ideas. They are at work in the Edda itself; most
clearly they are heralded in *Voluspá* (The Wise-Woman's Prophecy), the chief work of all Old Norse poetry. This history of the
world and its doom is obviously influenced by the new religion
from the south. But a believing Norse heathen—possibly a woman
—has conceived and written it, and the forces behind it are not
borrowed.

The vision begins in majestic pictures of the creation of the
world: the dead silence over the yawning gap of Nothing, the
awe-inspiring movement of the molding forces, and the freshness
of the new-born earth, clear and glittering in the morning light.
The landscape is easily recognized: cool waves on the sand, green
grass with growing leeks, and "the sun from the south warming
the stones"; but the well-known things have an undertone of
earnest foreboding. The gods seek their seats, the world of life
originates; and with life, inevitable and threatening, comes unrest,
strife, evil. Dwarfs swarm over the earth, giants are born. The first
conflict begins; and in a crescendo of rising horror the world rushes
into the supreme destruction of total war:

> Brothers shall fight and fell each other
> And sisters' sons shall kinship stain.
> Hard 'tis on earth with mighty whoredom,
> Axe-time, sword-time, shields are sundered,
> Wind-time, wolf-time, ere the world falls,—

till the sun blackens, the stars are whirled from heaven, and the
earth sinks with gods and men in a flaming ocean of chaos and
despair.

But this is no longer the play of a blind destiny, whose purposes
are forever inaccessible to us. The Norns are still "setting the
fate" for gods and men; but the sibyl's voice has a growing ring
of deeper wisdom: "Would you know yet more?" With increas-

ing clarity the collapse of the world takes on a tone of ethical judgment, serious and inescapable. The marshaling of destructive forces to the battle of all against all, the total moral confusion symbolized by Loki, "the lover of ill who fills the air with venom," are not simply a negation of the old and narrow principles of honor and decency; there is a violation of deeper laws. Questions are raised which have not before been put into words; new light is thrown on the ideals of olden times, foreshadowing the self-destruction of the heroic world with its lawless presumption. The forces of good which are gathered against it, symbolized by Balder, "the white God" with his curious lack of warriors' virtues, are equally far beyond the one-sided standards of the heroes and the selfish rural utilitarianism. To the exalted eyes of the seeress the history of the world turns into a clash between universal ethical forces, not anchored any more in the family or the social group alone, but in life itself.

When the earth again emerges from the waves, it is a new world, morally reborn. Broken is the arbitrary rule of the individual gods. "The High and Mighty" comes to sit in judgment and hold all power everywhere; and his realm is not that of everlasting combat, but of justice and peace. There are southern influences, both political and religious, behind these dreams; and they point far into the future. But the soil is prepared for them and minds are opened by the forces which are obvious in the Edda itself: that serious conception of life, that deep feeling of responsibility which in *Voluspá* is conceived as the law of the world.

The poet has no feeling of introducing anything strange and alien. In the wonderful concluding lines he returns as a matter of course to the landscape of his own country, fresh and cool in the morning sun; and his new experience transfuses it with a deep and almost Hellenic serenity after the misty chaos of disorder:

> Now do I see the world anew
> Rise all green from the waves again;
> The cataracts fall, the eagle flies,
> And fish he catches beneath the cliffs.

VOICE of ELD

Then in the grass the tablets of gold,
The far-famed ones, will again be found
Which they had owned in the days of old.
On unsown acres the ears will grow.

KINGS and POETS

When the god Rig in the Edda has finished his walk through the ranks of Old Norse society, the world of the thralls, the farmers, and the rulers, he gives his poem a significant climax. To the earl is born a son "more crafty and wise" who is no longer contented by being a chieftain; a greater future is prophesied for him. Here the poem breaks off; but the name of the hero indicates what is in store: he is called *Konungr*, king.

It has been suggested that this song of Rig is a discreet homage to King Harold Fairhair, who toward the end of the ninth century managed to weld the militant provinces and social groups of Norway into one realm. The allusion would be natural. Few events in Norwegian life have been more momentous; and through many centuries the kingdom became the center of literary creation.

The very unification must have made an overwhelming impression, actually the first common experience of the tribe; and the strong personality of the founder, the splendor of the new monarchy, and its background of European ideas soon made the royal court the focus of intellectual endeavor. In Norway as elsewhere the new form of life called forth a new kind of literary activity, different from the anonymous lays of gods and heroes: a personal and professional court poetry, created according to the law of supply and demand.

The new kingdom needed poets, for propaganda and entertainment; the singer became the servant of the monarch and his aims, totally dependent upon the royal favor. If he was accepted as a *skald*, and his continued work lived up to expectations, he often gained a brilliant position. Proudly the skalds describe their splendor: "You can see by our garments and golden rings that we are friends of the king; we have red fur cloaks with pretty stripes, swords rounded with silver, shirts of linked mail, gilded shoulder

straps, chiseled helmets, rings on our arms which Harold gave us."
They sit in the High Seat opposite the ruler himself; often they are
admitted to his council as influential advisers. But everything de-
pends upon keeping the king's attention and remaining in his good
graces; their position is uncertain and can be challenged any time.
There are rival skalds; there is even the low competition of the buf-
foons with their earless dogs and nonsensical talk, "miserable twad-
dlers who ought to be kicked behind," but who nevertheless "manage to make the king laugh."

Poetry created under such circumstances may easily stoop to
disgraceful bootlicking. In Norway, too, the work of the skald
was often a delicate task; but in general his poetry remained the
expression of a free man.

His personal behavior before the king had little of obsequious-
ness. Most of the Norwegian rulers were connoisseurs of verse, and
some were even poets in their own right; from the hand of the
first King Harold we have a somber verse about his deceased
Finnish mistress. This common craftsmanship made the king feel
somewhat like a colleague toward his poets; but the main thing
was their own sturdy feeling of self-respect. The skalds maintained their license of tongue at court; and as a rule the kings
tolerated even severe reproach ("especially when they were in
good humor," adds one skald). The poet never sold his art. He de-
served a decent reward; but if he praised his master it was a
voluntary gift.

Once accepted, however, he was faithful unto death. The plain
speaking of the skalds, their numerous and dangerous efforts as
peacemakers at court, are proofs of their sincere loyalty. Again
and again skalds refused to sing of a foreign king if the homage
might seem a disloyalty to their own master, even though refusal
was hazardous. When the Icelandic skald Bersi had been captured
by his enemy—the Norwegian king, Olaf—and was allowed to
sing before him in order to mollify his anger, he began by reciting
a poem to his former protector, Olaf's mortal foe, the Danish king
Svein: "Never I followed into battle a more brilliant fighter. I am
no cringer to forget my old friends and benefactors." This daunt-

less instinct of liberty speaks in their songs as well as in their deeds.

What the king expected from his appointed poet was a chronicle of his royal achievements, especially his warlike feats, a most natural desire in times when written records were rare. Most of the skaldic poems are therefore a kind of military biography in verse. The subject is a limited one, and only the best skalds managed to make it very entertaining. Skaldic poetry was no personal art, even though the poets wrote under their own names and were jealously proud of their work. The technique early stiffened into convention, a skill which could and must be learned. They tell us over and over of how the mighty king piled up corpses, crimsoned the swords, satisfied the wolves, fed the ravens, and gave the eagle its brown drink, clichés without much observation behind them; and they enrich their verse with a peculiar kind of intricate metaphors which is far from the main stream of Norse tradition. Even in his poetry the poet wore his coat of mail.

This conventionality makes many skaldic songs rather unpalatable to us. But they have other virtues. They represent the first attempt to approach actual events of the present; and behind the artificial form there is much concern about facts, much sound moderation and sobriety of mind. Truth meant something to the skalds. Partly it was a virtue of necessity: they wrote under the eyes of the king, who himself had fought the battles they sang. But truth was their own ideal as well, as is apparent in their picture of the hero. There is, of course, much talk of the king's gallantry in combat, his contempt for death, and his splendid generosity toward the faithful skald. But apart from these invariable formulas (which were probably more or less applicable to most Old Norse kings), there is little smirking and adulation. The skald seldom distorts his facts willfully. He keeps his sober objectivity even when he talks about the king's enemies. Rarely does he praise his master by vilifying his adversaries; more frequently he displays understanding, even a sad compassion for their fate.

The pompous songs of homage were the test pieces of the royal skalds. But in the retinue of the Norse kings, poetry was part of the daily fare; a good skald was expected to improvise at any moment, lending prestige or humor to the trifles of everyday life. Walking in the ship yards of Bergen, King Eystein saw a vessel stand proudly out of the fjord with swelling sails. "Is there any skald here?" he shouted; there was, and he had his stanza ready about the splendid sight. Such detached stanzas and epigrams we have by the hundreds; they show what lived under the armor of literary technique. In these unstudied fragments we meet again the swift pictorial power of the Edda and the same closeness to life and landscape, bright mornings when "the sunny mountains shine over the sea," stormy nights when "the prow breaks the clouds and the flaming waves hit the moon." "I was no lazy dog when I pulled this one over the gunnel" reads a verse carved in runes on the fragment of an oar, "and red and sore it made my hands too!" This freshness may even break through the literary convention of the songs of homage, because they are born of genuine feeling. And in the best of these poems there is something more than praise of Viking virtues: an awakening understanding of the deeper significance of the Norwegian kingdom.

With Harold Fairhair, the founder of the dynasty, fought and sang Thorbjørn Hornklovi. The exultation of victory still shouts in his poems, albeit with much grim humor. From the east came the longships with their gaping dragon heads, seeking battle, and soon the victory was ours: "The wounded tumbled under the seats, their rears up and their noses to the keel; in furious haste they scuttled over the shore, shields flashing on their backs, we pounded them with stones—they longed to get back to their mead drinking." His picture of the victorious Harold follows closely the familiar style. But the poet is already seeing in him the ruler of a nation, "Lord of the Norsemen"; and vaguely he also regards him as the upholder of national peace, the executive power behind the law, the enemy of "mischief-makers and thieves." The European idea of monarchy is here suggested, the king as "the people's friend," representative of a national system of law-bound liberty, an idea which was gradually to transform the private usurper of royal power into an exponent of the community.

In a more personal way the same ideas were expressed by Ey-

vind, court poet of King Hákon the Good, who in 961 was killed
in battle against pretenders backed by the Danes. Eyvind was himself an attractive personality, independent and faithful; he "never
played with two shields." His poem about the last battle of Hákon
is a masterpiece, a splendid picture of "the cheerful warrior under
the golden helmet" who had a jesting word for each of his men,
the national ruler who fought the Danes and "defended his country." But the highest praise is given by implication in the last
stanza, where the peacetime reign of the good monarch is pictured
by a hint of what came after him, in words which significantly
echo the ethical earnestness of the High One:

> Cattle die and kinsmen die,
> Laid waste are people and land.
> Since Hákon went to the heathen gods
> Enslaved is many a man.

Toward the end of the tenth century skaldic poetry was taken
over by the Icelanders. Verse making became a kind of national
livelihood on the island; for centuries poetry was "its only article
of export." All these Icelandic poets wrote in the common Old
Norse, and carried on the poetical traditions created in the home
country. Nevertheless, they are more properly included under Icelandic literature.

Throughout the Old Norse period, however, the court of the
Norse kings remained the chief forum of the skalds; and there
were Norwegian poets throughout, even though most of the later
ones left only epigrams. They maintained a national tradition in
their literary technique, different from the subtle art of the professionals; they were akin to the Edda and used a simpler language.
The members of the royal family continued to be active as poets.
The love songs of Saint Olaf quiver with a very earthly passion;
that unhappy and engaging pretender Sigurd Slembe coined an
Edda-like stanza about his life in exile, which reveals his character
in one sentence: "Man was the joy of man, there as everywhere."

KINGS and POETS

It is a literature with the wide horizon of warriors and seafarers. The verse of Harold Hardrada, king, poet, and experienced critic, is a running commentary on his tumultuous life, ranging from princesses in Russia and summer sailings below Sicily to the fateful morn of battle at Stanford Bridge. Young King Magnus Bareleg sighs forth his love to a hard-hearted beauty in Dublin; Earl Ragnvald of Orkney sings of Viscountess Ermengard of Narbonne, a lady wise in conversation and "with silky hair over her shoulders."

The political influence of the skalds was bound to decrease with the growth of the royal power. Most of the professional battle singers had little to say about the deeper constructive aims of the monarchy; their narrowness gradually isolated them, and other branches of literature took the lead. But there was one skald who made his most personal contribution in this very field, Sigvat Thordson (995–1045). He was born in Iceland, but went to Norway at eighteen and never returned to his native island except for one short visit. He was closely attached to King Olaf the Saint and his work of unification, and he was himself one of the noblest expressions of that process of national coalescence which was the achievement of the great king.

There are few skalds we know better than Sigvat. He was never economical of his verse—youthful Viking songs from the years when he went west and saw the world, recollections of travels as a royal envoy, poems of homage from his manhood at the court, besides numerous epigrams. The man behind the poetry is deeply attractive. He was no poet of passion: "Death for love is not worth while." But he had charm: an almost southern vivacity, a sparkling power of observation, and a genial humor, gentle and amiable; there is no poet he more recalls than Horace. The reader can actually see him, with his black hair and his "black Icelandic eyes—people pay attention to them!" He was a man of the world; his cheerful delight in life was receptive to everything and threw a luster over whatever he met. In his "Poems of East-faring"— composed on his mission as special envoy to Sweden at the age of twenty-one—he exuberantly makes verse about all that happens.

The ferry over the boundary river was dreadful, the march through the endless forests gave him two sore feet, the heathen farmers denied him shelter for the night and "I told the trolls to take them"; but splendid was the sweep through the sounds, and joyous the evening of arrival, when the hungry horses trotted through the village in the dusk and beautiful ladies peered out after the clouds of dust.

But he is no vulgar sybarite; his graciousness is not a disguise for fatuity. He has deep feelings: a strong sense of justice, an openness to friendship, manly courage, and a kind heart. And everything in him is controlled by a sound, equable poise which we have met before, and which never becomes trivial because of the tension behind it. In all his dealings he has a dignified composure, a free and noble self-respect; he is independent because it is a matter of course to him; he is peaceable because he does not need to assert himself. He can afford to understand life, and smile at it, because of his own quiet self-reliance. His attitude of mind is reflected in his style: "I always speak clearly." Again he follows the tradition of simplicity; he is a Norse humanist to the backbone, A. D. 1000.

The predominant relationship of his life was that with King Olaf; and it shows the whole man. He was well fitted to be a collaborator in the civilizing work of his master. He had much of the same background and had shared in good part the king's experiences; loan words in his language reveal his Western affiliations. His intelligence and consideration gave him a swift rise. As a young man he was appointed the king's marshal, and in the course of his life he was engaged in many fields of government; he reminds the king of his duty to give "a law valid for all citizens of the realm." But the foundation of all was the sincere friendship of these two men. Fidelity was obvious to Sigvat; "One master at a time is a decent rule" he answered the Danish king when he was summoned to his service. But total liberty of mind was equally a matter of course. When Olaf's enemy, the mighty Erling Skjalgson, was killed in battle against his king, the skald undauntedly

sang the praises of the dead chieftain: "I did not join in the drinking party the day his death was announced. I bowed my head in
grief. There never was and never will be on the earth amidst the
roaring seas a more courageous warrior." He speaks to the monarch as an equal: "You have a faithful servant, I a good master. We
are both lucky men!" He never suppresses his sober judgment.
Even when he writes about the bloody end of the beloved king, he
tries to understand: "I do not reproach either of the parties."

Against this background his complaint over his dead friend
takes on an undertone of deep personal sincerity: "Suddenly I left
the games of my comrades. I remembered how often he and I had
played together before." Sigvat received the news on returning
from a pilgrimage to Rome; he words his grief in one image, great
and clear as those of the Edda: "The high cliffs of Norway seemed
to smile at me everywhere while Olaf lived. Now the green mountain slopes are less kindly to me than before."

He does not speak much of politics in his songs. But his principal poem, "The Plain Speaker's Lay," reveals how intimately his
personal relationship to the king has been founded on Olaf's basic
ideas. Here, after all trivial praise in the songs of homage, he shows
in a glimpse what the fallen saint really stood for.

When Olaf's young son Magnus had been called back by the
repentant Norwegians, only five years after the violent death of
the king, he began to persecute the adversaries of his father so
vehemently that soon the people grumbled and began to doubt the
wisdom of their own decision. The friends of the young monarch
asked Sigvat to tell him the truth. He did so, in a poem which is a
masterpiece of considerate frankness. He begins by reminding the
king of the history of his forefathers; and in a swift outline he
sums up what had become the core of Norwegian kingship: justice, peace, and equality before the law. This is the heritage which
Magnus now betrays by his arbitrary violence; and his people are
not going to acquiesce. Take care when the peasants grow reticent
and hide their noses in their cloaks: then it is time to change your
course! "Let poor and rich enjoy your laws, *sinjór* (seigneur) of

KINGS and POETS

Norway," if you will again rule in happiness the realm of your
fathers! In this poem, which really succeeded in changing the
policies of the king, Sigvat gave a noble evidence of his own character, and the first poetic program for the Norse state of justice.

The SAGAS

The king looms high in the songs of the court poets. But the real monument of the forces at work in Old Norse society was erected by the historians. More than anyone else they incorporated the ideas of the new era into the living traditions of the nation.

From time immemorial story telling was a beloved art among the Norse tribes. From generation to generation through the Middle Ages runs an undercurrent of oral traditions, matchless both in quantity and form. In a lawsuit in eastern Norway around 1270 an assembly of jurors gave an account of the pedigree of the leading family of the valley through almost three centuries; and this was no extraordinary performance. For special reasons, however, Iceland became the storehouse of the tradition; in the lonely, subarctic island the art of popular story telling developed to a degree which has no parallel in Europe. This special gift of the Icelanders created the pride of their literature, the family sagas.

In general outlook these tales are strictly Icelandic. They depict a society different from contemporary Norway, that of a recently settled island, loosely organized. Without a king or an executive authority, without a strong clergy or a centralizing town life, it becomes split up into countless conflicting groups. The sagas tell the story of the local chieftains, their endless fights and lawsuits over honor, wealth, and women, their caricature of freedom. Their ideals are totally heathen—the morbid susceptibility in matters of personal honor, the legalistic passion for justice, the merciless revenge. Often these tales echo a belated continuation of the spirit of the Edda with a special flavor of their own, a picture of Norse society without the organizing power of government.

Still, in many ways, Norwegians recognize themselves in the sagas. Norse farm life on both sides of the sea always had fundamental traits in common; the Icelanders depict them in a fullness unmatched by any other source. The art with which the sagas were told became a living force in the homeland. In fundamental traits they carry on the style of the Edda. The saga man, too, was talking before a group, judging with their standards and hiding himself behind events. His aim, too, was truthful and direct communication, close to the spoken word, and his main interest the psychological analysis, the revelation of dramatic episodes which struck the imagination. Only the level was lower, closer to everyday life, and the style more homogeneous. We discover again the world of the High One, not that of the heroes; the voice we listen to is clear and forceful, concise and austere, matter of fact on the side of understatement, without much mysterious undertone, but with a mighty power of suggestion. It is an art where actually "the form merges with the content," a classical style, grown naturally from its own home soil. Nothing could be further from the foggy turbidity which modern ideologists have proclaimed as "Nordic"; in its vigorous simplicity it has often and rightly been compared to that of Homer.

The family sagas remain nevertheless a local Icelandic creation; they were unknown even in Norway throughout the Middle Ages. But from them another literary creation grew, the sagas of the Norwegian kings, which became an integrating part of Norway's own traditions and of the very life of the nation.

The Icelandic saga men gathered information not only about happenings on their own island, but just as much about events in the mother country. The traffic back and forth was constant and everyone who "came out" (that is, to Iceland) had something to tell. These traditions early began to cluster into rounded sagas about the individual kings, in the manner of the family tales and in their style. They were told principally for the pleasure and entertainment of the Icelanders. But the Norwegian rulers were no less interested in the story of themselves and their royal house and early began to encourage the saga tellers. Again the demand created the supply. The skaldic songs of war were short and could not be repeated indefinitely. In order to keep their position, the Icelanders at court needed something which would last regularly through the long and tedious winter evenings in the hall. Nothing could serve their purpose better than the story of the Norwegian kings themselves; and they early developed an astounding repertoire. A young Icelander who came to the court of King Harold Hardrada in the middle of the eleventh century spent the evenings of an entire autumn telling about Harold's ancestors, one saga after another. Finally, after some understandable hesitation, he entered upon the king's own saga; it lasted through the full two weeks of Christmas, and everyone was amazed at the accuracy of his information.

Soon the recording of the past became something more than a pastime. When, toward the end of the twelfth century, these sagas were written down, the Norwegian kings gave the direct impulse, as did many of the great rulers in other European countries. In the thirteenth century, they again and again had Icelanders write the story of their own reigns. Of Sverrir, the most important ruler of them all, it is explicitly said that he "sat by and told what should be written," giving the official version of his own history and making the past an instrument of his policy. For the saga of King Hákon Hákonson the royal archives were opened to the author.

The interest of the saga men naturally was focused on the personality of the kings, their virtues and vices, victories and defeats. Usually they did not trouble themselves with the deeper moving forces of history; and the artistic quality of their work varies, as does their reliability. But the general trend is one of sober objectivity, as in the family sagas: unbiased search for truth, keen interest in psychological motivation, and a clear, forceful, oral style, genuinely Norse in character. Thus they pave the way and prepare the materials for the great national historian, who was something more than a good story teller and who welded all the scattered information into a framework of great ideas.

Snorri Sturluson was an Icelander, one of the great chieftains of his age. Throughout his whole dramatic career he was a leading figure in the wild family feuds which finally brought about the union of Iceland with Norway, not without the obliging assistance

of Snorri himself. He enjoyed this life fully, as a passionate player
of the game—a Renaissance type, who loved power and women,
honor and gold (all of which he got in abundance), a shrewd and
ruthless maker of intrigues, not too squeamish about his methods.
And when the game was up he duly paid the stakes, being killed
by one of his own relatives and rivals while hiding on his farm in a
frosty September night of the year 1241; he was sixty-three years
old.

But behind this career of blood and intrigue there lived an
artist's temperament, with the eternal marks of the artist: complexity and sensibility. He was no ruthless molder of life; he was
subjected to it. In every moment of waking existence his eye regis-
tered and his brain attempted to understand, not by choice but
spontaneously, not one thing alone but the entire picture, not one
side of a character but the whole motley pattern of personality.
This desire for comprehension reflected his own tangled nature,
the struggle of disparate forces in himself, where brutal calcula-
tion curiously mingled with tenderness and pity. It made him unstable in decisions, hesitant, and susceptible to influence; he never
had that power of simplification which belongs to the successful
politician. But at the same time it gave him the wide range of
understanding, of recognition and compassion, which made him
one of the great chroniclers of human life. It is by this amazing
power of impersonation that Snorri, the Icelander, became the
founder of Norwegian historiography and a molder of the nation's future.

He was born in one of the centers of Icelandic story telling and
garnered in his infallible memory the traditions of centuries; he
had himself come to know Norway intimately, and had played a
part in its contemporary politics. In scope, his work therefore
widely surpassed that of other saga writers: it was a complete
history of the Norwegian realm, from the misty origins of the
royal house down to Snorri's own times.

But still more it surpassed them in the art with which it was
told. Quietly Snorri proceeded from episode to episode, drawing
freely on the work of his predecessors; his technique as well was

based on that of the early royal sagas. But all of it was recast by his own forceful personality. Again, as in the Edda, the tale moves in sudden, dramatic glimpses, striking the eye almost with the power of personal experience; and again the mark of the author is his intellectual honesty and his masterful grasp of the human mind. Snorri can reveal a character through a single movement, a single remark; he can play two personalities against each other in a glitter of facets, and build a king's saga of hundreds of pages into a careful monograph of a soul. Throughout, his own sensitive mind vibrates behind the words, but only behind them. The hallmark of his style is quiet lucidity, impartial and sober, a subdued force which is the secret of all classical art and the secret as well of his psychological mastery. If the character of Saint Olaf becomes the obvious center of Snorri's work, it is not only because of the space Snorri devotes to this king but still more because of the cool objectivity with which the author slowly and deliberately reveals the mind of his hero, his grandeur and his very human limitations, till the sturdy man himself strides forth from the page with his red beard and his stubborn neck and lives before our very eyes.

But all Snorri's mastery of analysis and description is made to serve a higher purpose. When we read his work, we soon feel that our guide is a man who knows, a man of the world, no peasant and home bird; and gently, but decidedly, he is leading us in one direction. It was his own artistic temperament which showed him the way. He, the Icelander, began to write the history of Norway, which was decidedly not his country; but the subject captured and enthralled him. As he wrote, fascinated and driven on by his own understanding, he gradually grew to identify himself with the nation he was writing about and to grasp, not only the personality of her kings, but the ideas of her history.

He became a Norwegian patriot as he wrote. The history of Norway in the early Middle Ages was a continuous struggle for national independence and unity against foreign invaders; Snorri sided with the Norsemen. Again and again he expressed a national pride; he made his heroes belittle the neighboring nations, he pictured the foreigners as awe-struck by Norway's grandeur. As a matter of course, the kings thus became the center of his work, the defenders of the nation, the advocates of national organization. And slowly through his tale we are made to share the deeper importance of their kingdom as well, their role as upholders of a state of law and righteousness, closely connected with the Christian church. The turning point of Snorri's work is the battle of Stiklestad. Not only did it prove to be the end of the period of invasions and the beginning of secure national freedom, it also meant the establishment of the new politico-religious reign of peace and justice where, according to an old pious text, "the rich do not plunder those who live in poverty." What Sigvat vaguely pointed out to his contemporaries: the development of the kingship from arrogated power to the authority of law, is here made the red thread of a broad and documented analysis of three centuries of national history.

But the power of his dramatic imagination compelled Snorri to depict the opposing forces as well. He knew no "democracy" in the modern sense, nor did his times. All through the Middle Ages "liberty" predominantly meant liberty for the few. When it came to the test, Snorri's viewpoint was decidedly that of the chieftain, without too much respect for the "tanglebearded" farmers; history and life he regarded from the heights of power. But again his subject captured him. In Snorri's eyes the history of the Norwegian state had been a protracted struggle between the kings and the chieftains of his own class. It is possible that here, unconsciously, he projected the problems of his own times into the past. To himself the interpretation was obvious; and it filled his work with dramatic force. Behind the local rulers fighting the authority of state he saw the indomitable will to freedom and individual expansion which was still the unchallenged power in his own island. Again and again he showed how the chieftains rose in revolt against the organizing power, till gradually their forces were led into the channels of social order; and he depicted them with broad sympathy, sometimes almost with love. His understanding led him to transcend his social limitations: again and again he showed how the very people, the uncombed common man himself, arose in wrath or enthusiasm to support a good king or wipe out an offender of his rights. In Snorri's long line of characters the kings liberally mingled with their opponents in the bright sunshine of his description—from the rugged peasant leader Asbjørn, who spoke against the ruler in the *thing*, imbedded in his social group like a rock in the soil, to the luckless and gallant chieftain Erling Skjalgson, a freeborn gentleman to the bitter end. In this historical drama, conceived with the fullness of life itself, Snorri grasped the theme of the future. In the clash of social groups of his own age he outlined the forces which, through slow widening of the foundations, were to create through centuries the modern Norwegian people's state.

The influence of his work has been immeasurable. With only brief interruptions, the Royal Sagas have been in the hands of Norwegian readers ever since they were written, and have imbued them with Snorri's ideas. He was the first magnificent expression of the nation's self-assertion, of its pride and its will to exist. In unforgettable pictures he called to life its obstinate desire for individual freedom, for political and social independence; and with equal vividness he depicted the ideals of unity and order which were to bend stubborn wills into coöperation. In his plain and forceful prose he even modeled the ideals of Norwegian style. He formed the nation's conception of its past, and to a great extent its dreams of the future. When the Norsemen six centuries after Snorri awoke to a new age with deepened ideas and problems of freedom, they could largely express their aspirations in his words. No literary personality of the Middle Ages has so deeply influenced the future life of the nation.

The SUN from the SOUTH

Behind these political and social powers, however, and sheltered by them, other forces were at work. They are only vaguely indicated by the court poets, and even in Snorri they play no predominant part. But they were gradually to change the general attitude toward life more deeply than anything else: the ideas of Christianity, not as an organizing power within the state, but as a transforming force in human souls.

The kings introduced the new religion in Norway and assured its victory. Their soldiers protected the British missionaries and liquidated the most obstinate objectors; their authority stabilized the church, by common law of God and king and to their mutual advantage. At Stiklestad Saint Olaf's men went into combat with the battle cry "Kingsmen, crossmen!" and his martyr death brought kingdom and church permanently together. In spite of their fights and rivalries, they worked along parallel lines toward the pacification and civilization of the country. But the fundamental aims of the church were different; in spirit it was not of this world. Within the political framework deeper and purely personal problems arose almost immediately, problems which have their center of gravity in the conflict of law and freedom within the individual. While the church was still fighting for its existence, this spiritual influence was bound to be weak. The missionaries had to be content with minimum results, mass conversions, and formal adherence to extrinsic rules. But as soon as the church had passed the missionary stage and gained time for work on the home front, it became clear, and increasingly so, how much more was implied in its principles.

The deities of the Edda were puppets in the hands of a blind destiny. They were just enlargements of the common man with all his petty passions, often slightly ridiculous, and most of them void of ethical idealism. The advice they gave was only too human and did not bind anyone; even at its height their moral system was a group standard, strictly limited both in range and obligations. Instead, the Christian church pointed to God the Almighty and his sacred universal law, common to all beings as far as civilized men lived. This law, overwhelming in authority, was unlimited in subject. The Christian world was split in irremediable dualism of good and evil, virtue and sin, down to the very trifles of existence; every feature of life had its ethical importance and was a matter of moral choice. And in this lifelong struggle of the high and the low the individual was isolated in a way unheard of before. Even the Eddic hero felt and acted as a member of a class, a family, a brotherhood-in-arms. The Christian did not make his choice as one of a group; he faced his responsibility alone, in terrifying personal freedom of decision, with his conscience as the only measure. Finally, Christianity gave this liberty a new meaning because it gave life itself a new significance. The aim of human existence was not cunning individual self-assertion, but a voluntary giving up of everything into God's hands, in humility, repentance, and self-sacrifice, symbolized in Christ. But whoever thus lost everything by the law, regained everything under the law, in a new, reborn freedom beyond human understanding. In these ideas, regardless of dogmatic difference of detail, was embodied the program of a radical change of human outlook, an immeasurable deepening of the problems of the individuals, and a new direction of their joint life.

In medieval Christianity these principles were rarely grasped in their full significance, except by the heretics. From the very beginning the church maintained its authority over the individual conscience, breaking the edge of freedom in favor of the law; and even the reduced requirements were never made active in all fields of life. It would seem unreasonable to expect more in a recently converted borderland like Norway. But even there the beginnings are clearly to be seen, and the results are sometimes surprising. Resistance was bound to be violent and penetration slow. But there is no question of the old tradition being overwhelmed by force, except in the very beginning. Modern theorists have maintained that the conversion of the Teutonic tribes meant an introduction of basically foreign elements which could never be absorbed by the organism; such theories are not supported by facts. The principles of Christianity have been strange to all nations, even to the people in which they originated, because in their ideal purity they exceed the possibilities of human strength; and obviously the new creed denied some of the basic conceptions of Old Norse life. Nevertheless it soon took root; in its main intent it did not mean a destructive break, but a pointing out of new aims to existing ethical forces, which in *Voluspá* had sought direct contact with Christian thought. The solutions were new, the problems old.

This development was not mainly expressed in books, but in life: in the gradual humanizing of the minds, the tempering of manners, the refinement of the conception of mutual obligations, as it was symbolized in the contemporary development of law. But the expression was most individual and direct in literature. Icelanders and Norwegians shared the field here; the homeland was strong in devotional prose, Iceland in religious poetry. But the differences count far less than elsewhere: the basic feeling was common. The Icelandic author of *The Lily* was a Norwegian monk; an Icelandic poet recited his *Beam of Light* before the brother kings of Norway in the Christ Cathedral of Nidaros as a member of the same universal and national church.

First of all the old ties had to be loosened; and sometimes it happened that the development did not go beyond this. Quite a few Norsemen in the transition period confessed that the only thing they believed in was their "own power and ability"—a morbid brand of individualism. But the profounder minds are early seen to be struggling with the problems of moral freedom raised by the new creed. They cut through the extrinsic demands, the "system of deeds"; they are out for the real thing.

The basic issue to these generations was bound to be the principles of manly honor which were idealized in the martial heroes of the past and symbolized in the system of personal revenge. Many men of the age could have subscribed to the words of an Icelandic

woman: "The Gospels are little fun; there is no fighting in them."
The church was slow to challenge these warlike conceptions, and
preferred to adapt itself to the primitive sense of justice behind
them. In an Icelandic family saga God himself temporarily re-
stores his sight to a blind man in order to enable him to kill his
father's slayer. But higher ideas were at work on their minds from
the very beginning; it can be followed in the titles attributed to
the Heavenly Majesty. What most appealed to these bellicose
souls were such names as "the Mighty Ruler," "the powerful King
of Rome"; even in religion they regarded themselves as warriors,
with the limited obligations of the soldier. But there are also other
appellations: "Christ the Pure," even "the King of Mercy." In such
names, more or less clearly, lives the idea of a common moral law
of paradoxical absoluteness, which not only exceeds the accepted
ideals of practical wisdom, but sometimes even runs counter to
them.

The poets exhibited this conflict most strikingly because they
still worked with the old poetical forms, in a language resounding
of combats and heroic deeds. The contrast did not always reach the
surface, but its presence is felt as a vague uncertainty, as an uneasy
questioning about the value of the old ideals. Earl Ragnvald, hero
of battles and gallant adventures, stands a pilgrim before Jerusalem,
cross on chest and palm branch on shoulder, overwhelmed by new
feelings: "Here all strife should die away!" The religious poets
look the contrast in the face. Ruthless courage had been the chief
mark of a freeborn and noble personality; but now a poet can
sing: "Afraid is the man of evil deeds, the righteous are unafraid."
In the teaching of the High One, the ethical approach is narrowly
pragmatic: unbridled desires are to be condemned, but only because they are foolish. To the new poets they are sin. We can
measure the distance from the Edda in a religious poem from the
thirteenth century. It chooses for its hero a man of patient and
unrevenged suffering; here certainly "the sun from the south has
warmed the stones" and opened new horizons to the liberty of
choice.

These are glimpses only. A thorough realization of such ideas would have meant a revolution and revaluation for which few were prepared. There are instances of revolt against accepted standards: "It is a sign that your work is *not* well done if it corresponds to the deeds or opinion of the majority." But such traits are not typical. The main feature of Old Norse Christianity is a feeling of fellowship, which makes the new religion a livable dwelling for human beings. Undoubtedly it is based on a compromise; the explosive force of revolution is dampened down. But something was given instead: new bonds to replace those broken, equally strong and less narrow, a milder mental climate where the new ideas could grow, and where some of the essentials found shelter from the very beginning.

To the medieval Christian the whole civilized world was one great home, where the churches everywhere taught the same simple and sublime lessons in words and sculpture and offered the same cordial welcome to everybody. The crusader from the north joined in a common enterprise of all good men, the pious pilgrim shared the spiritual values of the whole world. And what began as a community of law, developed into a community of love, which became one of the moving forces in medieval life. To the Eddic man, freedom is his own personal privilege; at most, it extends to his closest associates. The Christian feeling of community involves the idea of freedom as a common good, to be shared voluntarily with others. The religious poets always have this fellowship in mind, even if they still fail to grasp its political and social implications. "May my poem serve as a blessing to ourselves and to all those who remember us in their prayers": behind the mountain walls we see the lights of a friendly world with good will and mutual responsibility. Some of these invocations certainly have not become obsolete in our age. "Let us pray, good brothers and sisters, to God the Almighty," says an Icelandic homily, "that He may free the world from its errors, arouse those stricken by disease, feed those who are starving, open the prisons, unbind those who are in fetters, give homefaring to those in exile, good harbor to those at sea, and healing to those who are wounded."

Of course this is "foreign"; but it is being assimilated. Again the style reveals the structure. There is little in Norse Christianity of ecstatic emotion, and much of deep, simple feeling; such is the language in which it is expressed. The Norse legend is less wildly fantastic than its southern patterns, more subdued and restrained. The edifying literature is closer to life, even in its pictures of Heaven and Hell, near to the everyday existence of the common people for which it was written, as plain and straightforward almost as the saga. The poets, many of them, return to the austere Eddic tradition, cleansed of its entangled heathen decorations, welding their new wisdom into the lucid, majestic forms of the past: "Each man harvests the fruit of his deeds; happy he who does the good." One of the poets again adapts the old image of the hero, imbued with a new meaning: Christ is "the stag of the sun, his feet on earth, his horns reaching toward Heaven."

For much of this we must rely mainly on authors who themselves, professionally, belonged to the church. But scattered information is to be found everywhere; and one of the most important witnesses is again Snorri. He must have been a lukewarm Christian himself; his reference to the pious words and deeds of his heroes may seem rather conventional. But in one essential point, his portrait of the sainted King Olaf, the hinge on which his whole work turns, it is different: again he is carried away by his psychological imagination and his feeling for leading ideas. He wrote in an age when Olaf's role began to be established; the sources at hand were a mixture of history and pious legend. Snorri combines them, making the political growth of the final unifier of the realm simultaneously a history of the growth of a Christian character. He openly depicts Olaf's irascibility and brutality, his lack of self-mastery, all the unbridled forces of lawlessness that were in him. Against this background he describes his fight against the forces of wildness, those in himself as much as those around him, and shows how the reverses and the years of disaster change and purify him, turn him to humility and self-chastising, and make him morally worthy of the final triumph. With his accustomed mastery Snorri makes the details work together, loaded with psychological significance. The legends told how Olaf once, thoughtlessly, cut wooden chips on a Sunday, and punished himself for this breach of church regulations by burning the chips in his palm; by a miracle he was not hurt. Snorri drops the miracle, makes the item purely psychological, and dates it during Olaf's exile, a proof of the new humility created in him during the days of darkness.

From a historical point of view this whole interpretation of Olaf's character must remain uncertain, perhaps even improbable; he stands at the first primitive beginnings of Norse Christianity. But nothing has contributed more to building him up as a historic force and symbol. In Snorri's work the sainted king gradually stands forth as the representative both of the new ideals of state and society and of the mental forces which were to fill these forms with new meaning. In the dramatic and victorious climax of his life he crowns not only his work as a king, but his development as a human being. When in the concluding chapter, coming back from his exile, Olaf rides down the mountain slopes toward the fatal battle of Stiklestad, looking out over the land he was going to win by his death, no longer mastered by his own passions and ambitions, but free from them, quiet in the liberty of Christian devotion, he gathers in one mighty symbol a development which was gradually to be shared by his own nation, pictured with a serene splendor which has never since lost its grip on the imagination of his people.

The NEW CULTURE

From this soil, prepared by state and church and tilled by new ideas, there gradually grew, toward the end of the Middle Ages, a new form of Norse culture.

Through the channels opened to Europe a flow of foreign impulses found their way into the country. The medieval church was not alone a religious institution; it was the main bearer of the literary traditions of the West, worldly and clerical. In Norway as everywhere cathedrals and monasteries became the centers of knowledge, braving the isolation and the hardships of climate. They did not confine themselves to religious tracts; they passed on the learning of past and present, and increased it to the best of their ability. They handled the classical texts, time bombs which were to explode in the Renaissance; in far-away Iceland of the twelfth century a young student furtively read his Ovidian *Art of Love*. All over Europe Norse clergymen went, for education and study, for new manuscripts and new ideas. And they could follow the paths of an increasing foreign trade, which brought back not goods alone, but all the imponderables that go with them, from legends and anecdotes to worldly fashions. The North was no longer a remote corner of the world. Recent excavations of the Norse settlements in Greenland have proved that new Parisian hats reached this far-away outpost in amazingly short time; and ideas traveled faster still.

The center of the new worldly culture, however, remained the royal court. Always the Norwegian kings had been open to foreign ideas, but the invasions and civil wars had made relations unstable. After the consolidation of the dynasty by Sverrir, the strengthened kingdom eagerly sought contact with the great powers. Legations from the Norwegian king began to appear in the most unexpected places, and strange ambassadors found their way to the North; King Hákon Hákonson politely sent hawks to the king of England; Emperor Frederick bestowed upon Hákon the rare gift of five "blue men" (Negroes). European learning became a necessity at court for practical purposes; early the foreign sources tell of how the young Norse kingsmen "learn to exchange their coarse mother tongue for the fluent beauty of the Roman language."

This development soon became part of the deliberate policy of the kings. The main task of the rulers of Sverrir's house was to stabilize the state after the storms of internal strife, and nothing could serve their purpose better than the new culture which took shape on the continent toward the end of the twelfth century. The ideals of chivalry reconciled tradition with the future: personal independence with loyalty to the king, martial courage with Christian humility, a worldly culture on religious foundations, centered in the idea of balanced human dignity under a refined law of honor. These ideas swiftly penetrated the Norwegian court as well, around 1200, not only in titles and honors, but as a general pattern of life. When in 1247 Cardinal William of Sabina came to Norway to crown King Hákon Hákonson, the worldly-wise prelate in his banquet speech expressed his surprise at the countless multitude of guests and their unexpectedly polished manners.

This development called forth a new kind of literature which corresponded to the new standards. The initiative was with the king himself—the same Hákon Hákonson whose long reign is the climax of the Old Norse empire. He was a well-educated man who knew and quoted his Latin classics; the famous Anglo-Norman historian Matthaeus Parisiensis, who came to see him as ambassador, called him "well versed in literature." But his literary activity was not a matter of personal taste only. In *The Pretenders* Ibsen has described him as the bearer of a great "king-thought": to gather all Norwegians into real unity; and the kind of union he dreamed of was that of moral principles. In his conversations with the learned foreigner he talked about the "violence and lack of moderation" of his people; the strong and peaceful state he tried to build should be the home of better ideals. For this purpose he introduced into Norway the fiction of chivalry, which had developed on the continent in the centers of the new culture. On his personal order the French romance of Tristan and Iseult was freely rendered into Norwegian prose in 1226. Other romances and poems followed—one of them translated by Hákon's own son—a whole literature of "knight's sagas," mainly adapted from Western and Oriental sources. From Norway they gradually spread to the other Scandinavian nations, imbuing the national genres of fiction with the modern continental style.

If we come from Edda and saga to this "court literature," the difference is striking: here is really something radically new. Original creation is not to be expected in works of this kind; the innovation is in the approach. Here is little of the simple realism of the past. The chivalric romance is fantastic and exuberant, moving freely in the fairyland of the unbelievable. Here is no impersonal restraint. The authors speak, eager to reveal their own sensitive personalities; the center of their interest is not the violence of war, but the tender secrets of the heart, the dreams and longings of love, often close to sentimentality. Forgotten is the concise austerity of olden times; the authors indulge in loquacious and exaggerated descriptions, vague and elaborate, sometimes highly artificial. The world seems to be regarded through different eyes.

Modern theorists have condemned this new taste as irremediable decay, a foreign pollution of the sources of national culture. And undeniably the court literature shows a loss of spontaneity, a temporary taming of the forces. But the creative power is not lost. It is only led into other channels for a while; and in itself the process is nothing new. Foreign influence is at work in alternating waves of assimilation and creation all the time from the Edda on, in a continuous widening of the foundations of the national culture. In the court literature there is mostly absorption and adaptation; and some loss is inevitable. But the gains were soon to come, and are heralded even here.

The new genre did not need to advertise itself; it was entertaining. The sagas no longer satisfied; it was not only King Sverrir who found the new "lying stories" more amusing. In the romances other fields of life emerged with the freshness of discovery, an enchanted world of feeling and imagination, breaking the harsh rigidity of tradition. And there was more than entertainment: behind these seemingly fantastic novels there was a new attitude toward life. Joyfully the hero threw himself into the wildest adventures, as did his ancestors in the Edda. His morals might be rather dubious, but in principle he was a Christian warrior. His standards were not only those of martial honor, but those of the religion of love; he had a deeper freedom, and a more serene joy. He never forgot the noble balance of a real knight, at least as an ideal; he was no savage, but a servant of God. "That is the greatest of all victories," says one of the romances, "to triumph over your own anger and help those who need help, even if they do not deserve it." Here we are equally far from the somber fatalism of the ancient heroes and the rustic utilitarianism of the farm philosophers; and it does not necessarily mean a decadence.

This is true also of the style. The new way of writing may have a bookish flavor when approached from the oral simplicity of the king's saga. But this language is capable of saying different things. A mollification and dissolution are going on. But what is lost in sturdy force is gained in the range of possibilities, in the undulation of the melody, the graceful whispering of the words. The mind is not changed; it has just found new forces in itself, and new means to express it.

All these things exist together. They do not eradicate, they fertilize each other; their mutual interplay is the new culture. The "modern" prose is less "popular" than the oral traditions, but it is still Norwegian; the poet Bjarni sings in the manner of the troubadours, but is still a skald. When in 1263 old King Hákon lay on his deathbed far away in the Orkneys and had his courtiers read to him, day and night, through the long hours of disease, he omitted the light foreign fiction he had introduced in his youth and stuck to the serious classics of tradition, "beginning with the Bible and other Latin books, and then, when he got tired of listening, Norse books, first the lives of saints, and next the sagas of the kings of Norway, one after another." But all of it belonged to his own life's work, and together his literary favorites nicely circumscribe it, elements of that continental and national culture on Norwegian soil which he had been so eager to build.

✻

It took time before the elements coalesced into original poetic creation; the monument of the new intellectual life is a prose treatise, the *King's Mirror*, one of the highlights of Norwegian literature. The book is anonymous. But it was probably written by Archbishop Einar Gunnarson of Nidaros (died 1263), primate of the Norwegian church, collaborator in the great law reforms, a leading man of his time and an upholder of its highest ideals. His work is the outstanding witness to the progress of the amalgamation.

The *King's Mirror* is a dialogue: a father gives his young son all kinds of information and advice which may prove useful in life. But as the author quietly walks on, his book turns into something more: a sketch of the whole social set-up of medieval Norway—king, courtiers and officials, judges, warriors, and merchants; only death prevented him from adding the concluding chapters on yeomen and clergy. And this is no extrinsic description. Everything has a background of ideas, of philosophical and religious principles; we gain a full picture of the intellectual atmosphere of the country, and of the author's own personality.

As a matter of fact, Old Norse literature has hardly produced a more personal work. If we read it against the background of previous centuries, the most striking thing about it is the consistency of its development. We move within a wide circle of personal experience; this writer is no simple farm philosopher. He has acquired the highest education of his time, attaining the topmost rung in the. church. He masters the worldly knowledge of his age, including science; the Latin name of his book, *Speculum Regale*, intentionally connects it with famous contemporary works of learning. He is an expert in law and well at home in matters of business, speaks with authority about the details of naval and military action and is thoroughly versed in court life and the secrets of high policy. He is a trusted diplomat, far-traveled in Europe, a man of the great world. But through all of this he remains himself and the representative of a national heritage. In the songs of the High One, the eternal contrasts of spontaneous nature and restrictive rule were still fighting primitively, so to speak, on their own virgin ground; here, they are expressed in the general terms of modern Europe. But their balance rests on the same ground: a secure belief in common sense and sound equilibrium, equally far from ecstasy and sterile rationalism. Such is the basic law of healthy nature: even the animals display an amazing degree of "forethought, insight, and practical wisdom." And such is the law of healthy human life, not only within the narrow village circle but in the whole enlightened and progressive world of which Norway now is a part. Continental and Norse traditions meet here, in the personal culture of the author, as naturally as in his rich and cultivated language, where the literary flavor of Latin and the elegance of French chivalry are welded into a forceful, broad Norwegian, close to the spoken tongue.

This natural unity of elements is apparent in the author's intellectual approach. Here speaks a really free man, who has made the standards of quiet independence a part of himself, discussing clearly and dispassionately, weighing the arguments with moderate skepticism, seeing things from many sides, careful to define exactly the limits of the knowable. But the broad foundation of his mind is still more obvious in his ethical judgment, where the basic principles of his life are brought into the open. In the first place he is a Christian: "The chief point in all conduct is to fear Almighty God and love Him above all things." But he gives it a Norse motive, taken directly out of the group mind of the Edda: shun the vices, "lest they bring you an evil name . . . for one's honor lives forever, though the man himself be dead." And there is no opposition here. The ethics of the church and the law of common sense are identical, as far as normal beings are concerned; even Christian charity is unthinkable without a healthy mind. The basic virtues are moderation and self-mastery, because they will nat-

urally create righteousness and decency, "the capacity to determine judiciously what one owes to every other man." A mind
of the thirteenth century is speaking here, with its limitations, but
also with its strength; there is no moral mountaineering, but much
of confidence in human community. If there is no high-strung
emotion, there is no dejection either. The author believes in the
forces of good both in life and in man and is not afraid to enjoy
them in a dignified manner: "Strive never to be downcast, for a
downcast mind is always morbid; try rather to be friendly and
genial at all times, of an even temper and never moody." In the
heart of this prince of the church there is a deep-felt humanism;
harmoniously God and honest men walk the good ways together
under the universal law.

All this is reflected in the description of society, which is a leading purpose of Archbishop Einar's work. Like Snorri, he is certainly to our time no democrat, not even in spiritual things: "Those
to whom God has given wisdom and rectitude are few only and
not the mass." But still less is his ideal totalitarian. There is a scale
of power in his society; but within the frame everybody has his
well-defined rights, "in the estate in which he is placed," protected
by the strong hand of authority.

The horrors of the recent civil wars with their senseless destruction of values form the unmentioned background of his work.
It is hardly by chance that the author opens his book, not with the
warrior, but with the peaceful merchant; in his advice to the
young commercial student he outlines the new ideals of life, based
on constructive everyday work. The picture closely corresponds
to that of the ideal farmer in the songs of the High One, but
adapted to modern conditions. The good merchant is active and
enterprising, but discreet, cautious and foresighted, honest in all
his dealings, polite and agreeable toward everybody; he is always
eager to learn, observe, and study, from books and from foreign
customs, without ever losing his roothold in the home soil. "If you
wish to become perfect in knowledge, you must learn all the
languages, first of all Latin and French, for these idioms are most
widely used; and yet, do not neglect your native tongue or speech."

The NEW CULTURE

The warrior follows next. Even he is deeply influenced by the new spirit: a master of his mind, "resolute in combat, but not hot-headed and least of all boastful," fighting "as if in the best of humor, though filled with noble wrath." But high over such professions looms that of the judge, representative of the basic principles of society. Parts of these chapters are included word for word in King Magnus's law; and there is a deep passion for justice in them, a vibrant indignation against the forces of violence which sometimes even in the very court enable the rich to "find protection in their wealth and thrust the poor aside." To make truth alone prevail is the high ideal pointed out to the judge; and in the details, the author's own refined and human sense of justice is admirably revealed. He has his difficulties, especially in the problem of retaliation; but if after mature deliberation you find it proper to seek revenge, "take it with reason and moderation and never when heated or irritated." He returns several times, doubtfully, to capital punishment, emphasizing that it must be inflicted "with great reluctance." In the crucial discussion of moral guilt, nothing is left of the literal legalism of ancient times; it is up to the judge to decide "in a tolerant and rational spirit . . . as he thinks is right," investigating carefully "the circumstances." With delicate psychological consideration the author defines how the guilt of two personalities in the Bible cannot be judged from the extrinsic details of their crimes, only from their whole character and attitude, "because the men were unlike."

This whole dissertation is climaxed in the king and the court, focus of the new culture. The ideas of the author about royal authority are those of contemporary Europe: the anointed majesty is sacred, to honor him is to honor God, obedience is the main political duty. But again everything moves within the framework of the law; in his fullness of power the king is "merely a servant of God," executive of the Christian state. In examples from Scripture the author brings out with fine distinctions how the king and his associates have to "guard the bounds of equity among all the men of the realm"; and he sums it up in the prayer he has written for daily use by His Majesty, gathering the ideals toward which so

many generations had slowly striven: "Give me the right understanding, self-control, and sense of justice, eloquence, purpose and
good intentions, so that I may be able to judge and determine the
causes of rich and poor in such a way that Thou wilt be pleased,
while they rejoice that justice is done among them."

From this center everything radiates; therefore everything
about it is important, even the details. Numerous chapters of the
Mirror are devoted to meticulous description of court manners,
an Old Norse Emily Post. When going before the king, you should
wear coat, mantle, and brown trousers, hair and beard carefully
trimmed according to fashion. You should leave your mantle behind when you approach the throne itself, holding your head up
and your whole body erect, striking a dignified gait, but not walking too slowly. When addressing His Majesty, you grasp your
left wrist with thumb and forefinger of the right hand, being careful to use the plural in all phrases referring to him; and if you ever
have to ask, do not say "Eh?" or "What?" or make a fuss about
it, but use only the word "Sire." Modern heralds of national purity
have ridiculed these "pedantic" details; it is a misinterpretation.
They have a value in themselves, teaching that most delicate balance between law and freedom: how to behave "correctly and yet
in a natural way." But above all they are symbols of the new community, the feeling of general standards which had replaced the
coarse independence of the fathers. "If you ask the reason why,
it might be a more than sufficient answer to say that well-bred
people have found it so from the beginning." This is more than
"manners." In his proper behavior the courtier shall be the example of a Norse gentleman as an ethical type, with the fundamental human virtues of the new culture: "able to discriminate,
moderate and righteous."

In its essentials, this picture of society is ethical; and the
author explicitly states that these are the fundamentals. Sometimes dearth comes upon a people, he says; and still worse,
"there may come failure in the morals, the intelligence, or the
counsels of those who are to govern." The fine equilibrium of
forces is shaken; "everyone makes his own moral code accord-

ing to his own way of thinking." Then the decline of the nation is near, and we can only struggle to uphold it until God wills that times shall improve. The author has himself seen such a decline, and the rise from it by virtue of moral forces. His work is the contribution of a good and honest citizen toward ensuring that these forces may never fail again.

The *King's Mirror* was a popular book in its time; numerous manuscripts show how widely it was read. Few contemporaries reached the heights of the author; both in character and abilities he was far above the level of his age. But nobody summed up so personally and exhaustively the ideals and aspirations of the period, the inheritance which, over the abyss of centuries, was again to mold the nation. Edda and Sigvat, Snorri and the *King's Mirror* blaze the highway for Norse culture into the future.

The STREAM GOES UNDERGROUND

There is a hidden anxiety in the *King's Mirror*, and dark forebodings. They proved to be well founded.

The literary flowering of old Norway rested on king and court, nobility and clergy; with the beginning of the fourteenth century these foundations swiftly crumbled. The Norse empire fell to pieces. King and court left the country; the realm drifted into the union with Denmark which was to last until 1814. The nobility was denationalized; the Reformation broke the backbone of the church, German merchants prevented the development of a national middle class. Epidemics decimated the literary men, fire and plunder destroyed schools and libraries. As a result, written literature practically died out for centuries; the connection between old and new seemed to be totally severed. When in the sixteenth century literary life slowly began to stir again, even the written language had vanished in favor of Danish.

The pessimism of contemporaries is understandable. When about 1570 the humanist Absalon Pederssøn proudly described Old Norway's might and splendor, he sadly had to state that nowadays "she has lost her power and is getting old and gray, so heavy that she cannot any more carry her own wool."

✵

But the traditions were not really broken. The stream goes underground for centuries; it does not dry out and disappear. As in political life, the strongest connecting link is the farming class.

In many ways, the decline of the Norwegian state made it hard for the yeomen to keep the gains of the past. All unifying forces were fatally weakened. The national crown was suddenly represented by foreigners. The inherited system of justice was meddled with; the church and its established standards were replaced by an enforced, unpopular Lutheranism; common cultural life almost disappeared. Dispersed people lived in the lonely valleys, on the narrow shores, in an isolation of body and soul which can remind one of the Icelandic saga times. There was bound to be a resurgence of the primitive mind, of ferocity and ruthless self-assertion; the precarious balance of forces which had been created in the late Middle Ages was seriously shaken.

But it was never totally lost. The nation did not relapse into submission or lawlessness. All through the centuries, the farmers kept their stubborn sense of independence as a human privilege expressed in the inherited law; and in their relentless fight for their own rights they defended and maintained the nucleus of the nation's heritage. In their isolation they clung to the values they felt to be their own: their tales and traditions, their customs and standards, superstitions and beliefs, the whole system of life which connected them with the fathers. In this heritage, literature carried on the deepest traditions of the past.

The beginning decline of the Norwegian state coincided with a new poetical flowering. The period of assimilation was over, foreign and national had coalesced. Again came the stage of creation; from the ready soil grew the ballad or folk song. Early the clergy began to complain about the "voluptuous songs for dancing" introduced from England and France. In Iceland they never took root; in Norway they had been prepared for through almost a century, and they released the creative powers with the force of an explosion. The ballad began as an art of the upper class. But it was early taken over as the legitimate property of the farmers, and its further development belongs to them. The impulse to the folk songs came from foreign countries; some of the oldest of them took their subjects from the translated court literature. But their spirit and tradition is national; in amazing fullness they express that fruitful interplay of forces which was the real outgrowth of the Middle Ages.

The UNDERGROUND STREAM

Here, as in the Edda, Norse landscape is the setting; and again it gives to life a note of wild grandeur, boundless, somber and mysterious. The ballad is the playground of grotesque fancy, born in lonely glens under towering mountains, filled with anxiety and forebodings as in no other nation, teeming with the shapeless monsters of evil and mystery, trolls and dragons, nixies and gnomes. Behind everything looms the evil and misty realm of darkness "where shines no sun," projecting its gloomy shadow into the bright world of man. Through this forest of secretive forces strides the hero—as he still stares at us, bent over his sword, on the sunburned carvings in remote valley churches—the great and lonely mind, nephew of the Eddic warrior and the knight of English and Scottish ballads, master of ruthless courage and unbelievable adventures, combats, abductions, and revenge, a symbol of unbridled individual independence. All the primitive self-assertion of the tribe resurges in these ballads, expressed with the gigantic proportions of passion:

> That was Falkvord Lommansson,
> He rode his foes to meet.
> Grass did not grow in fifteen years
> Where his steed put down its feet.

It is easy to understand how Norwegian yeomen, heirs of the old nobility and fighting for their freedom under not too different conditions of life, could identify themselves with these defiant heroes of the past and continue to sing about them for centuries. In the newer ballads, the hero is himself a farmer's son, armed with the farmer's favorite weapon, the wooden club, scaring kings and courtiers over the fence with his grim laughter.

It is the same spirit which speaks in the yeomen's historical traditions, in their new-born sagas filled with the self-reliance of old families residing for centuries on their farms, in their proud tales of thwarted invasions and heroic revolts against foreign officials. The frightened clergymen of the sixteenth century often complained about the terrible people among which they were doomed to live, and the local traditions bear them out only too well. Sometimes, the farmers directly connected their sheriff killings with the heroic feats of the Edda times.

But with all this, the ballads themselves are not Edda. They do not merely tell about the eternal underground of primitive forces. They also bear witness to that many-sided development which through centuries had striven to tame the forces and make them work together—all those standards which were once embodied in the *King's Mirror* and struggled for expression in the borrowed forms of the court literature, and which now finally got life and blood in a great national poetry.

The hero is no longer a mere Viking type; he is a Norse knight, with the refinement of European culture. There is an atmosphere of courtesy and good breeding in the ballad, and of unforced natural humanity, freed from the sentimental note of the French novels; the elements have merged. The amazing feats of arms still catch the interest. But still more than in the Edda, the poet concentrates with sympathetic understanding on the psychology of the heroes and quite especially that of the heroines, their delicate feelings, their unhappy love, their gallant fidelity or infidelity. At close quarters even the magic powers show milder traits; mermaids and elves sigh for human love, even the trolls sometimes try to behave with clumsy courtesy. The widened range of feeling makes the landscape sing in new tones as well, softening the Eddic notes of somber ruggedness, calling forth the traits of airy serenity which are also there. Cold and gloomy the barrow closes over Sigrun and Helgi's ghostlike love in the Edda. When the couple of the ballad have paid with their lives for their short delight, two "lily trees" grow from their graves and meet over the church portal.

Behind the gracefulness and the apparent ease there are serious morals, all the norms of the "new culture." The ferocious hero is purified by a struggle for standards, by fidelity and willingness to sacrifice himself, the virtues of a freeborn Christian character. It is symbolic that so many of his battles are against the foggy monsters of lawless evil, and that his frequent partner is the mild wife, "the lady of the kind heart." More and more the conflict moves in the moral sphere of Western civilization.

In the religious ballads the sources are pointed out: Norse ideas of inescapable destiny peacefully combined with the Christian concepts of sin and retribution. But the strongest note is that of forgiving mildness; again and again the victims of masculine brutality implore divine clemency for their torturers. In *The Dream Chant*, one of the treasures of medieval literature, an unknown poet has exalted these standards in a mighty picture of the Last Day. It is borne by a deep conviction of the momentousness of every action in life: trembling "as aspen leaves in the wind," the souls are confronted with their own deeds. There is little talk of formal offense; sin is a violation of the basic code of altruism: to wrong the right, to move the landmarks, to be hard of heart and narrow of mind. The virtues are those of kindness within the frame of Norse everyday existence: to give a cow to the poor, shoes and grain to those in need. Again, as in *Voluspá*, the simple laws of life seem to emerge from the severe landscape itself, with the overwhelming power of eternity: "The tongue will speak and truth reply on Judgment Day." Through ages when official Christianity had little to give Norwegian minds, these songs kept the gains of a whole era alive in the souls of the nation.

As poetry the ballads can stand comparison with the Edda; and even in form they carry on the essentials of the past. The folk songs are still in the Norwegian language, .as it continued to be spoken in the countryside regardless of the defection of the clerics; and they are still in the Edda line. The diction is more supple and flexible, singing in the new tone. But as compared to the court literature, the style is tightening again, filled once more with tense and watchful power, a direct and striking tale along grand, simple lines, bursting into sudden flashes of overwhelming emotion. Again the subdued feeling loads the plain words with intensity and makes a world of human fate emerge from one sharp detail. All the pity of thwarted passion is in the picture of the lover Tarjei's bridal horse running empty out of the courtyard of the death-stricken wedding house. And with all its historic patina this is modern poetry in language and expression, directly accessible to Norwegians today, a living link to the past.

✤

Down to the nineteenth century these songs survived in the memories of Norwegian farmers; nothing shows better their inherent power. But they tell mostly of the culmination points of human existence, lofty ideas and sublime feelings, worded in the solemn language of poetry. There were other forms of literature which came closer to everyday life and expressed the ideals of the common man in earthier fashion. If the ballad is the song of the hero, the fairy tales again speak with the voice of the High One.

Even more than the folk songs, these tales are the playground of the fantastic imagination of the people, a willful pageant of the troll world, enhanced by feats of gigantic heroism and colored with grotesque and primitive humor. But here, where the people itself frankly speaks in the words of ordinary life, it is still more obvious how solidly this playfulness is rooted in mental health, a sound sense of reality. There is much of brusque independence in the fairy tales, as in the ballads. But there is still more matter-of-course self-reliance, grown from the world of the many, which makes man feel secure. As early as 1200 A. D. a Norse historian complains about the fairy tales that they always "belittle the king." In the later tales His Majesty himself is a big and genial farmer, who is approached on an equal footing with the sober self-assertion of men who are masters of their lives. They can afford to play into the burlesque; they have balance in themselves.

There is still solid respect for a good, smart blow in the fairy tales. But the real hero is Oskeladden (the Cinder Lad), a youngster often to be met in Norse tradition, born from the people's daydreams, and at the same time a symbol of their closeness to life. He does not fight so much; his is a victory by other means. He is the great realist, who begins despised and ends in triumph, because he has a sound intellect, open-minded and unprejudiced, curious and resourceful, inaccessible to bluff and slogans, looking through the disguise of things to things themselves. But what makes him finally victorious is his moral solvency, his sincere and steadfast character, his noble heart. Those are the qualities which he brings out in others, too, and which make them triumph over the fakes and cruelties of life: courageous patience, truthfulness and justice, helpfulness toward everybody, all the virtues that make joint life tolerable. There is little talk of religion in the fairy tales, and the representatives of the church are not too well treated. But the standards of guilt and justice are there all the time, even if they are not talked of; life would be unthinkable without them. Even in the mythical world moral law is omnipresent; there is no victory for the trolls. The only pagan god that is still vaguely remembered is the strong Thor with the red beard, faithful helper of man against the powers of evil.

There is little of sublimity in these tales, and much of the sound art of living. This accounts for their biting sarcasm, not a sterile grimace, but the smile of those who know; it accounts for their broad humor, which is also to be found in many ballads. It is a laughter out of human surplus; as in the Edda, the narrators can afford to smile at the heroes, even at themselves. The equilibrium is expressed in the very art of telling with its dramatic vivacity and drastic concretion of detail and its "sound coolness" at bottom, imperturbable in the wildest turmoil. And again the fairy tale is modern, like the ballad; it speaks without translation even to the generations of the motor age.

This is still folk art, anonymous and isolated, not yet moving on the level of the nation and the world. But it is not petrified; it is part of a living culture. These are the same farmers who simultaneously reflect all successive phases of European art, especially the rococo, in carvings and colorful painting. Their tales and songs draw their power from life itself, lifting up the ideals of the yeomen's own existence. If we piece together a picture of everyday life in the Norwegian valleys through these centuries of seclusion, not from the poets and raconteurs, but from the countless historical traditions, we find often, besides the proud independence, a wildness that is less noble: caviling, disputatiousness, and small-minded suspicion, all the fruits of isolation. But behind it we see a society striving toward the same principles of righteousness and common sense, the same ideals of joint existence, which are so strong in the literature they cherished. Behind the admired hero, there is always the "home law," the inherited system of venerable custom, which puts him in his place. Behind the ruthless violence, the standards of mutual help and trust remain; behind the whims of individual imagination there is always the wisdom of the proverbs, the simple love of truth. These powers with their insoluble mixture of foreign teaching and primeval popular wisdom carried on through the anonymous centuries, deep under the surface of ideology and confession, and made them a whole; when the stream saw the light again, it still was a stream.

The people never totally lost the feeling that in maintaining such traditions they carried on a heritage. The memory of the Norwegian state mostly faded away, and so did the deeper conception of national freedom. But St. Olaf lived, the good protector, exterminator of giants and serpents, builder of roads and churches, representative of peaceful civilization. Everywhere people sought the springs he had made run, and showed the footsteps of his horse, marked at night by tongues of flame.

These are the traits that deepen as we get closer to our time. Law and church are working on the mind; the bellicose ballad is replaced by mild lyric songs, the primitive heroic ideal adapts itself to modern life. In the newer traditions, the saga teller does not forget for fighters and athletes those men and women whose only distinction was to be peaceful, wise and honest, faith-keeping and straight, "who had no enemies and themselves loved all." The purest type is remembered in the tales from a southern valley, in the saga of Ketil Kyrvestad, "the man that was always well spoken of." His life story radiates an almost apostolic mildness: he always repaid good for evil, he liberally shared his riches with all in need and did not even summon the thieves—a man of stainless integrity, who met life and death with the same dignified kindness. But at the same time he was a man of this world, with penetrating judgment and observation, a model farmer and breeder, a master of pregnant and colorful conversation, famous for his genial jokes, "a humorist unmatched in all times." Here again we touch the marrow of the tradition. If we compare this type of pious natural dignity with the human ideal of the Edda, we measure both the distance covered and the things which have remained.

❧

To give this folk culture the literary organs of national consciousness and foreign contact became the task of the literate classes through the centuries of union.

They worked under terrific handicaps. When life began to stir in Norway again, the center of culture had moved to Denmark. Educated people came home from their studies with a foreign language and with foreign traditions, to a country which was, in many respects, a mere province, lacking practically all facilities for higher intellectual life.

But in these men lived the idea of Norway as a nation. They had witnessed the downfall of a great realm; however vaguely, the hope of resurrection never died in their hearts. They needed support for their dreams; with moving enthusiasm they turned to Norway's glorious past and to the present folk life, as a soil in which to take root. The Norse humanists of the sixteenth century are no Renaissance types, but zealous and serious men in search for foundations of a new Norway. The same Absalon Pederssøn who complains so discouragedly about the downfall, has words of steel when he fulminates against the German intruders, who "have gotten the country's sand into their shoes and never want to quit it again." His voice quivers when he tells of Norway's "sacred soil" which he would like to "seize with his body, kneeling with kisses"; and he ends with a confident ring: "Within, these hard mountains are filled with good butter, silver and gold, and other precious things, and the nation still has something of the old virtues, manhood and power."

In this spirit his contemporaries and successors worked, through the sixteenth and seventeenth centuries. They did not yet formulate any clear idea of national freedom. Still less were they able to lead into Norway the great literary currents of liberation from abroad; Humanism, Renaissance, and religious Reform had lost most of their explosive power before they reached Norway. But these good officials and clergymen never ceased to feel the country as something apart, and to believe in its power of development; their task was to prepare the ground patiently for growth to come. They translated from Old Norse, trying to heal the break and resuscitate the national pride. They struggled to make their Danish language an instrument of Norwegian expression. They studied the modern living conditions of the country; they tried to lead the surviving religious life into the channels of the new church. Toward the end of the seventeenth century, they had managed to create a literary milieu again, certainly provincial and narrow, but an organ of assimilation and expression.

How far this process of amalgamation had advanced about 1700 is demonstrated in Petter Dass (1647–1707), a clergyman of Scotch descent in the storm-vexed fishing districts of northern Norway "toward the world's end," the first creative genius of Norse literature after the Middle Ages.

To us, he certainly seems to be no man of freedom at all, but one of inflexible law. The modern ideas of an independent Norway, of political liberty and social equality, would have been as unthinkable to him as any kind of intellectual rebelliousness. He was the almighty local representative of the autocratic Dano-Norwegian king and rigid Lutheran orthodoxy; and the portraits indicate that he enjoyed his role, heavy and massive in the cassock, with square-cut beard over the ruff and imperturbable, authoritative eyes.

But the freedom of Petter Dass was on another level. Reality to him was not the theories of dogma and constitutional law; it was the life of his own parishioners, "the slaves of the elements," among whom he was born and lived and whose existence he shared to the last detail. He was himself a fisherman as much as a cleric; together they faced the common vicissitudes of luck and failure, the same joys and hardships, the same inescapable death under the vigilant eyes of the mountains and the sea. It filled him with a deep feeling of human fellowship: in the essentials of life he and his parishioners were equals; and the core of their community was their simple Christian faith. The merciless struggle for life was no senseless toil. On the barren shores of their Arctic homeland the basic standards of human existence should shine the more brightly, conquering the wildness of nature and mind by righteousness and good will. Here again everybody was equal and everybody free, sharing the liberty of personal choice and the common safety of the good decision—a religion not of ecstasy, but a father's house as it had been in the Middle Ages, a trusty helper in everyday life and a faithful hand when the Arctic night of storms closes over your frail boat.

This freedom under the law gave to Petter Dass his broad human security, and made him a great national poet. His description of life in northern Norway is filled to the rim with trivial details, tools and clothing, houses and food. But they are seen with a loving eye which makes them shine and glitter by an inner light. The wedding customs of the peasants and the crisp foliage of the spring birch, the surf over the skerries and the delicious fat liver dishes of the Helgelanders are all expressions of a life he knew and trusted because it had meaning and proportions. And his closeness to this life made him national without knowing it. The old realm of Norway was little more than a Danish province to him. But in his pictures of life at home as he knew it, struggling under the rigorous necessity of nature, he unconsciously continued one of the main lines of national tradition, which was soon going to call forth more radical demands. His religion, severe and strong, seems to grow from the landscape itself as that of the *Voluspá* and the *Dream Chant*, filling once again the forms of official Christianity with the deepest life of the nation. He is no folk poet; but his Danish speaks in Norwegian style, with its mixture of drastic burlesque and forceful, dramatic simplicity. And so does the mind behind it, struggling for mastery of its passions, glittering with genial humor, and at bottom undisturbedly serious.

In Petter Dass as in the folk tales, the broad range of feeling is the sign of a free soul. There is no discrepancy between the robust sketches of his youth, the courageous hymns of danger and death from his manhood, and the subdued whispering from his last sick-bed, when through the agony of pain he peacefully bowed to his fate. His people understood him. Up to the end of the nineteenth century the fishing boats of northern Norway carried a black stripe in their sails, in commemoration of their poet.

Here, as in the popular traditions, there is abundance of power and possibilities, which need only expression in terms of the modern world. Three years before Herr Petter died a young Norwegian student had quietly left the country for Western Europe. He was going to throw the doors wide open.

The LIBERATION of THOUGHT
LUDVIG HOLBERG

Most Holberg portraits show an elderly scholar at the end of an unprecedented career, a dignified and somewhat tired face with drawn features and quiet, skeptical eyes under a full wig—Baron de Holberg, writer of world fame, former president of the University of Copenhagen, entail holder and testator, a chilly and hypochondriac old gentleman, pretty particular about his diet and expenses and the other troublesome trifles of life.

But this was not the man himself, only the remnants of him. The true Holberg was the precocious boy with sparkling eyes who in the 1680's promenaded through the town of Bergen, Norway's most international port, "a Noah's ark with all kinds of creatures," open and fresh from the western winds. It was also the adventurous graduate of divinity who, nineteen years old, escaped abroad from theology and relatives armed with sixty dollars and an inexhaustible curiosity, who roamed through great parts of Europe on the passport of a friend, giving lessons in violin and flute and filling his mind with the wonders of a new world. It was the mature man who in solemn professorial disguise was the first great journalist of the North, flooding the public for more than thirty years with books and pamphlets which, unlike the dusty folios of his venerable colleagues, it was impossible not to read, to enjoy, and to learn from. It was above all the gamin whose very thought moved in teasing jokes and paradoxes and who sometimes roared with laughter in the street at his own fancies, the poet of a compulsive imagination, who in one single year of creative trance wrote that series of master comedies which founded the stage of his nation. Back of all this, and most surprising, it was the revolutionary, in satin and shirt frill, who started out on his life work with the purpose of changing the mentality of his people, and succeeded in doing so.

That this proved possible, however, was because at bottom Holberg, like many great originators, was no revolutionary at all, but the real carrier of the tradition. He could awake his compatriots to modern life because he gave expression to thoughts that had for centuries slept wordless or inarticulate in themselves. After his definite escape from Norway, his career belonged to the Danish part of the monarchy; he never returned to the country of his birth. But Norwegians as well as Danes call him the father of their modern literature, and for the same good reasons.

The complexity of his activities points to the secret of his mind and of his influence.

The first impression in reading Holberg is that of a cautious and skeptical intellectualism seasoned by dry humor, a strict adherence to "the law of reason," which corresponds well to his Voltairian features. But his rationalism is not flat and sterile; behind his quiet reason there is a mumbling chorus of other voices. His intellectual curiosity was matched by an almost ruthless honesty, "the right characteristic and distinctive mark of my nation," and an equally violent desire for freedom. From the very beginning, his intellectualism was revolutionary; and it did not stop before the limits of intellect itself. When he turned his searchlight into his own soul (which he loved to do), he saw a confusion of contrasts which reason could classify, but never explain. He called it his "bizarrerie"—the nervous changeableness of body and soul, the sudden waves of emotion and passion, his fits of dejection or excitement under the influence of music and poetry, his feeling of helpless awe before the chasm of the firmament and the riddles of life. And when he looked to his fellow creatures, he saw everywhere the same tendency toward being "unlike oneself," of going to extremes, regardless of the solid teachings of reason. In one of his epistles he tells the strange story of a highborn Danish noblewoman who repudiated the love of the most brilliant and courteous gentleman of the country and found quiet and satisfaction in marriage with a wretched ferryman, a drunkard and a brute. Holberg had him-

LUDVIG HOLBERG

self talked to her in her paltry cottage; and in telling about it, his voice is deep with understanding: we do all belong to that puzzling race of mankind.

This insight molded his general attitude with its exceptional broadmindedness. His guide in life and death remained reason, sound common sense, common to all healthy beings, with its laws of logic and its dream of the great medium. The more he felt his own lack of stability—and he believed it to be a characteristic of the whole Norwegian nation—the more tenaciously he clung to this only possible counterpoise. But reason always remained a challenge to him. It egged him on to attack all that hampered the freedom of the human mind; but it also prompted him never to acquiesce in his own conception of reality, always to distinguish, to reserve his judgment, to leave room for the imponderables. It made narrowness and cheap systematization unthinkable to him; wherever he had to establish his rules (and there always have to be rules), he saw to it that life itself was admitted in freedom as far as possible. It is easy to follow the growth of this vigilant realism along the line of Norse tradition, from the High One through the *King's Mirror* down to contemporary fairy tales. But there is in Holberg an additional touch of skeptical self-analysis which we are used to calling "modern," and which in Norwegian literature is born with him.

This pattern of thought and feeling settled his task in life and made his youthful ramblings abroad a diplomatic mission. Half-forgotten Norway had no ambassadors any more, even Holberg himself hardly felt that he was representing a national tradition on his travels; he had something important to tell his nation, and was just looking for tools and arms. But in bringing them home, he contracted and reëstablished alliances which were to prove more durable than many a treaty on paper.

He did not confine himself to his own times. He was the first in either of his nations to give classical antiquity its modern meaning as a symbol of balanced humanity, in support of his own ideals; he caught up with modern movements of liberation as well, from Humanism and the Reformation on. But his main travels sought

LUDVIG HOLBERG

out the contemporary world, the Western lands, "where the habits of living are free." Holland and Great Britain were his ports of call, those hearthstones of intellectual liberty. When on April 18, 1706, he inscribed himself at the Bodleian Library in Oxford as *Ludovicus Holberg Norvegus*, a connection was reëstablished which has never since been broken. All through his life he had a touch of the intellectual independence and the political sobriety of the British, their sound humor and judicious realism, and their gentleman's ideals of education; "I liked that nation and they liked me."

But his chief resort remained France. The beginning Enlightenment was the model of that crusade of thought which he himself entered upon at home. He shared with the French philosophers their veneration for the dignity of man, their hatred of prejudice, their confidence in the sensible laws of nature; and he admired the way they expressed it, without preciosity and metaphysical cloudiness, in a style which made literature pleasant and dangerous. He saw with amazed delight how in modern France such ideas had penetrated culture to the core, how the "absurd ornaments" of Gothic architecture had been replaced by a better taste and how the poets willingly obeyed the laws of sense and order. But the new liberators never made him forego his freedom of judgment. Their cheap optimism and elegant frivolity never lured him to discount his own serious standards and his sober knowledge of human nature; his poetic creation was never distorted by the narrower ideals of the French.

He took Germany in the same unbiased way. He was ready to burst with laughter when he heard a professor in Leipzig discourse at serious length on whether the blessed in Paradise took both luncheon and supper. He never missed an opportunity to ridicule the pedantry and bodiless speculation of the Germans. But he openmindedly accepted their formulations of "natural law" because they suited him; he was just a realist and did not classify verity according to its birth certificate.

Thus equipped, twenty-seven years old, he proceeded to the work of reshaping his two nations.

He did not underestimate the difficulties. In the comic epic *Peder Paars* he measured his strength against the task; and the picture he gave of contemporary Dano-Norwegian society was not encouraging, with its massive dead weight of blind authority, superstition, and ignorance, in state and school, religion and morals. But the poem also indicated what sharp and dangerous weapons this young man handled, how biting was his wit and how lucid his thought. He was not bent on fighting people's opinions. He would change their way of thinking, teach them "to distinguish sharply between semblance and reality," to break the obsolete standards and establish new ones by free personal choice. He had no system to offer, just an attitude of mind; the library of books he wrote is a motley collection of styles and genres, epics and treatises, comedies and novels, essays and epistles. They seem to lack any underlying plan. But in their cheerful mixture of earnest and fun the same spirit was everywhere at work, unseen; and beneath the modern slogans that spirit was not new in Norway.

He started out by showing people the world in which they lived, in "Introductions" to modern history which in purpose come close to the writings of a modern columnist. Holberg was no champion of political liberty in our sense of the word. To him, it was intellectual freedom that counted; political life must have a frame, autocracy might be a convenient arrangement. But his way of reasoning was a high explosive. He always had to dodge censorship; in one of his books he even seems to have deftly inserted some subversive reflections after the censor had done his task. His very impartiality felt like a liberation, the concern about facts, the careful weighing of pros and cons, and still more the undertone of skeptical humor playing with many possibilities. He approached the subject as Oskeladden did the king, imperturbably calling institutions and men before the tribunal of common sense. He once wrote that "a good critic never censures in anger"; his own quiet way was much more dangerous.

Moreover, Holberg's political conservatism had nothing to do

LUDVIG HOLBERG

with slavish submission. It indicated a new pattern of life: that of the growing burgher class with its ideals of peaceful coöperation, not too far away from the thinking of his contemporaries in the Norwegian countryside. If he defended absolutism, it was because he believed that it worked toward equality. He was not blind to the martial virtues; he often returned to the puzzling role of "enthusiasm" in history, quite especially the heroism of the old Norsemen, "something unequaled in our time." But "peace is the natural state of man," the quiet, constructive work which takes the violent forces into the service of the common good. He called the father of twelve educated children more of a hero than Alexander who sacrificed men by the millions. He spurned the Vikings as freebooters and praised the times of Hákon Hákonson for their morals and "wonderful thoughts"; he lauded Christianity, which is even strong enough to "break the special love of the fatherland." His ideal among princes was Peter the Great of Russia, who went abroad to learn and came back to teach his nation how to build a civilization in the wilderness. In his political novel *Niels Klim's Journey to the Subterranean World* (the first modern Scandinavian work to win world fame) he showed how hypertrophy of any special feature of society, even freedom, throws life out of balance; but he praised the state of Mezendore (probably North America) where the motley population could work together each according to his gift, and sang the eulogy of the imaginative model state of Potu, where the inhabitants were trees and all forces were balanced by the sensible laws of nature, and where even the autocratic monarchs "knew how to combine authority and liberty."

To Holberg, this was only the frame, however; at the bottom, all real problems are moral. He once tried to show that all his works had a moral nucleus; he was himself most at his ease in his essays and epistles, where he could unforcedly concentrate on his main interest: the human soul.

Nowhere does the reader get so close to Holberg himself as in these moments of meditation, when he picks up one detail of life and experience and lovingly causes it to glitter in the light of his reflection and his humor. There are few fields of existence which he does not touch: the character of cats and the right method of killing flies, the mysteries of ladies' fashions and the real nature of God; and again the approach is often more important than the thing itself. Holberg somewhere tells of a scholar who was reared on goat's milk and could never afterward keep from cutting capers; he was himself closely akin to that disrespectful and very Norwegian animal. But at bottom he is always serious; here laughs a man who knows where he stands and would like to help other people find out the same thing for themselves. He never shows us more impressively than in these casual remarks what a great and independent spirit he really was—from his perfectly modern ideas about "education for life" to his large-minded defense of the abilities and rights of woman.

These reflections often have their starting point in some "bizarrerie" in man (and in Holberg himself); and again his honest realism is impressive. There is no varnishing of facts: "sound reason" is not as almighty as some people believe, "human wickedness and inconsistency far surpass those of the beasts." He may speak with a sad smile about the progress of mankind. But in his heart he is an optimist. The aim of life is not to quell the unruly forces, but to canalize them, transform, and manage them; and Holberg never sincerely doubted that it could be done, through the basic health of the normal mind.

To that health, however, belonged also a stern sense of duty. Few feelings were stronger in Holberg himself, formidable worker that he was; and this sense of responsibility was to him a part of reason. It is hard to say here where moral ends and religion begins; like the author of the *King's Mirror*, Holberg recognized no unbridgeable gulf between God and the man of good will. Even in religion he was no narrow rationalist. He fought unbelief as much as superstition; he often found that he had to "suspend his thoughts" and recur to revelation. Well he knew the depths over which he was balancing, "that shining abyss without bottom and limits in which the soul is drowned." But for all practical purposes the law was given to us within ourselves, together with the power to grasp and obey it. Tolerance and free research were God's delight: "it is the duty of every Christian to inquire before he believes." Who might venture to approach the Almighty in his thought without fulfilling "the first commandment of philosophy, to know oneself"? Certainly the Lord will judge sincere errors more mildly than indolent adherence to accepted truth. He is not the God of fear, but of confidence and honest work, and "will be worshipped with a cheerful heart, if one's last night is to be happy."

All this is good theory, and beautifully expressed. But what makes Holberg a genius is that to the discursive faculty of the practical philosopher he added the eye of the dramatist and the imagination of the poet.

Every page of his work shows how comprehensive was his observation and how vigilant his feelings; again and again a debate over ideas becomes a play of characters. In his dramatic art, the individual facts regroup themselves spontaneously into a moving picture of man in function. Holberg can write only comedies. But somehow everything is in them, apparently without effort: his studies and thoughts, his knowledge of books and men, even the deepest and most serious aspirations of his life, walking and talking before our eyes in blood and bones.

The immediate purpose of Holberg's comedies is simple: they are weapons in his fight for the liberation of the mind. Whether they are social comedies or merely studies of an individual character, they usually pick out one special human weakness, one "bizarrerie," and expose it in the distorting magnification of the stage light, till the onlookers relax in relieving laughter over the general ridiculousness of mankind. The range of types is wide: the fickle-minded and the bustler, the braggart and the garrulous, the inflated scholar and the scientific humbug, the armchair strategist and the much-traveled snob. But common to most of them is that they cannot "distinguish between semblance and reality," that their judgment is disturbed, especially toward themselves, leaving them unnatural, affected, pedantic, out of balance. Holberg says that most of his plays are moral, "teaching people to reason about

virtues and vices, which was unknown to many of them before."
His gallery of figures teach his ideals with the smashing power of
the cartoon.

But they do very much more. Holberg's incentive in writing
usually was his irritation at some special human frailness; he complained himself how the bark of a dog could throw him off his
hinges, how much more then the Political Tinker or the Much-
Speaking Barber. But as he got to writing and anger subsided, the
characters gradually caught life under his hands. A mottled swarm
of observations knocked at his door and demanded their place in
the picture, no longer that of a single fault only, but of a live human being. Most of his figures remain within the frame of a human
type, accessible to understanding and reason. But the form bursts
with colors and individual life, and with humor, a broad comicality
of situation and reply, moving from the gaminlike raillery of the
fairy tale to the burlesque power of the baroque.

At the same time this art is full of sympathy. There was hardly
one of the human bizarreries which, sooner or later, Holberg did
not also recognize in himself, at least as a secret trend. It gave his
satire a ring of self-irony and hidden understanding, and his laughter an undertone which sometimes is not far from pity. His master
stroke is the comedy of *Jeppe, the Transfigured Peasant* (built on
a motif which Shakespeare used in the prologue to *The Taming of
the Shrew*). In this social play he depicts the pack horse of Danish
society as Squire Holberg himself knew him at his worst, brought
on the stage with naked objectivity, a bundle of vice and misery
shrouded in a cloud of spirits. And yet this human wreck is presented to us without total loss of dignity. Something of value is
left in this old drunkard sleeping on the dunghill, some touch of
warmth and strength, some remnant of those qualities which made
Holberg praise the peasants' "reasoning about solid and important
things" and in his old days let him talk indignantly about their
"abominable state of slavery" in Denmark. These pictures of man
with their delicate interplay of morals and realism, judgment and
compassion, observation and emotion, are the monument to Holberg's broad humanity and its value as a power in life.

LUDVIG HOLBERG

His chef-d'œuvres are the fifteen comedies he wrote during 1722–23, "the year of abundant bloom"; one of them gave the program of his work. In *Erasmus Montanus* he presented a spokes- man of the highest modern culture, a student home from the uni- versity, bursting with reformer's zeal and sterile ideology. He is confronted with his simple farm parents, relatives of Jeppe, sturdy exponents of the village tradition, and is completely crushed against the wall of their imperturbable common sense, not because he is wrong about the problem in question (he isn't), but because with all his correct theory he is a headless faddist, while they in their bigot ignorance represent that healthy closeness to life for which there is always hope. To liberate both parts from their chains and make them work together under the banner of free, responsible reason was Holberg's program. He showed in *Erasmus* both the hugeness of the task and the tools with which it had to be tackled.

✵

When a few years before his death in 1754 Holberg tried to sum up the results of his life work, he said that he had "recast the common man of these nations as in a new mold." As usual, he did not exaggerate; and quite especially his words hold good for Norway.

Directly, he had little to do with many of the ideas that were to guide the following generations: the deepened understanding of national independence, the new conception of democratic free- dom, the rising interest in the world of feeling. Indirectly, his in- fluence is omnipresent. His books became popular reading through- out Norway almost on publication, not only in the new and growing burgher class, but among the farmers as well; and to all of them his writing spoke with a voice they understood. He opened the world to his fellow-countrymen and made it seem comprehensible and near, Greece and Rome, England and France, a new cosmos of ideas. But they understood it so well because in the things he told them and in the way he told it they recognized themselves. In Holberg the underground stream again approached

the surface as a conscious national tradition. He taught his compatriots to think independently and to know themselves; and the
whole resurrection and future unity of Norway was in it.

His work had the limitations of his times. He did not express the
whole national heritage, only a part of it; if we compare him to
the popular traditions, we soon feel his classical lack of individualism, his "unromantic" emotional life. But so strong and general
was his influence, that even in the approach to new problems, he
was still there.

The two generations after Holberg were the ones which prepared the sudden liberation of Norway in 1814; and both the
strengthening of national hopes and the increasing demand for
political liberty would have been unthinkable without him. When
Gerhard Schøning, "the Arch-Patriot," wrote his Norse history,
glowing with admiration for the frugal, courageous, and liberty-
loving founders of ancient Norway; when the officials began to
worship the "natural" and freeborn modern farmer, even trying
to write poetry in Norse dialect, they acted in Holberg's spirit.
When the farmers themselves began to read Snorri again, it was
because Holberg had taught them to read; when the religious folk
movement of Hans Nielsen Hauge could sweep the country with
a pietism contrary to many of Holberg's ideals, it was because he
had encouraged the common man to act on his own responsibility.
When the merchants began to "look west" for new political conceptions, when the Norwegian liberals began to make the Copenhagen government feel uneasy, it was because Holberg had accustomed them not to be afraid. The deep simultaneous concern about
everything national and about the ideas of the great world which
makes eighteenth-century Norway look like a different country
from that of Petter Dass was in the main a result of Holberg's
work.

Especially deep was his influence on literature. Soon after his
death the first wave of preromanticism reached the North. Here
a movement was signaled which in its consequences not only upset
Holberg's century, but has not yet reached its balance: the great
conscious revolt of instinct against reason, of feeling against rule.

Holberg's broad view prepared the younger generations for taking the new movement in their own way. There were traits of pre-romanticism in himself, and his disciples were not less open-minded —there was enough to support them in the traditions; Norwegians were among the first in the North to greet the preromantic ideas. But from the very beginning they were on their guard against excesses, the turgid bombast and the sickly emotionalism: they had a basis from which to judge. They learned from the new, but did not submit to it. The immediate successors of Holberg followed the line from him and from Petter Dass, giving strong, realistic pictures of Norwegian folk life in a severe and simple style. The "Norwegian Society" in Copenhagen which remained the stronghold of separatism during the last decades of the union, sailed under the stars of the Greeks, the West and Holberg; the witty poetry of Johan Herman Wessel (1742–85) as well as the humane philosophy of Niels Treschow (1751–1833) are filled with *his* spirit.

The very liberation was prepared by him. It was Holberg's paling morning star which still, on the threshold of the new century, greeted that dazzling sunrise which bore the name of Henrik Wergeland.

The GENIUS of the HEART
HENRIK WERGELAND

The literature of modern Norway was born with the free constitution, given at Eidsvoll, May 17, 1814.

Even to the members of the constituent assembly the liberation always had something of the miracle about it. Conceived under the dark skies of war, fought for and maintained in defiance of all reactionary Europe, the constitution somehow seemed to be connected with the triumphant suddenness of the Norwegian spring itself, with the thaw and the white May sun and the fresh foliage of the birch groves around the old manor of Eidsvoll, born in one of those happy moments when heaven is close to earth and old hopes unexpectedly come true.

In itself, however, the liberation was no product of hazard, but of long and self-sacrificing toil. The "generation of Eidsvoll," the group, consisting mostly of officials, who together saw the work through, were the Spartans of modern Norway, disciplined by faithful civil service, hardened through seven years of war, blockade, and famine, and welded into one by ideas which really matched the situation. Their outlook was serious, almost severe, marked by Holberg's rational independence and his stern sense of duty. Their ideals were those of the French and American revolutions, beautifully expressed in the austere Roman style in which they built their houses—Cato, Mirabeau, and Benjamin Franklin—and their task was to found a new forum of lawful liberty in the North, based on the free Norwegian yeomen. Such ideals enabled these officials of an autocratic state to build, in a few spring months, a constitution which in its mixture of freedom and discipline has since remained the elastic frame of Norwegian life. It kept the actual power in their own hands, but it opened unlimited possibilities for peaceful democratization. It is understandable that after this tour de force some of the generation settled down a little. They had generously arranged for the nation's future; now they should like to do some governing themselves for a while.

Such was their attitude in literature as well. These strained and busy men were also the generation that received the tremendous impact of European romanticism. They were cosmopolites as a matter of course, well acquainted with the German, English, and even French ultras; as early as 1819 Byron received an admiring letter in English verse from "Drontheim in Norway" and was moved and encouraged by this homage from "wild and strange places." They studied the new ideas openmindedly, as good pupils of Holberg; but they were not swept off their feet. They grasped the importance of romantic thought to religion, poetry, history, and national life; they themselves began experimenting in all these fields, even trying to explore the folk traditions and folk language which still lived unnoticed in the countryside. But their main attitude was that of cautious observation; after all, they were the governing class, struggling under heavy burdens of responsibility. They caught little of the explosive force of romanticism, and it could hardly be expected. Again, many of them show a slight complacency; for the time being there was surely no urgent need for new reforms.

Into this little world there broke, in the middle of the 1820's, a youngster hardly out of his teens, who seemed bent on playing havoc with all solid tradition and set out with the power of a whirlwind, making the country revolve around him through his short and hectic life.

He had early made people talk about him, the mad son of the vicar of Eidsvoll, with his newspaper activity from the age of thirteen and his continuous fallings in love (the most recent one ending in a grotesque attempt at suicide). On turning up for studies in the capital, he soon became the horror of all good burghers in the townlet of 20,000. Perhaps he was not worse than the average student (which at that time meant a good deal). But his color-

ful personality and his total disregard of convention focused attention on him; and he really seemed to lack the "golden mean" to an
amazing extent. His morals and behavior were a constant shock to
good society, high-lighted by café brawls and lawsuits, frolics and
practical jokes; he was never regarded as worthy of holding the
pastorate in the church for which he was educated. He always
remained unpredictable; a short time before his death in 1845 he
could still, at a students' banquet, crush a filled wine bottle against
his forehead in a sudden fit of despair.

Worst of all, he could not be ignored. On the contrary, he filled
the nation with ideas corresponding to his life. Every other one of
his countless articles proclaimed that kind of people's revolution
which has never been appreciated in vicarages and state depart-
ments. Among his companions were not only outcasts and de-
bauchees but outright subversive elements, who openly incited
the lower classes to discontent with their lot. And he garlanded his
activities with an incessant flow of "romantic" poetry which was
definitely unsuitable for tea parties and ladies' almanacs, wild and
chaotic, rude and formless, defying all established good sense. It
is understandable that many gagged at his antics and acquiesced in
the sweeping judgment of one of the numerous ladies who had repudiated his love: "He was so terribly coarse!"

But from the very beginning there were people who thought
otherwise, who maintained that his faults loomed so great only
because of the close range, that actually this young Hotspur was
the heir of the realm, the fulfillment of the tradition of centuries
and the guide to the future. Their number increased steadily; and
they were right.

Even those who detested Wergeland had to feel the tremendous
power which radiated from him, and his unmistakable air of genius. This tall and broad-shouldered youngster with the hooked
nose was a giant, not only in body. The twenty-two huge volumes
of his collected works were written between his official debut at
nineteen and his death at thirty-seven. Merely as a physical performance these ten thousand pages written without a typewriter
represent a terrifying achievement. But all through them are lines,

stanzas, and whole poems which, regardless of their amazing pre-
cocity, can only be compared to the gems of world literature;
there is a profusion of ideas, evidence of baffling foresight and
flashlike understanding and a feeling-at-home in most fields of
human tradition. And with all this, his writing was just one portion, for long periods only an occupation of spare moments, of a
life filled with a thousand other activities. This force of nature
with its untutored energy was bound to foam over, often and
violently, erupting brusquely into people's faces. The waterfalls
of spring are not always delicate.

But the focus of his powers was not wild self-will. To us it is
obvious in nearly every detail of his life and work, and nowhere
more clearly than in the chaotic poetry of his youth.

The distinctive mark of Wergeland's mind and the motive force
of his actions was sympathy, an extraordinary power of living in
and identifying himself with all forms of existence; he himself once
called it "the genius of the heart." He was a passionate lover of
nature. From early years, his living quarters were crowded with
all kinds of natural objects, from flowers and stones to moss and
craniums, including his pet, the old blue rabbit with one eye. He
lived in a kind of direct and continuous communication with
everything, a feeling of secret fellowship: "There is a spirit hidden in the darkest dust grain." What to everyday minds was trite
and commonplace spoke directly to him: "I see the bantering
faces of the waves, read the handwriting of the leaves, feel the
pulse in the veins of the grass and hear the heart-beat of the roses."
"My cat, rubbing against my cheek, smothers all heart sores, into
my dog's eye I lower my sorrows as into a deep well."

It was the same spontaneous sympathy he felt toward man, often
witnessed by his friends behind the storm clouds of passion and
temper: his childlike openness of mind, his awkward kindness and
infectious joy, his spontaneous willingness to help. And this feeling
embraced the whole of the universe. His soul "clung like a butterfly to the star-clusters" and heard from the depths of ocean the
pulsation of the earth's globe; and in everything he felt the same
unifying power: eternal, all-embracing love, the community of

the good heart. The mirror of his rabbit's eye reflected the cosmic host of life, from the flaming suns of the firmament down to himself and his pet animal, all playing through the fantasy of the same gracious creator. "The most beautiful moments of the worm are also those of God. See sky and insect flaming from the same delight! There is a moment when the master of earth shares the joy of the flower as that of a sister, and when nobody would be able to crush a caterpillar."

This universal sympathy with its conviction of a loving plan behind everything is the real foundation of Wergeland's indomitable desire for freedom. If there is a spark of divine goodness in everything living, an eternal power of love and reason (to Wergeland again there is little difference between the moral and the intellectual good), then the fight to unfold this individual nucleus against hindrance and oppression is the real struggle for life. Into this militant religion of love Wergeland gathered all the ideologies of liberty on which he had been reared by his radical father: the brusque traditions of the ancient Norsemen and of the revolting farmers, the skeptical independence of Holberg, the flaming ideals of 1789 and the reborn radicalism of the liberals, the dark defiance of Byron and the romantic worship of the gigantic individual. But the moving force remained his own spontaneous feeling of universal love, close to the sublime spirituality of Plato and Christ; and it gave his gospel of liberty its boundless range and its burning intensity. Everywhere in life he saw the same divine battle being fought, in the revolt of oppressed nations and in the unheard sigh of the haunted animal, even in inanimate nature. For freedom longs the little wave rising by the wind from the endless ocean; in the undulating serpent "an angel is struggling to unfold his wings." Liberty is the breath of God, because God is love.

It is easy to connect this attitude with that of other poets along the radical romantic line, from Shelley to Whitman. But what distinguishes Wergeland from most of them is that in mind and background this romantic and revolutionary dreamer was at the same time a rugged son of earth, close to its real life.

In spite of all differences, there was no generation toward which

HENRIK WERGELAND

Wergeland felt more of veneration and loyalty than that of Eids-voll: they had basic conceptions in common. Behind his luxuriant emotion he himself had much of their austere seriousness and belief in sound reason; he was himself a man of duty and action. To him as to them, Greece, Rome, and ancient Norway were not only the classical grounds of liberty, but the traditional home of discipline and sober thought. Holberg certainly was the radical reformer, but quite as much the man of dauntless realistic honesty and sense of obligation. For the Christian religion of love Wergeland never forgot its somber sense of responsibility and its background of bitter human self-knowledge. With all his lofty ideas, he was amazingly sober in his approach to life, far from inane optimism and vague literary fictions. Certainly the world was governed by eternal powers which carried their law in themselves, the forces of "true liberty" both in the rationalistic and the Christian meaning. But he knew only too well how many of the forces that pressed on for liberty in himself were not noble children of love and reason but just mad, perverse lawlessness, sin. He called himself a unity of "cherub and beast"; Byron early came to represent to him this doubleness of proud independence and sterile, isolating wildness. He saw the same picture everywhere in the history of mankind: how much of its struggle was not against oppression and tyranny, but against inner forces, misused freedom, ignorance, and evil. But in Wergeland this insight never developed into pessimism and escape from life; it turned into a program of action, based on the moral responsibility of the individual. The task of man is struggle, not only against tyranny, but for the good powers in himself, and a struggle to help and direct, enlighten and augment them in his fellow creatures by active humanity.

To make these ideas clear in the terms of 1830 was the main purpose of his early writing, especially of that poetic monster *Creation, Man, and Messiah,* a verse-drama of 720 pages, published when Wergeland was twenty-two. It is a unique piece of literature, "gigantic as the Milky Way," comprising the origin and development of cosmos and history down to the death of Christ. Taking everything into consideration, however, the most amazing thing about the book is not its lack of clarity and moderation, but the grandeur of the ideas and the power with which the youthful author has made the subject serve them. The work begins with the creation of man, "the germs left in the slime by spirits," endowed from the very conception with the birthright of free moral decision. Through the centuries of prehistory and history Wergeland follows the slow development of individuals and nations toward real liberty, their fight against kings and clergy and their struggle to understand themselves and realize their common ideals of freedom, truth, and love as symbolized in the Saviour. In this immense historical pageant, filled out by his contemporary poems, he musters his allies in past and present, from the prophets, Socrates, Plato, and Christ to Washington, Kosciusko, Lafayette, and Bolivar; from North America, "where the seed of my own liberty grew in the shelter of the sycamore," to France, "the land of life," and the white cliffs of Great Britain, "freedom's stronghold mid the ocean." But all of it converges into a program for his own work. Poets are no articles of luxury, but servants of their nation; he mentions the skald Sigvat as an example. Their task is not only to point to the future, but to work toward it in the everyday toil of their compatriots, making their own human growth a part of the growth of the people.

In the *Creation* he had shown where *his* work awaited him. "The aim of my continued efforts," he wrote, "will be to make my life a commentary to my poem, as faithful and prosaic as possible." In one huge arch he spanned the universe and the world, past and present, to end with himself as man and poet and his task in the small Norwegian nation.

❈

He had fifteen working years after writing these words. The highest praise possible is to say that he really managed to live up to his program.

He awoke to manhood under the thunder of world-wide revolutions, and these horizons never closed to him again. His ideals remained universal; his fight in far-off Norway always had a note of international fellowship. His hopes got their shining brightness against the somber background of the totalitarian prison-states of his days; he found comfort and encouragement in knowing that "United Nations" fought with him all over the globe in the same battle of freedom—Greeks and East-Indians, tortured Spanish republicans, and slaving American Negroes, all "created for equal honor with us."

> I hope for Poland, because I must.
> There is a God, and he is just.

In a direct and personal way he managed to make his compatriots feel their local struggle as a section of the common front of fighting humanity. But the mark of his own work was increasing closeness to the immediate tasks. The more he came to grips with the factual problems at home, the better he felt that he was serving the world.

The frame of this work was Norway's free constitution; it is not an exaggeration to say that Wergeland worshiped it. He had lived his childhood in Eidsvoll; his father had been a member of the assembly, he knew all the traditions about it, he wrote its history, it grew into his life. And love made him seeing. With strange acumen he grasped, more clearly than anybody before him, how in spite of all foreign patterns the constitution was no importation but a realization of the deepest ideals of the people from ages of old, faithfully guarded through the centuries of oppression. Norway's real heritage was not romantic antiquities, but a way of thinking and living, not the Viking ideals of plunder and robbery ("the spirit of lawlessness was outlaw in ancient Norway"), but "the original, Gothic liberalism, which created the lawbound freedom, founded on reason and moral conceptions, even before Christianity," "that righteousness, that patriotism, that natural good sense which never has been lacking in the Gothic tribes," and which still was a living force in the farmers of his own age. In the constitution these ideals were expressed in our terms and in amazing fullness, as a program to be given concrete existence by the new generation.

But to Wergeland this program had a much deeper and wider meaning than to any of his contemporaries. The constitution was not merely a political arrangement, a charter of the freedoms and rights of the individual; much more it was a father's house of common duty and mutual help. Behind its dry paragraphs he saw a society built on the Christian principles of life, where all citizens should collaborate peacefully as "citizens of God's realm," in that kind of liberty which involves the law. He knew only too clearly that in this respect the constitution was still little more than a list of possibilities; it was necessary to make these realities. With all his radicalism he detested revolutions, except as a measure of extreme emergency; in Norway the foresight of the fathers had made bloody revolts superfluous if only the needs were met early and realistically enough, without complacency, in the spirit of the constitution itself. To work in that direction became the program of his life.

The condition of everything was to safeguard the freedom of the democratic state. From his early student days, Wergeland became one of the champions of Norway's unscathed independence within the union with Sweden. He coined the slogans and ran the risks. He made the day of the constitution, May 17, a national festival, in open defiance of the Swedish king; he became a symbol of freedom, people cried "Hurrah" when they saw him walk down the streets with his brisk step and lifted head and the eternal carnation in his buttonhole. When in a great speech in 1833—at twenty-five—he consecrated a national monument which had been boycotted by all cautious burghers, he became the very mouthpiece of the nation's youth and of its self-assertion.

But national independence was just a condition to him. The real task ahead was to raise the people to inner freedom; he joined the fight of the farmers for political power. Nothing shows better the purity of his ideals. It was Wergeland's class which still governed Norway. In challenging their political and social monopoly he brought down upon himself the full ire of his own group, of those who at all times think that there is always enough of democracy. He gladly accepted the challenge: "I belong to the fish who live in foaming waters, not in stagnant ponds." Earlier than anybody else he grasped the historical significance of the farmers' march into political life: they had carried the nation's liberty through the period of oppression, and were to carry it further on. But still more important was his feeling of justice, his simple confidence in the common man, and his desire to help him. He had lived among farmers, he knew their struggle with the soil, their hardships and problems; again this young man became a mouthpiece to whom the nation had to listen. He had his triumphant share in the first great victories of the people in the 1830's.

Beyond the political results he saw social liberation. Regardless of personal security, he threw himself against the economic injustices which were still inaccessible to political procedure: the grinding and exploitation of the people by sheriffs, moneylenders, and solicitors. He became a kind of people's tribune, a social security system of his own; his articles hit the mark without respect of persons, his biting farces won the laughter to his side. He duly paid the price for it; some of the lawsuits he ran into pursued him to his deathbed, ruining his economy and embittering his joy. But the more clearly did he understand the people he fought for. In some of the literary sketches from these years of struggle there is a social indignation which shows how far he had already transgressed the cautious limits of liberty visualized by the constituent fathers.

He did not stop there. True democracy was a matter of the whole culture of the nation. The distinctive mark of old Greece had been "the universal character of its intellectual life"; in our times as well nations had to be judged by the degree to which they managed to make the broad masses participate in culture. Modern Norway corresponded badly to such ideals, with its thin crust of Danish language and half-foreign traditions, borne by a narrow literary elite. Again Wergeland saw the democratic program beyond the limits of his class. Only the traditions and the language of the nation itself could carry a homogeneous Norwegian culture, and again he pointed to the farmers, "the folk life in the broad people, which was and is the characteristic stamina of Norway."

HENRIK WERGELAND

He called for a Norse theater, a Norse poetry and music, reared on the native traditions. He tried to write in the dialects derived from Old Norse which were still the spoken language of the people; he approached his own Danish to the vernacular. Even the intimate instrument of his mind he felt as a trust from the many.

With all these efforts, however, democratic liberation was only one part of Wergeland's program. Still more important than giving the lower classes their rights was to make them deserve their freedom and to enable them to use it. Too well he knew how many of his compatriots were just sitting around, "empty of thoughts, each in his corner"; and "ignorance and serfdom mean the same thing." His work for changing the people's outlook and bringing the world of ideas home to them is one of the noblest chapters of Norwegian tradition.

He began immediately after his *Creation* was published asking a patriotic society to use him for their educational drive: "I will do something, and I feel my powers. Please, pile, heap work upon me!" In eloquent manifestoes he aroused the farmers to interest: "Read and learn, and you will not any more feel yourself cast away to a joyless by-place, even if you are sitting in a cottage behind snow and mountains and barren moor! You will follow your plough as an enlightened and free individual; your body is tied to the cliffs of Norway, but your spirit is created for a free flight around heaven and earth." The main instrument of progress is the free book: time will come when the poorest working man is sitting outside his cottage on Sundays with a pamphlet in his hand. All through his life Wergeland worked for public libraries. He personally opened one in Eidsvoll, giving the books himself or begging them from relatives and friends. He toured the countryside, lecturing and organizing, scolding and encouraging, irresistible. Soon his reading clubs were frequented by "farmers, cottagers, hired people, youngsters, even some of the gentler sex"; their bookplate was a rising sun. When good reading on a subject was unavailable, he wrote himself, one volume after another: textbooks in orthography and history, guides to useful herbs, a catechism on the duties of a citizen; his articles teem with practical advice about subjects important to the common man. He organized patriotic societies for all kinds of good work. He began a Sunday school in Eidsvoll, and a high school for grown-up farm girls and boys, teaching himself; he gathered young and old to "citizens' festivals," to songs and games and information. One aim went through all of it: to arouse the proud sense of responsibility of being a citizen of free Norway.

But behind it was a general program of justice, not class politics. In working for the farmers, he soon discovered that they themselves were an upper class toward their own cotters. Without tempering his fight for the former he took up a parallel fight for the latter, the proletarians of the countryside, unprotected in the "terrific war between poverty and wealth, misery and greed." When the struggle in the rural districts began to yield results, his interest switched over to a new social layer which was hardly recognized as existent yet: the working people in town. Here the point of view was not yet political, only humanitarian; but the appeal to self-consciousness and self-respect was the same, and so was the untiring energy. The six volumes of his periodical *For the Working Class* are still moving to read, filled as they are with his endless eagerness and patience. There is no explaining away of realities; he does not mince words about dirt and laziness, vice and drink. But he saw too well how much of the depravity of the people of the East End sprang from their slum life, their lack of "clean and sanitary houses"; and his heart ached for them. Unwearyingly he pointed out what might make their existence more tolerable, even under present conditions, from good books on the shelf to ivy on the wall and a loom for the housewife. He opened a public library for the working people of Oslo in his own home, himself serving and advising the readers. He, who "could climb to Heaven on the flickering thread of a cobweb," did not feel above the most commonplace work, if only it served the great aim: to make Norway a happier place to live in.

HENRIK WERGELAND

To cut Wergeland's work into sections and compartments is to do him an injustice, however; he did not feel or act that way. To him, the promise given ·to the nation at Eidsvoll was unlimited and the task boundless; he just put his shoulder to the wheel wherever he saw a need. During his summer walks, he used to carry pine seeds in his pockets, strewing them wherever he found a barren spot in the woods. Such seeds abound in his writings as well, regardless of political and social distinctions.

The final aim of his work was a general liberation of the mind. His life was a running fight against intellectual and religious prejudice, and like his master Holberg he could give powerful blows because he combined radicalism and respect. No one more than Wergeland could be penetrated by the universal love which is the nucleus of Christianity. The more violently he turned against those who would narrow religion down by zealotism and put up "the motley curtain of dogma" between God and man. On graduating in divinity from the university, he denied the dogma of eternal punishment; when the examining professor asked on what authority he based his assumption, he pounded his chest and cried: "I have it here!" To him nothing could more involve liberty than the teaching of Christ: "Were the angels not free, then revolt in Heaven!" Real Christianity is not stagnation, but progress, liberating the individuals from their bonds and thus first reuniting them in love. "To be oneself in part and whole," involving the entire field of thought and belief, is a duty not only to the intellect, but to God; nobody knows better than He how little the form means and how much the conviction. There is humility in this attitude, but also strength and pride. When well-meaning people sent Wergeland on his deathbed a prayer book of the traditional type, he returned it with the words that he found more comfort in one of those glances with which he painfully turned in his bed to look for a star.

And there was a deeper emancipation still. The worst result of bigotry and prejudice was to make man callous and cruel. Wherever Wergeland turned his eye, he saw these forces at work. In fighting them he showed what wide obligations were involved in his ideal of freedom and how it made him seeing.

All through his life he pleaded the cause of suffering animals. Again and again he pictured the senseless pain inflicted on them by neglect and cruelty and thoughtless habit; among his works is "Speech to Humanity in Humankind by the Pony Brownie," appealing for mercy in the name of Him who blessed the sparrows under the sky. Under the hill on which Wergeland lived, he posted a poem: "Cast off, the road is steep!" and was not afraid to add striking arguments to the poetical ones if the drivers did not pay immediate attention. He saw the plight of children, in a society that was not made for them. His writings teem with appeals on their behalf, protests against cruelty and mismanagement, cries for help. It was not just pity, but a deeper realism: society could not afford to let the germs of genius be lost. One of his pet ideas was that of picking out the intelligent children and having them educated at the expense of the state. He saw the plight of women, pinned in their corners by prejudice, contempt and lack of education. He pleaded the cause of unmarried mothers, not concealing his self-reproach (he himself had an illegitimate child, which he later adopted); he condemned the current sexual morals, dominated by the brutal self-interest of man. He even foresaw the general uprising of the average, "happy" woman against "the masters of the earth" when once they get to understand their real status and refuse to remain any longer "a charming interlink between man and the animals."

Not all of his proposals were adopted by his contemporaries, or even regarded as sensible. Details might be impractical; his general aims were often far beyond the understanding of the age, and his unending enthusiasm could be tiresome. When he, nevertheless, in his short lifetime, won among the people a position of confidence and affection which has never been equaled, it was because the common man instinctively realized what was the moving power of all his work; as his father put it: "Nobody has loved the people as sincerely as he did." When they saw this upper-classer wear simple clothes, eat simple food, and harden himself by Spartan exercises in order to share the general living conditions of his nation; when they saw him walk with petitions from house to house, begging for old clothes to give the poor, giving his own money, coat, and blankets; when they saw him faithfully keep his friendship with degraded outcasts in whom he still saw the spark of humanity, or gather books for the patients in the hospitals and the hopeless life prisoners; when they saw how among his thousand occupations he was always accessible, always had time—they grasped what he meant by calling humanity "the heart of freedom."

He often used a lofty language; the man in the street did not always understand his speeches and his poetry. But even the poorest farm lad knew that this youngster with the fiery eyes was his friend, who approached him with sincere respect as a fellow-citizen of the free Norway they were building together. When in 1832, at twenty-four, Wergeland walked through the country with his little knapsack, the common people gathered around him everywhere to see him and speak to him; "the magnates in their state coaches would hardly have excited such attention." In his later years he used to say that if he left his gold watch with his name on a bridge in Oslo's East End, it would remain untouched.

The symbol of his position was the celebration of the Seventeenth of May which he annually arranged for the children, himself writing the songs, giving the speeches, and directing their innocent enjoyment in the bright spring evening, sitting high on his beloved Brownie in the middle of the exultant crowd—a vision of Norway's future which has never been forgotten since, filled with the thought of the man and the naïveté of the child, and its deep seriousness.

From this life his poetry grew, and would be unintelligible without it. His practical activity outlines his human maturation. His poetry reveals the sources and the deep unity behind it.

He had violent forces to cope with; his first poems show the battle. Hardly in any literature is there a poetry of comparable

volume and quality in which the unbridled imagination of genius
breaks forth with such an overwhelming, almost terrifying might.
His myth-making fancy moves in leaps of association through all
times and worlds with sovereign arbitrariness. The violent rhythms
burst with ideas and images; everything is high-strung, swelling, and luxuriant, like "the thought of demented angels." He
himself felt as if he were in the hands of the powers when his
visions came, whirled away "like a mote among motes." Nothing
could be farther from the main line of Norse literary tradition,
not making exception for the most bizarre skaldic verse.

But this difficult poetry has a unique charm: seldom in literature
has the primitive spontaneity of genius been so nakedly revealed.
Sometimes the reader has the feeling of being present at some
majestic event in nature. And in every feature there is what
Wergeland himself called "the wildborn dignity" of his mind—
a mixture of spirituality and concretion, of earthbound sensuality
and dizzy seraphic flight which soon left his stimulator, Shakespeare, behind and is wholly his own. The wide plains of romantic
feeling are opened to Norwegian poetry in his verse, never to be
closed again.

Through the struggling confusion, moreover, there is from the
very beginning a fight for clarity, in idea and form; the teaching
of Holberg had not been lost on his pupil. Wergeland's thoughts
are not soddy and muddled, there are just too many of them as yet.
Here is no trace of that weakish vagueness which he ridiculed in
many romanticists; everything is power and energy. Through the
drifting clouds of formlessness there are sudden flashes of blinding
lucidity, which are not unknown in Norse tradition, and a patient
toil for mastery of the unruly verse. And the struggle for form is
the expression of a moral fight: Wergeland's painful liberation
from that bitter and misanthropic Byronism which for years dark-
ened his youth. These poems show how hard he had to work for
his own personal liberty, and how dearly he paid for the optimism
which was to carry his humanitarian work.

In the creation of his maturity these forces of counterpoise
gradually won the upper hand. It cost him long and patient self-

education, which for years made his poetic writing shrink to a trickle; but he emerged as a different man. He always remained a "romantic" poet; his basic experience was always that of universal sympathy, conceived in a realm of his own where colors and proportions were not of this world and mute things spoke in celestial voices. But more and more the spontaneous act of conception involved the form and the law. Something of the tropical exuberance was lost; but other things came instead. It is the testimony of an almost incredible perfectibility that the lucid and simple nursery rhymes of the 1840's were written by the man who one decade before had indulged in the *Creation*.

Still deeper goes the ripening of his feeling; the universal sympathy comes down from the universe and goes into the huts of men. Again something of the seraphic splendor is lost. There is a new depth instead, and a new stamp of reality. Some of these efforts are pathetic. He struggled to become a folk poet, and the obstacles often were insurmountable; too long had he lived among the stars. But nobody would wish away from his works all these songs for the common man, ditties for miners and chanteys for sailors, "ballads," and versified commandments. Again they testify to the unity of his endeavor: no simple task was too simple, if only it had to do with the fundamental things. In recompense, things came closer to him; the feeling of fellowship broke the barriers. In the social poems of his later years the romanticist is already close to realism, not that of the eyes, but of the heart. In his series of commemorative poems, ranging from the leaders of the country and the world to the ruined genius found dead at the roadside, the individualization is not too sharp; but the hidden kernel of nobility and grandeur is brought out with the force of the sculptor.

His most intimate expression remained the soliloquy with nature: a tree, a flower, a child. The filmlike motley of his youth has disappeared. The absorption is complete: he is engulfed in a depth of goodness revealed to him alone. But this isolating concentration is just momentary; around him are the whispering voices of life's active, daily community, without which he could not exist. Often he connects the two worlds himself, or they insensibly mingle: he

is talking about the same things. The rain quenches the thirst of
the tree, the dew from the leaves bathes the drying shrub, and the
hind with her fawn kneels in the grass, licking the full drops in a
hazy understanding of this miracle of love. Should man have less
of love toward his fellow-beings?

This continuous contact with eternity gave him his defiant
courage, through all delicacy of emotions, and that manly resignation which was the definite sign of his ripening. He often felt
bitterly alone, singing in a tiny language to a recalcitrant little nation in a corner of the world, isolated as the Lapp minstrel before
his handful of souls in the chilling fields of ice. But how to despair,
knowing what he knew? "The world must still be young," just
hinting at the first of her boundless promises. For thousands of
years the moss has sprinkled its tiny silver calixes over the barren
cliffs, to give food for one single fir tree; should not we be as
patient and confident? What are the vicissitudes of life to one
who has once seen and understood the reality behind it?

How Venus sparkles to-night! Have the heavens also spring?
Now the stars have shone all through the winter;
　　now they rest and rejoice. Hallelujah!

What riches for a mortal!
My soul rejoices in Heaven's joy of spring, and shall
　　take part in that of the earth.
It sparkles stronger than the vernal stars, and
　　it will soon open with the flowers.

Glorious Evening Star! I uncover my head.
A crystal bath upon it falls thy sheen.

There is kinship between the soul and the stars.
It steps in the starlight outside the curtain of the face,
　　whose folds have disappeared.

HENRIK WERGELAND

There were many who did not believe him, who refused to see more of his life than the trifles and the inconsistencies. His answer to them was his deathbed. On a chilly seventeenth of May he contracted pneumonia followed by phthisis. The disease needed fourteen months to break the strength of the giant; those months he made a sacred memory to his nation.

Tradition has turned it into a tale of roses; it wasn't. There was much of trivial anxiety, even hatred and persecution, and still more of pain; the greater was his victory. He early guessed that he would have to die; there was a feverish haste over his work: so much was left to do! But in the depth of his heart there was a sovereign serenity. He had never feared Death, rather regarded him as a faithful friend and collaborator in the good work of nature. In face of the final test he would show his nation what he had really lived for.

He once wrote that if you have the heart of a good man, you shall have on the day before your death "the same smile and the same song on your lips as before"; so he had himself. To the very end, the bed in his sickroom overflowed with the activities of his days of strength, poetry and prose insolubly mingled. He filled the newspapers with articles on good reforms: better prisons and less noisy hospitals, measures to protect the animals and laws to protect religious nonconformists. He sent seeds to the gardens of the cotters in Eidsvoll and a silver drinking bowl to be emptied in commemoration of the constitution; he published his working-man's periodical, a poem of homage to the flag, and a song for the children's homes. Among his last publications were a leaflet about a new, useful Russian sawbuck (with an illustration and verse to sing with the work) and a sailor's chantey called "Last Voyage." He used many of his precious months on the fight for opening Norway to the Jews, a reform which was not passed till six years after his death; he bombarded the parliament with petitions and the public with moving poems, urging them to see clearly in this crucial test of Christian democracy. In the midst of all he wrote, as recreation, one of his most luxuriant works of fancy, *The English Pilot*, with fervent declarations of love for English liberty and incisive pictures from English high-life. He wrote hymns of humble and undogmatic confidence in God; he had power left to begin and finish his autobiography, scrawled under the eyes of death with a self-irony and humor which draws from inexhaustible depths of health. And meanwhile, the newspapers published, again and again, small lyrical poems of a lucid beauty which suddenly made even his old enemies understand what they were going to lose.

The keystone of this miraculous year was his remodeling of the *Creation*, "to show them my real intentions." There was much to correct in the form, nothing in the basic ideas; he had always believed in them. But in a new concluding canto he returned to the great views of his youth, telling the world about the future he dreamed for it. Looking into coming millenniums, his visionary eye saw a community of happy republics, only divided by hedges of roses, where war was abolished and prisons turned into granaries, where religion was a common good and race differences forgotten, where the workers lived as happily in their cleanly quarters as wealth in its palaces, and men, women, and children equally shared the rights of life, guided by the goodness of the human heart. Who could ever doubt that "once the demoniac delusions will vanish in a world which is embraced by the arms of forgiveness and filled with the light of understanding"?

His work was done; in the flower songs of his last months he retired into his own world, writing poems where all was soul, and the limits of life and death insensibly faded away. In his last poem, the opening rosebuds "betray to him the religion of Heaven": he had indeed been right all the time about the secret behind everything, all promises are going to be fulfilled, he is even going to see Brownie again and ride him "up along the mountains of thunder and across the streams of lightning." From such visions his eyes closed in the last sleep.

In the evening of the night on which he died people of the working class gathered outside his house, waiting solemnly and silently in the pale Nordic twilight. From the morning on, an endless line passed by the coffin, many weeping loudly; he was soon buried in flowers. Many brought their children, and lifted them up so that they might see him.

※

It is still too early to evaluate his influence; he belongs to the living present, not to the past. But the essence of it can be outlined already.

He was born in one of the great revolutionary periods of history, in a small and recently liberated nation struggling to found a new existence; he became one of its great bridge builders. He took up into himself all the traditions of the past, national and foreign, restrictive and revolutionary, merged them, and turned them toward the future as a constructive program of modern life, where the country's deepest national heritage was reborn. He made democracy an ideal of everyday life, with immediate tasks for everybody; he made his compatriots feel their freedom as a mutual responsibility. He taught them "to be themselves," but never to forget, that liberty without community is senseless; he opened to poetry the hidden forces of emotion and fancy, but taught it to seek its justification in real life. He made radicalism a tradition in his nation, because its task is never finished; and he did all this with a believing optimism, at the same time naïve and close to facts, which made his vision prophetic. He guessed the secret needs, not only of the present, but of the future; there is hardly any field of good work in modern Norway where he has not put in the first spade. His voice is still heard, stumbling from eagerness, warm and strong.

He could do it because of the mental health that beneath the turbulent surface balanced his tremendous forces and gave them aim and direction. But the secret of his influence was the depth of love that was in him. He said on his deathbed that he was "nothing but a poet"; it meant that everything in him drew its strength from the heart. This spontaneous goodness overflowed into all he worked for and made his life a national legend, the wonderful symbol of his ideas; even those who know little about his program and never read his poems, have their share in the warmth that emanated from him. His fellow-countrymen still feel something like an embarrassment in trying to make clear what he really means to them, as a secretly shared happiness, which is as factual as life itself, but can not be fully explained. He is always there; his life has just begun.

TENSE INTERLUDE

In his visions Wergeland had glimpsed the landscape of the future. But he well knew that many in the nation did not share his dreams; the great problems of progress could not be solved without a struggle. All through the period of his contemporaries, the generation dominant from 1830 to 1860, these contrasts were shaping up for battle; and more or less consciously the armies were grouped for or against his ideas.

Leading circles in Norway were not on Wergeland's side either before or immediately after his death. They represented the governing class, the venerable traditions, the old and honored names, and they were an impressive group. Norway has rarely seen such a sudden lining-up of intelligence. Behind their arrogant sophistication, moreover, there was a genuine idealism, a sound respect for intellectual order and regular work; they resisted Wergeland and his followers because they felt it as a moral duty. But there was something anemic about them—"a generation of silhouettes"; they belonged to a social group on the defensive. They had much of Holberg's ironical reserve, but little of his broad mind; and they totally lacked Wergeland's virile closeness to life. They did not believe very much in the people and were frightened by his vision of Norway's democratic future. To them the constitution was no song of promise; they were rather nervous about what they had. Gradually they were isolated. From the 50's the group began closing its ranks into a reactionary block to which law meant the preservation of their own privileges, looking to the common Swedish-Norwegian king as a conservative guarantee against the rising wave of mobocracy.

But before the ossification got under way, this generation was called upon to fulfill one of the greatest tasks of the century. By the irony of history it devolved upon these cautious and finical urbanites to bring to the surface again that broad stream of popular traditions which had gone underground in the late Middle Ages, and which was soon to sweep them away in its accumulated flood. Wergeland had early maintained that Norway's strongest line of tradition was not the Danish written literature of the upper class, but the heritage preserved by the farmers; but he anticipated more than he really knew. About the middle of the century, within a decade, this whole folk culture suddenly emerged from oblivion. The youth of the silhouette generation had longed for something to give them a greater sense of being at home in the land, and their boldest dreams came true.

There is a Norwegian folk tale of the time of the Great Plague about a depopulated and forgotten village in the woods which was rediscovered after long years by an errant hunter; he shot his arrow into the forest and heard from the thicket the ring of the silenced church bell. In the same sudden way the traditions of the country were retrieved; the nation awoke and found itself rich. Feverish and eager scholars hastened into the countryside and brought back in inexhaustible plenty the ballads and folk songs, the fairy tales, the historical traditions, the language, the folk music, the arts of architecture, painting, and wood carving. There were no detached fragments, but a homogeneous culture of striking character. They followed up the collections with a scholarly research in history and language that caught the attention of the world. On their search they also discovered the country itself, a virgin land of lakes and mountains, as it can still be seen, untouched and moving, in their sketchbooks. After centuries of foreign unions, when the national mind had to grope for expression through all kinds of inappropriate mediums, this generation suddenly saw in their hands the longed-for prerequisite of real independence: an unbroken tradition back to the origins of the tribe.

Still more important than the discovery itself was the interpretation of what was found. There was a romantic "national renaissance" all over the Germanic, Anglo-Saxon and Slavic worlds in the nineteenth century; eagerly nations sought support for their existence in folk life and historical traditions. But these renaissance movements had various purposes. In some nations they laid new foundations for democracy; in others they created a chauvinistic ideology, a worship of muddy instincts and cryptic "race characters" which broke with the liberal traditions of the West. The generation of national renaissance in Norway kept clear of such aberrations. They were rather lukewarm toward the program of political reform; but they were still more distant from any primitivism. What thrilled them in the traditions was not dead antiquities, but the mind, and not only the mysterious underground, but quite as much those constructive powers which had made Norway a part of the general European development: the intellectual honesty, the sober feeling and sound humor; "even in the most arbitrary creations of fancy the Norse will have common sense." They felt that they were maintaining a national tradition when they opposed Wergeland's formlessness (even if they did it in a pedantic way); actually, they were not too far from his own ideas in his later years. It is difficult to overestimate the importance of this interpretation to the whole development of Norwegian national feeling.

Their own poetry fitted well into the picture. Compared to that of Wergeland, it may seem narrow; their moral standards were rather Victorian, their pictures of folk life sometimes dangerously idyllic. But they managed to open the national sources of romantic feeling and absorb the shock even of Wergeland's youth poetry without losing their sense of proportion; they never totally forgot that Holberg had lived. Young Wergeland apart, Norwegian literature has no romanticism that can be compared to that of the German extremists. The poets found an inexhaustible reservoir of material in ballads and folk tales. But the strongest impulse of the tradition came from its spirit and style, and from the landscape behind it, which really was discovered by them; and it gave their poetry a clear and tender note which still grips Norwegian hearts with a peculiar intimacy. Most of these poets were believing Christians, and, like Petter Dass before them, they made the standards of Norwegian folk religion resound from nature itself, finding again, in the words of their foremost hymnist, "that stillness, lucidity, and depth which most appeal to the minds of our people."

The representative man of the group was J. S. Welhaven (1807–73). He was born in Holberg's native city, himself an intellectual type with a devastating power of irony; his master in contemporary literature was Heine. But he lacked the revolutionary fervor of his idols. His impertinent manner concealed a shy sensitiveness, a sincere belief in the strength of classical form, and a pure Christian idealism. But his ideas did not open him to human contact, except for critical purposes. There was something inhibited about him; he lacked surplus. His feeling, clear, but tenuous, filled his verse, but not very much more. The watchword of his aesthetics was relentless retouching, "till all is clear and all the mists have vanished"; to a man of that type Wergeland could be nothing but a horror. He used much of his youth in attacks on the "rude" giant; honest in purpose and often correct in detail, he was blind to the deeper meaning of his enemy's work. He always remained aloof from the progressive movements of his age.

The enduring part of his creation is to be found among his personal lyrics; these make him one of Norway's great national poets. He brought his joy and sorrow to the mountains and the forest; and he heard out of them a melody which still resounds with unbroken charm. It is significant that some of his best poems with foreign motif take their theme from Greek mythology; in his pictures from the valleys there is a delicate, vitreous clarity of feeling and expression, close both to the ballads and to the Norwegian landscape, which may rightly be called classical. In his late songs, after the literary feuds have faded away, there is a deep, resigned calm molded into a form of marblelike firmness, which draws from the noblest traditions of the nation.

With all their merits, there was something static about these men; they were complacent, and increasingly so. Soon after the middle of the century, however, the smooth surface began to be agitated by the pressure of forces below, a new democratic line-up, parallel with the resurge of radicalism and the deep transformation of economic life all through Europe. Many of the rising ideas had not found literary expression yet. But there is an increasing uneasiness about the role of literature in modern life, a feeling of new realities and new responsibilities. To the whole coming generation the revolution of February, 1848, brought a deep shock: over the national idyll flashed the glaring light from the contrasts of the great world.

Leading in the movement was the farmers' group; and it soon became clear how deep was their challenge to the established order. Their self-confidence had been growing steadily since 1814. The religious movement of Hauge and their first political victories had given them a feeling of independence hitherto unknown; they began to carry their demands into new fields. From the 1840's they advocated radical democratic reforms in the educational system. The "national renaissance" was bound to increase their feeling of importance; their own culture became a focus of research and literary creation, a subject of the nation's pride. Most important, however, was the realization that their own language, the spoken dialects of the countryside and of working people in town, was no degraded patois, but a coherent, homogeneous idiom, directly descended from Old Norse and the carrier of the nation's literary tradition in ballads and tales since Edda times. This discovery was made by one of their own, the farm boy Ivar Aasen (1813–96), a self-taught philological genius, who about 1850 created a common spelling of the New Norse dialects for practical use. Literary circles greeted his learned works with a romantic enthusiasm which did not last long: this inconspicuous scholar with the gentle manners was a revolutionary. His goal was to give Norway back a language of her own; but quite as important were to him the social aspects. He knew from bitter experience how much the lower classes were hampered by the Danish language taught to them amid sweat and tears from the first day in school. By gradually introducing New Norse instead he would help the people in its struggle for education and development. Little by little the broad masses should thus be made the "chief cornerstone" of culture, in a democratization much more radical than anything visualized even by Wergeland.

Hardly anywhere has the idea of social and cultural equality been set forth in more thorough-going fashion than in the writings of Aasen. His idea struck home. His works released a violent struggle for the introduction of New Norse and, simultaneously, for a radical Norwegianizing of the Danish language in Norway, a controversy which has not yet abated. Into this struggle he threw his songs. They were no fighting poetry, but through them a new section of the people spoke on its own behalf. Many lines of tradition converge in his verse, from the Edda to Holberg, from Christianity to Goethe; his lapidary style is akin to that of the proverbs and ballads as well as of Welhaven. But in his central poems Aasen reached below "literature" down to the nation itself, speaking in its own voice in majestic simplicity about its long struggle for life and its strong wisdom, its urge for freedom and its sense of justice, its spirit of endurance and its manly resignation under the law. Past and present merge in these songs; sometimes the High One himself seems to be talking, in the same language and against the same landscape, reduced to its eternal elements of space and grandeur, mountains and sea. By its very existence this poetry was a promise of the future, when all the nation's powers could be fully set free.

Behind the farmers new social forces raised their head. Around 1850 the first efforts were made to organize working people, no longer for humanitarian purposes, but for political struggle. The fright of the governing group showed how desperately dangerous the attempt was felt to be. It was crushed by reckless force. But the episode spelled the end of the quietistic conception of society. No great poetry was born from it; but the influence was deep. Three young poets were connected with the movement and had a narrow escape, the leaders of the next generation.

Aside from the political and social demands there were signs of a growing intellectual revolt fostered by the new ideas of triumphant science, against the whole bourgeois system of moral and religious conventions. To the reigning class, nothing could be more execrable; in church and school orthodoxy turned an unbroken front against the new radicalism. But it became increasingly clear that the rising wave would also reach this basic scale of values; long before the clash of the main armies the attack was heralded in one important field by a brave and lonely fighter, Henrik Wergeland's sister Camilla Collett (1813–95).

She had not the wide range of her brother, whom she did not understand too well; by her long and unrequited love to Welhaven and by her marriage to one of his friends she was even closely connected with Henrik's enemies. But there was at the bottom of her soul a passion of almost terrifying power, and a burning sense of justice; when death left her lonely, she consecrated her forces to the cause of subjected woman. She had no program of inaugurating literary realism, but as a matter of fact she anticipated it; the task forced the weapon into her hand. In a long series of novels, pamphlets, and treatises from the early 50's on she pitilessly tore the veil away from the injustice done to women in the very midst of "civilized" society, quite especially in her own class. With the shrillness of a cry she struck at the hollowness of accepted standards; the diaries of her own tragic love show how mercilessly honest she was both toward herself and others. Outside the question of women's rights Camilla Collett remained a conservative; but her influence pointed much farther than the special problem to which she devoted her energy. Her pathetic figure, vexed by lonely strife, by passion and sorrow—"the condor" she has been called—became, like that of her brother, a general symbol of liberty and a constant reminder of the new responsibilities of literature in the struggle for freedom.

The great expression of this brooding tenseness in all fields of life was the poet and journalist A. O. Vinje (1818–70).

From his early childhood in one of the mountain valleys of Telemark, this precocious farm lad displayed an amazing intellectual voracity, a sensitivity of feeling and a passionate desire for independence which was almost comparable to that of a native. His touch of skeptical irony was sharpened by early reading in Holberg and Heine, both of whom he felt as national allies. His life-long and hopeless fight for bread and for recognition in the literary circles of his time gave him a personal note of violence and detach-ment. He became the great literary buccaneer of contemporary Norway. He fervently joined Aasen's language movement; and in this as in most other respects his New Norse weekly *The Dales-man*, caustic in form, reckless in opinions, and sparkling with tal-ent and wit, pathos, and guile, became the anathema of the gov-erning group. This newspaper, which lived and starved with its editor and finally died with him in 1870, became a mouthpiece and a transformer of the increasing disquiet which pressed on in the Norwegian society. His range of interest was fantastic, his curi-osity insatiable, and his horizon the whole world. There was hardly a problem, political or social, religious or moral, on which he had not a highly personal opinion or at least a witty remark. He was the first to introduce Darwin in Norway; one of his books was a ruthless attack—in English—on the social backwardness of Great Britain, and it was one of the sorrows of his life that he was unable to subject the United States to the same treatment. More danger-ous than the details of opinion was the spirit, the unfaltering in-quisitiveness, the disrespectful approach; here the general revalua-tion was already at work.

But his own standards were stable enough. Vinje's background was motley, and so were his reactions; even when he was most consistent, his way of thought was often just his own. But there was one set of values he never questioned: that solid morality, that common sense and "health of mind" which he had found in the farmers of his native valley, and which to him reflected the good sense and faithful character of life itself. Here was the core of Norway's national tradition, from saga to Holberg, the law to which he himself clung through all his changeableness, and which he tried to apply to the bewildering problems of the modern world; at bottom, this skeptical individualist was a classicist. He admired Byron for his proud independence and emotional splen-dor, but condemned his lack of balance and harmony. He praised Wergeland for his good heart, but called his wild poetry un-Norwegian; he lauded the clear Welhaven as the most national of poets in spite of his Danish language. His own literary ideals were the Edda and Homer, Goethe and Aasen; his poetry is subdued and clear, with the serenity and long vistas which he had learned to love in the mountains of his childhood.

There was much of discord behind his balance. His composure is forced, the periods of equilibrium short; sometimes the reader feels as if he is walking on the thin crust of a volcano. The more impressive was his struggle to master his powers. Actually, this radical farm classicist with his seething background of modern problems is one of the strongest testimonies to the strength of the tradition and its power of adaptation. He believed himself to be the founder of a new literary epoch; in the long perspective, he was not too far wrong.

To formulate the problems anew, as clearly as they had appeared to Wergeland, was the task awaiting the new generation. Vinje saw the direction, but did not find the catchwords. It devolved upon Ibsen and Bjørnson to coin them, in a way which was of importance not alone to little Norway. When in 1854 the younger of these two announced that a new youth with new thoughts was knocking at the gates of literature, it was our own times that began.

The ETHICAL IMPERATIVE
HENRIK IBSEN

It has always been regarded as significant that Ibsen's most personal poems and dramas play in the clear and chilly atmosphere of the Norwegian alps, beyond the petty details of everyday life. Nowhere does this fact seem to be more fraught with meaning than in the field of human liberty. To Ibsen the conflict of law and freedom was not just a point of view, but the crucial problem of human existence, to be faced in the inexorable light of eternal moral principles. It was one of the achievements of his poetic work to make his nation feel as he did, lifting their problems up to his own level.

There was in him an urge for independence more violent even than in most of his compatriots, founded in his character, reared by an unhappy youth, and fostered by the ideas of his times. This desire for liberty was combined with an ethical earnestness, which was the moving power of his soul. Above all, life was serious to him, heavy with responsibility and retribution, subjected to laws that knew no compromise. This conviction was no philosophical theory to him, but a religion, closely connected both with Christian ideas and with the moral gravity of all Norse tradition: freedom means freedom of ethical choice. But the penetrating intensity of his moralism came from the eye of genius, sharpened by the struggle of contradictory forces in himself. To Ibsen inner life meant everything, the rest very little; freedom was the liberty of self-realization, of being true to oneself to the utmost limit, an honesty deeply imbedded in tradition, but conceived with a passion that was his own. "Freedom" really means "law," and the most severe of all.

This attitude explains his thoroughgoing influence, in his nation and in the world. He was bound to raise problems on a wide front.

But he turned them inward, as an ordeal by fire of the individual soul.

He was aroused to adult life by the thunder of the revolutions of 1848. He was in the right mood for revolutions, a poor and ambitious pharmacist's apprentice in a townlet of 800 inhabitants, undernourished of everything that makes existence worth while, filled behind his big, black beard with the burning ideas of radical authors. He frightened the life out of his comrades by his nihilistic rebellion against established society. In his first verse there was the spirit of Byron and Wergeland, of the revolt in France and the rising in Hungary. When he went to the capital in 1850, he immediately joined the workers' movement, which a year later was crushed by the police. His first printed work was a drama on the Roman insurgent Catiline, leader of the lowly.

This revolutionary blaze did not last long; it was not Ibsen's destiny to become a "red" poet in the political sense. But the deeper direction of his life was pointed out here—a life on the barricades.

After his first attempts he seemed to calm down. The "national renaissance" was at its peak; Ibsen joined the movement, and for a while seemed to be totally absorbed by it. He eagerly studied the popular traditions, collected folk tales, and adapted his style to national patterns; he became the official poet of national pride, much used and badly paid. His first real creations grew from this soil, plays with subject matter from Old Norway's fight for independence and unity, influenced by the psychological mastery and laconic style of the sagas. In the last of these dramas, *The Pretenders*, he gave magnificent expression to the basic issue of the nation's history: how to bend the stubborn individual wills into collaboration, symbolized in the figure of the great unifier Hákon Hákonson. This was the first of his plays to bear the mark of Ibsen's mature genius. It seemed to herald a great positive poet of the country's traditions.

But behind these works the revolutionary forces slowly developed in him and gave his creation a sudden and different turn.

In all the dramas of his youth, the conflict was in the individual, fighting the world for his right to live. The issue was outlined as early as in *Catiline*—no play about the revolutionary masses, but the tragedy of a man and his moral failure. This attitude was influenced by the rising wave of individualism which swept the Western world with the break-through of modern capitalism; but the strong personal note came from Ibsen's own development. In the bitter struggles of his youth there was not just vain ambition, but a feeling of vocation which involved his whole moral existence: "Genius is no right, it's a duty." His first years of creation had made him realize the cost of carrying such ideals: years of defeat and of terrifying loneliness with a continuous feeling of never living up to his own standards, conflicts which had sometimes taken him close to moral disintegration. These years of trial created in him a compassionate understanding of the fight for freedom within the individual and of the forces in man which hold him back or divert him from his own direction. It was his own doubts and misgivings and his temporary triumph over them which had filled his drama of the victorious King Hákon with such a confident power. But simultaneously these years had built up in him a militant radicalism much more dangerous than that of his youth, a hatred against the bigoted and complacent bourgeois society with which he had to fight and its whole set-up of inherited conventions and considerations, its moral laxness and comfortable common sense. That general spirit of protest which was brewing under the lid in Norway during the previous decades now broke forth in Ibsen, not in a political or social revolutionism, but as a moral revolt.

And he felt ready to express it. For years he had tried to seclude himself in an ivory tower of aesthetics. Now he was over that period of petrification, or believed himself to be; he felt his art as a weapon. He had exalted Norway's glorious past and its present liberty; but more and more the question urged itself upon him as to what right his compatriots had to the country's great history, or how far their lofty promises had been fulfilled in their souls.

HENRIK IBSEN

Long ago Ludvig Holberg had asked his compatriots "to be them-selves," and Wergeland had repeated it as a general program of life. Ibsen raised the challenge again, in a narrower field, with the terrifying intensity of his passion.

He showed his new face in *Love's Comedy*, a cheerful but seri-ous Holbergian attack on the sacred foundation of bourgeois so-ciety, the conventions of marriage, openly inspired by Camilla Collett. In its playful form, this comedy speaks with Ibsen's own voice of moral indignation, against the "lie of society," the half-measures and half-truths, the spirit of compromise in the great decisions of life. It was no isolated attack: he saw the same bacillus of destruction at work in all Western culture. In his poem on "The Murder of Abraham Lincoln" he lifted his anathema against the general moral decay of Europe. It seemed to Ibsen that within the frame of political liberty the worms were hollowing the free-born will of man.

His fears were confirmed when in 1864 his compatriots refused to help the Danes against German aggression, in spite of their earlier heroic promises. On his way to Rome, Ibsen saw the cele-bration of the victory in Berlin, and it filled him with flaming hatred against Prussian militarism. But the poetry born from his experience was a sermon of doom against his own nation that had failed in the test: the great verse-drama *Brand* (1866). In this mas-terpiece of love and hatred, ice and flame, he pictured his nation, physically free but morally emasculated, deprived of all the noble privileges of real liberty. From this swampland the hero rises like a mountain peak, frightening in his fanaticism, but monumental in his freedom, because he knows no consideration except his moral law. The work is not Christian in a dogmatic sense. But it is filled with the ethical radicalism of Christ—Ibsen "exclusively read the Bible" while writing it—borne by a deep belief in the inevitability of choice and sacrifice, of Nemesis and retribution. It is one great negation of that "sound realism," that "Norwegian soberminded-ness," which was so lavishly praised by the men of the national renaissance and which to Ibsen was just a lukewarmness of the blood. There is nothing of that kind in *Brand*. In burning, prophetic fervor the drama has no match in Norwegian literature; and like *Voluspá* and *The Dream Chant* it seems to be born from the Norse landscape itself with its violent span of contrasts, of light and darkness, frost and sun, of somber valleys and white, eternal mountains.

Hardly any work of literature has struck the nation as *Brand* did. It was felt as a personal challenge to each individual; problems which had unclearly weighed on their minds for decades, were suddenly posed in shining lucidity. It was followed up a year later by *Peer Gynt*, where the theme is played through again, not as an organ fugue in major this time, but in rich orchestration of irony, lyrics, and humor. If Brand, in Ibsen's words, was himself in his best moments, Peer was his nation at its worst. But here as well there is a lot of "self anatomy"; it gives a special sting to the satire that secretly Ibsen also lashes his own hidden weakness. He loved to ridicule those who talk and act as free souls without really being so. In Peer he painted in full size a man who has forfeited his freedom, not by misusing it, but by never using it at all, who covers his moral evasions by a fantastic play of fancy till the original impress of his soul is worn out and he is ready for obliteration in the melting pot. Here, as in all his creation, Ibsen rarely answers a question. But his power of raising them and bringing them close to the reader is matchless; and there is a splendor of expression and a sun haze of poetry about the work which still has lost nothing of its power.

Almost overnight *Brand* and *Peer Gynt* became classics in Norway. The details could be questioned, even the justice of the whole attack. But no one could evade the cleansing fire of idealism which blazed through this poetry. The fight for freedom which had filled the history of the nation, gained a deeper significance from the moment these books were published. To Ibsen himself they made clear what should forthwith be the task of his life, "that which I firmly believe and know is imposed on me by God: to awake the nation and make it think great thoughts."

※

He arranged his whole existence for the work to be done. He did not return to Norway after *Brand*. He stayed abroad for twenty-seven years, jealously guarding his aesthetic distance and his liberty of attack. He turned his private life into a shell of protection, carefully nursing his growing fame and fortune. He cut his beard and even changed his handwriting; the uncombed radical became a neat bourgeois with an increasing line of orders in his lapel.

But behind this façade of philistine respectability the spirit of revolt became more and more outspoken; and his battlefield remained Norway. He deliberately narrowed his front of attack. He lost all interest in the cause of national freedom, at home and abroad; he distrusted the ideology of democracy, the worship of liberties instead of liberty. What he longed for was not special revolutions in the externals of political life, but "the real thing, the revolt of the human mind."

In bringing this gospel to his Norwegian contemporaries, he renewed their contact with the world. He opened his country to the wave of radical realism in science and philosophy, morals and aesthetics which made the 70's and 80's a period of intellectual housecleaning everywhere. He commanded attention because of his renown; but the secret of his influence was his dramatic vision. He did not discuss problems; they rose by themselves out of the clash of human beings, who bore in the very marrow of their souls the mark of reality. Through these years he reached the full mastery of his art, a form which is in itself a monument to his intellectual sincerity, reminiscent both of the Edda and of the Greeks, filled with passion and cool objectivity, with the vivid characterization of the baroque and the revealing conciseness of the saga, tense with restrained emotion, merciless in its logic of structure, ethical in its severe strength.

He began with *The League of Youth,* a comedy of the democratic heroism of phrases, Peer Gynt electioneering. He was greeted with applause by the conservatives; but Ibsen was no reliable ally. His only preoccupation was the freedom of the individual to follow his own law. His main enemy was the "dead" laws in the souls, the heritage of obsolete ideas, what he called "the corpse in the cargo"; he could never remain a conservative. His next blow was a revelation of the moral rottenness of bourgeois respectability, *The Pillars of Society;* and a still more dangerous attack followed when, in *A Doll's House,* he approached the problems of woman. To none was freedom of the soul more openly denied. Ibsen saw in this oppression the whole "human tragedy of our age," the fight between authority and natural feeling; and this time there was no reconciliation, but an inexorable rupture. His Nora suddenly made thousands of women realize their own situation; the prophecy of Henrik Wergeland and his sister came true. The slamming of the front door when Nora leaves family and home in order to live her own life marked, it has rightly been said, a new epoch in woman's history.

The applause of good society suddenly ceased; this only spurred him on. In *Ghosts,* the masterpiece of this period of creation, he horrified his public by bringing on the stage things which decent people preferred not to talk about. But much more important than the discussion of syphilis and heredity was the bluntness with which sacred principles and institutions were called to the test and found to be long ago deceased, a dead weight on the minds of the living. Ibsen knew from his own experience the burden of that heritage. Beneath the polemics, *Ghosts* is his most somber drama about human guilt and the debt of retribution, Norse destiny and the law of the Hebrews molded into the simple grandeur of Hellenic form.

Ghosts met a storm of disgust from conservatives and liberals alike. It proved to Ibsen how little political freedom had penetrated into moral life and how needed was his own work. He answered by *An Enemy of the People,* a drama of the risk run in telling truths which people find it more pleasant not to remember. And the resistance sharpened his sword. More and more directly he attacked the institutional carriers of tradition: church, school, and press; and the fight made him understand in a new way the necessity even of political and social revolt. He began to talk about a union of all the underprivileged. He looked hopefully to

HENRIK IBSEN

North America, the land of spontaneous freedom, and to women and workers who were not yet weighed down by traditions. He even vaguely called himself a socialist.

He got an answer in the interest with which his books were received, not only all over the world (from *A Doll's House* on), but in the homeland, both by foes and friends. There was suspense in the air for months before a new Ibsen drama appeared. It aroused the passions as if the persons had been living relatives and friends and the conflicts were experienced in one's own soul; public discussion revolved around them, his pointed sayings were on all lips. Wergeland had been right when he prophesied about poets who would be "leaders in the world of ideas, teachers of the peoples."

※

But in the secrecy of his creation another turn was being prepared, which was to give Ibsen's problem of liberty its last and most personal note.

It was the very power of his genius that pushed him on. Through all his dramas he had been guided by his stern ideals of "being oneself." But his principles had always been borne out in visions of living humanity; "poetry is to see," he said, real human beings, not marionettes of ideas. This intensive understanding proved to be dangerous to all theory. The characters in his plays revolted against his standards; they began to live their own life almost in spite of the author. Even the wrecks defiantly developed a human dignity of their own; the prisoners shook their bars. As his insight grew, he became more and more doubtful about his own merciless idealism. He saw how different were the conceptions of good and evil, in man and woman, in different individuals, in different periods, even in the same human being; he began to wonder if any ethical standards were generally applicable.

In the beginning 70's he had tried to solve the problem from the philosophical angle, in his great play about Julian the Apostate, *Emperor and Galilean*, but without very definite results. In the following decade of fighting his doubts were pushed into the background; but they were always there as an uncertainty, often softening the tones of reproach and condemnation. From the middle of the 80's, as he himself began to feel approaching age, his doubts arose again, and gradually gave his writing a new character. He did not drop his standards, but they lost their rigor; he began to talk about their "power of development." The clash of general claims subsided; he more and more "saw" without judging. His plays became difficult; the psychological intuition touched virgin fields, especially in the souls of women, forces below the threshold, not to be fully grasped till psychoanalysis came into use. He shrank from being called a "poet of problems." Liberation became a secret struggle to master the vague tendencies of the unconscious, defeat a submission to hidden trends of the mind. His language was filled with double meaning, symbols of a transient reality.

There is less of wrath than before, and much more of pity. All through Ibsen's creation, the law of duty had to fight the human desire for happiness in its deceitful disguises. Once, all his sympathy had been with the law; now he was not so certain any more. Perhaps, to most human beings, the lie was the only thing they could stand? Perhaps the exalted standards could only deprive them of something they really had, without giving them anything instead? These doubts with their mixture of bitter pessimism and pity shook the very foundations of Ibsen's moral world; it shows his reckless honesty that he did not hesitate to express them. The culmination is *The Wild Duck*, his masterpiece, in which the characters are uncovered unto the very marrow of their wretchedness without a reproachful word, in deep, tearless compassion. In this world of petty humanity the moral die-hard was just a destructive power; to Ibsen, the judgment meant a judgment of himself.

Toward the end of Ibsen's life, these ideas developed a more and more personal ring, and were concentrated on the problem of his own self-realization. He once believed he had broken the spell of "aestheticism," making his art a power in the world of reality. But as zest subsided, he was again filled with anxiety. He could talk disdainfully about his work: "Verse, verse, just verse!"—fiction instead of action, fruit of the same wasted freedom he had lashed in *Peer Gynt*. And there was a deeper self-reproach. Fifty years before, Wergeland had given his program as "Truth, freedom, and love." To Ibsen, the first two words sufficed; and he had given them a new and deeper meaning. But all the time he had felt the deficit of love as a fundamental human shortcoming, a lack of immediate contact with life. Brand with all his heroic idealism was close to doom because his heart was cold, Peer Gynt was saved from destruction only because there was left in him a tiny gleam of human affection. Again Christianity loomed behind Ibsen's thoughts, with its totally different ideal of self-realization: to be oneself is to sacrifice oneself. When he weighed the results of his life on that scale, it more and more seemed to him that he had sacrificed the fullness of human existence for a chilly world of poetic fictions.

He had always felt genius to be a duty. Now he asked with increasing anxiety for what purpose he had used his freedom, what kind of "self" he had realized, and what he had suppressed. His ideals remained untouched in their blinding eternity, he had just doubted people's ability to approach them; now he feared he himself had failed. In his last drama, *When We Dead Awaken,* he questioned his whole life work regardless of its fame. He, who had hidden so carefully behind his figures, spoke almost without disguise, in questions of terrifying frankness, his voice broken with stifled lament. In such self-doom his creation ended.

The judgment can never be appealed against; his personal account he alone could settle. To his nation, whose lives were molded and recast by the works he repudiated as futile, the case must look different. His last confessions are the moving testimony of the price he had to pay for his message. But they also remain the monument of that unflinching search for truth which carried him through, even to the bitter end, and which was the grandeur of his life.

Ibsen's work had many immediate results. But it is the atmosphere of his nation which he most deeply influenced.

His limitations are easy to discover; he himself pointed them out with increasing vigor. Great parts of his creation really move in thin and chilly mountain air, far from the dwellings of man. His worship of freedom may seem to break the bonds of human community; and at the same time, with all his talk of liberty he lacked free, natural ability for living. There is something superhuman, even unhuman, in his idealism, especially in his youth; his introverted, monomaniac sense of responsibility may seem hostile to life itself. There was nothing he lacked more than that "sound common sense" which he criticized so bitterly in others; Vinje rightly felt himself a representative of a national opinion when he ridiculed *Brand* as overstrained: "Happily life is far too healthy and sensible to act that way." There was an uncorrupted humanity speaking through the Britisher who cried from the audience during an Ibsen performance: "Give her a kiss, man, and make it up!"

But the limitations are inseparable from his genius. He did not intend to give a rounded picture of life. He wanted just to cry out the passion that filled his own soul; and within his limits he raised the issues with a clearness and sincerity never to be forgotten. He solved few problems; even his approach may sometimes seem obsolete now. But the basic things remain: the terrifying moral intensity simultaneously asserting the claim of freedom and the maintenance of law, the eternal tension, which is mirrored in the tightness of his style and which is only softened, not relaxed, by his psychological understanding. On this point he upheld a main line in the country's tradition; he attacked the national heritage and he recreated it. He became the second great originator of the century, pushing his nation on, calling its conscience on the alert, breaking its complacency. It would be hard to live always on Ibsen's heights; but once for all he has shown the nation the way to the mountains with their grand vistas and their invigorating severity.

All generations after him carry his mark, even those who reject him. He is still a living power among his compatriots, a fire in the blood and a thorn in the flesh.

The WARMTH of LIFE
BJØRNSTJERNE BJØRNSON

It was Norway's good fortune that at Ibsen's side stood a genius who supplemented him as Wergeland did Holberg. In the work of Bjørnstjerne Bjørnson the achievements not only of his contemporaries but of the whole century are gathered into the broad common stream of the nation.

Like Ibsen, he came to Oslo in 1850, a student from the province, old-fashioned in clothes and queer in manners; his comrades jovially teased him about his dialect and his unruly wave of blond hair, called "the mountain peak." But he soon gave them other things to talk about.

He was a born leader and knew it. This youth from the backwoods, whom no one had ever heard of, behaved like a chief and a conqueror, and somehow it seemed to be perfectly natural. He was handsome: a slim, strong figure with brisk step and head borne high, an open, shining face and the eyes of a lion tamer; "he seemed like a revelation from a different world." There was a confidence about him which fascinated, an air of vitality and genius; wherever he appeared, he was the obvious center—as with Dante, "no one left when he came, no one stayed when he left." He emanated an ingratiating charm, witnessed to by all who ever met him, electrifying and irresistible; "it was impossible to deny him anything." From his first appearance people spoke of his resemblance to Henrik Wergeland, "alike as the hands of the same man"; and he accepted the challenge. A friend once gathered the impression of him in two words: "Sun and storm"; it fitted them both.

There was a deeper parallelism, however, in their whole mental structure.

He was no problemless Sunday child; his triumphant exterior concealed a character of strain and contrast. His strength was a force of nature, which often broke its reins. There was a passion in him, a desire for life and a reckless, vehement self-assertion, which could suddenly sweep him away, carrying strange things to the surface. He who seemed so self-assured, was painfully sensitive, tossed about by "the hard blows of his impressions," raptured by a troll-like power of fancy, which in his childhood made him "the worst liar in the district" and which even much later could unexpectedly derail him. His life moved in waves, calm and tempest, despair and hope—"others can hardly realize how overwhelmingly I have been a man of emotions"; he rightly used to say that he belonged to the western Norwegians from the narrow fjords, the people of avalanches and eddy winds. And he displayed his changes with a southern openness which has always been rare in Norway, and which a generation before made his great predecessor a bugaboo to all good burghers.

But if these powers of disorder were strong, in him as in Wergeland, the counterpoise was even stronger—all that draws a straight line through a man's life. This sensitive soul had a cool, almost calculating intelligence; this emotional dreamer was a realist, a man of penetrating observation and solid common sense. He saw, understood, and remembered everything, words and actions, in others and himself; he could handle things and human beings with amazing practical touch. Behind his changeableness in minor matters was a will power, flexible and strong, which gave everything its purpose. This impulsive poet was a man of patient planning, who could postpone his debut for years in order to be fully prepared, who could save an inspiration for a decade in order to let it ripen, and follow an idea through half a century without ever losing the track. This man of effervescent power, this lover of life who improvised one of his most famous speeches in homage to "all that is after midnight," was at the same time from his student days a most methodical worker ("laziness is against my nature"), an early riser, who used his forces systematically and carefully to the last horsepower. At bottom he possessed a deep mental health which corresponded to his physical strength and stabilized his whole being. He never doubted that life made sense, that it was basically good and sound, governed by "the great, healthy laws of balance"; those laws he would struggle to live up to himself. Even in his wildest storms of passion he saw his actions in relation to those great principles, and early it was obvious that the constructive powers were the stronger in him, that the tremendous currents were not milling around themselves, but were running toward a goal.

But the force which pointed out that goal to him, which kept his powers united and made their balance active, was that same simple force which had also molded Wergeland's life: the goodness of the heart. Beneath all that was tangled and twisted, hard and unruly in Bjørnson there was a fertile soil of human sympathy, a spontaneous openness toward his fellow beings, an overwhelming power of understanding them, of suffering and weeping and laughing with them, of embracing them in compassion and fellowship. This youngster of turbulent forces whom his friends called "the Bear" had the delicacy of a girl and the watchful tenderness of a mother, and her soft hands. "Never," says a friend of his later years, "did I see a man get tears in his eyes so easily." In him as in Wergeland this sympathy created the same spontaneous urge to help and to be useful, to be where life needed him, the same feeling of universal responsibility: "I believe and love without any moderation." To his student companions it was demonstrated most strikingly that memorable winter morning when he appeared in their modest den with a shivering twelve-year-old German accordion player whom he had adopted, and whom he never afterward sloughed off; his life was an unbroken chain of such acts. Here was the power behind his powers, which fitted them into a pattern. He was less abrupt and ecstatic than Wergeland, less seraphic, more matter-of-fact in his whole approach; but the motive power was the same.

A mental endowment of such complexity was no light burden to start with in life. In Bjørnson's youth, when the ferment of the elements in him was just beginning, it would sometimes drive him to despair, the more so because of his merciless self-observation.

BJØRNSTJERNE BJØRNSON

The urge of expansion in him was almost irresistible, precisely because he was so strong; and it had the same categorical character as in Ibsen: it is the duty of the genius to realize himself regardless of considerations, in unrestrained freedom. But at the same time he soberly realized how dangerous were the powers he handled, how easily they could break their dams and turn his liberty into a caricature; at bottom he never doubted that his place was on the other side. He felt his dualism as a personal challenge; to reconcile the contrasts and make his powers serve the common good of mankind became one of his main tasks. It made him a moralist, often in defense against himself, sometimes more than even his admirers could swallow; it made his inner life a struggle which absorbed much of his power and brought him humiliating defeats. But at the same time, it was this many-sidedness with its unavoidable battles that gave his work its baffling breadth and gave his life its depth and dimension, its human fullness. He was no flat compromiser, but a whole man.

The foundation of his existence, to which he always returned from his crises, remained his feeling of human fellowship. Wergeland was so young, and often so alone; Bjørnson through his long life always seemed to have many marching beside him; they were always in his mind. He was not one to brood over his personal problems, as Ibsen did. He struggled with them to get through them, to become a better worker in the common cause of humanity, to battle through and march on. It gave him sometimes the terrifying briskness of a military commander: when he had reached his decision, doubts were not always welcome. But it also gave him his genuine humility: he never forgot that he served causes that were greater than himself. Here is the real source of his strength, of that deeper certainty, that feeling of directed power and hard-won poise which radiated from him and made him invincible. Till his dying day he remained "a frail, struggling, slaving, joyous, repentant, fresh-up-again man," always reborn from the secret springs of his mind.

BJØRNSTJERNE BJØRNSON

In this personality, at once simple and motley, Bjørnson's whole historical role was presaged. His victorious certainty did not just come from his feeling of power; he knew how he was going to use it.

The world was on fire when he awoke to manhood; and so was he himself. He had been a "trouble-maker" in the little town where he went to school. In college he had founded a newspaper called *Freedom,* and his first printed article was a "Speech of Liberty to the People of This Place." On his arrival in Oslo he immediately began to display his rare power of winning followers and raising enemies. But his real background was not revolutionary; he had not spent his formative years in ambitious dreams of revolt, in the manner of Ibsen. He had begun the conscious building of his own character. He had grown harmoniously into the heritage of the nation; and to a rare extent he had identified himself with the spirit of his people and the aims of its history.

He had lived a happy childhood in the vicarages of his peasant-born clerical father, east and west in Norway. He had seen the mountains and the ocean, valley and shore, and filled his soul and senses with the contrasts of the landscape—the wildness and the mystery, the calm and the serenity, powers of his own soul. He had lived with the farmers as one of their own and learned to love and understand them, with his peculiar mixture of sympathy and shrewd observation; he had seen in them the same tension of elemental forces; he had absorbed their language and traditions. He had grown into European traditions as well, above all Christianity, less a code of law than a cheerful confidence, which to his dying day remained connected with all that was constructive in him. He had lived in Snorri's Royal Sagas, scene of an eternal drama which to him seemed to play among his own farm friends; and he had filled his mind with Wergeland, who pointed to the same connections in the images of poetic genius. Early there was built up in him a grand vision of Norway's way as a nation, from the past into the future, an endless struggle for real freedom among the blind powers of nature, embodied in slowly built ideals, kept alive through the centuries of darkness, and emerging again in the promise of 1814, interpreted by Wergeland and left unfulfilled by him. It was Bjørnson's deepest conviction that "nothing can grow to power in a people which does not have root in its history." In Wergeland's broad program of liberty the fulfillment of the nation's historic destiny was translated into a clear and simple working plan, leaving the task with Bjørnson's own generation.

He knew that in this work *he* was called to shoulder Wergeland's burden. Like him, he felt a capacity for action in all fields of life; but his main task was that of a poet. To him poetry was not a niggling with the pretty feelings of the individual; it was the vision which points the way to nations. "The poet does the prophet's deeds"; he is the "leading instinct" of his people, lifting up its highest ideals and pointing to its deepest moral forces, as did the Edda poet, the ballad singers, and the tale tellers in their majestic anonymous simplicity. His deepest intent as a national *skald* was clarified to him when in Rome he saw the masterpieces of classical art. Their magnificent universality, born from the turmoil of struggling forces, was the ideal of his own literary tradition: "It is not the particular which is great, although it glisters most; it is the universal which is great, to raise aloft the emotions and ideas which will echo among the millions." Rome, he wrote, is "a health resort for rough-haired, tangled Teutons," the place to learn "that simple, honest thing of being human." In his first creations, his saga dramas and peasant novels from the 1850's and 60's, he answered the call, showing in great pictures the inner unity of Norse life, the warm stream of human health through its twisted history, the "moral order and noble freedom" which had been dominant whenever the nation had been able to unfold its own self.

In so doing, however, he made his creation a battlefield. The balance he talked of had never been a matter of course to Norwegian minds. He knew it from himself: "Beneath so high a vault it costs a hard struggle to reach mastery." Through his saga dramas rage the tides of passion: wrath and defiance, arrogance and self-righteousness, symbolized in the description of the spring flood in *Arnljot Gelline*, where the destructive powers of *Voluspá* again seem to engulf the world in their morbid nihilism. In the peasant novels there is sometimes a brutality which shocked Bjørnson to the bottom (not to mention his readers): he knew it only too well. The style is as tense as in the Edda; its directness "exploded like TNT" among contemporary critics, surging with emotion, bursting from restrained force.

The dominant trait, however, is not despair, but optimism. Through the darkest abyss of this poetry shines the light of that simple truth "experienced by a hundred thousand millions": that redemption is always possible, that human will is able to master the storm and build a free character, helped by the powers of good. Strongest among those powers was to Bjørnson Christianity. In his saga hero Arnljot the pride of the pagan warrior is broken before the mildness of St. Olaf, conqueror of destruction; to Bjørnson this conversion was not only the fulfillment of a personal fate but the symbol of Norse history. In his peasants the religious background is always present, amid the variety of character and plot, united with "the bottom in them, the strength that shall continue." Even in his style, mastery is the dominant feature, behind its explosive newness: always again the passion is brought back under control by artistic restraint, by concern for what is "universal." The more highstrung the feeling, the more tight and momentous the form; the tragedy of a life may be concentrated in one reply, one taciturn, sagalike short story, heavy with words unspoken, rounded as a crystal ball. Amazingly this style unites the features of centuries in a natural, modern expression, free from false archaism, saga heroes and present-day Norwegians meeting on a common ground.

The striking reality of these books, however, comes from Bjørnson himself, his warmth and strength, that mighty breath of life which was in him. His heroes are not the empty shells of a moral theory; they resound with his own factual struggle. Their "sound balance" is no cautious indolence, but duly paid for; in some of these novels, which were originally printed in newspapers, we can follow the shifting battle lines from day to day. But the core of these men and women is Bjørnson's own songful optimism, his brisk and cheerful resolution; they are rough and jovial as he was, vehement and charming, strong and humble, patiently growing through suffering and defeat. All the characters are conceived in the same fullness of individuality, followed with a cool but loving eye till they exult from real life, in a sun glitter of lyrical warmth. Through all of them sings his love of Norway; these prose works are the first of his great national anthems. His devotion may break forth as a direct sermon; his famous description of how the birch trees managed to clothe the barren mountain slope just because they always kept trying, is a hymn to the endurance of his people, orchestrated as playfully as the sough of the May wind through the victorious birches themselves. But the landscape is everywhere present, even in the psychological analysis, weaving its melody into the dreams and struggles and victories of man, fresh with the scent of the forests and the breeze from the mountains, the deep shadow of the hillside and the serenity of a summer day.

"This book," Bjørnson once wrote of a contemporary author, "reaches us like a clear call from a mountain top, redoubled in thousand echoes, making the air lighter, the forest fresher, the water bluer to those who listen." Nothing could better describe the effect of his own creation. No work of fiction has become so widely and enduringly popular throughout Scandinavia as the collection of his peasant novels; their ideas and their art spoke directly to the minds. In his own nation, few literary works have done more to build self-understanding and mold standards.

But to Bjørnson literature was never more than a part of life. In his first works he had outlined his basic ideas; but his vision was the future of a whole nation. The task was endless, writing could not do everything. His letters are crowded with impatient outbursts: "I am no indoor poet," "I cannot merely sit and think up characters," "I must have something to rule over, or I go to seed"! He was, as he wrote himself, "irremediably earmarked for action"; now already he began that "rotation of crops" which made his poetry grow in the breathing spells of a whirlwind of outward activity.

Activity to him meant something very special. With amazement, and not without anxiety, the good people of Norway saw what kind of volcano had opened among them in this poetic genius. He was the greatest orator the country has ever borne, "with a voice like an orchestra," combining the lofty pathos of the prophet, the versatility of the accomplished actor, and a terrifying power of suggestion; there was no stormy public meeting which he could not master by the mere impact of his personality. He was a prolific journalist, editor, pamphleteer, and propagandist. He could not keep to himself anything that filled his mind; through sixty years he flooded the newspapers with long, signed articles and countless "little anonymous devils," easy to recognize from their striking style and buoyant spirit. He was a skillful organizer, something of a conspirator, and a virtuoso of personal persuasion. He "carried the key that opens people"; he could force access to an inveterate enemy who refused even to see him, and leave with everything obtained—"There is nothing left of him." And he followed up his personal contacts by a lifelong correspondence which recalls the vast epistolography of Voltaire and Benjamin Franklin, approximately estimated at 30,000 letters, from open postcards of amazing frankness to extensive treatises overflowing with advice and encouragement, philippics and consolation.

His fighting spirit was as infectious as his laughter. He filled the country with his sayings and doings; never before had Norway listened to such a voice. But all of his activities were tied together, stirring each other and fertilizing each other by the unity of his purpose: to make real in all fields of life that freedom which was the vision of his literary creation.

He would build a free Norwegian art. He became the dynamo of architecture, painting, and music, pushing them on and holding them back, acting as their outspoken conscience. In the theater he did more. He was himself a director of genius, repeatedly the manager of the country's leading theaters; the creation of a na-

BJØRNSTJERNE BJØRNSON

tional stage in Norway was his work. His aim was not an independence in the externals, but in the spirit: to make Norse art again express those deep forces which had molded the nation's life. Such were his aims in politics as well, for years a main field of his activity. He was no politician, he never held a public office. His task was to be "the instinct" of the fight: to make the nation realize even in political life the implications of that self-possession which had been the burden of its history.

Few Norwegians have ever seen those connections as clearly as he did. That survival of Norway's liberty through the ages of union which Wergeland had just grasped in poetic outline, Bjørnson conceived in the complexity of its conditions with the penetrating eye of the scholar at an age when most young men are still struggling with their textbooks. There are important ideas derived from him in the works of J. E. Sars, the great contemporary historian of Norse freedom, ideologist and chief of staff of the army of progress. Bjørnson had the poet's power of moving his historic visions into contemporary life; his program of the future seemed to be born from the past as its obvious outgrowth. But at the same time his approach was that of perfect realism. Actually, his aim was not political, but moral. To him the individual programs and planks were just means of building the nation's self-respect and deepening its sense of honor, and there were many ways to the goal. Too well he saw the value even of those ideas he had to fight; too clearly he knew how tangled were the lines even of the simplest problem. He hated the "clear standpoints," the sterile abstractions, the "intoxication of consistency"; to him the ideal was never to lose sight of the final aims but to solve the immediate problems within the limits of the possible. With all his impetuosity he was patient; there was just one thing to do: to tell the truth, untiringly, again and again, till it took root. Like Wergeland, he saw Norway as a part of the great liberty front of his day, all over the world, from Garibaldi and Castelar to Gambetta and Lincoln. But his dearest hero was Victor Hugo, prophet and poet, who made his ideals live on earth.

This broadness made Bjørnson a political leader. He was not

BJØRNSTJERNE BJØRNSON

always easy for the professionals to handle; he always let the cat out of the bag; he could never be prevailed on to bring anything about by tricks. He swept resistance away by his force and splendor. From his first political speeches he displayed his marvelous ability to make the details of the day's work appear in the sunlight of great ideals, as a direct challenge to the individuals. His "policy of the heart" proved to be good realism as well. From the famous battle in 1859, when—at the age of twenty-seven—he turned the election of his district, to the winter ten years later when the scattered radical forces finally gathered in the great party of the Left with the clear program of full independence in the union with Sweden and full democracy and parliamentarism at home, Bjørnson became one of the spiritual leaders of the rising wave, center of the advancing storm and its directive force.

His adversaries called him a demagogue and an evil demon; they hated him. But his real power did not rest in his skill as an agitator. The broad masses began to listen to him as they had listened to Wergeland, because they recognized the vision behind his activity and felt that he believed in them. In his *Poems and Songs* (1870) he gave the program, his and theirs.

There are wonderful personal lyrics among them, and their tune is that of cheerful strength, perhaps more so than in any other volume of verse in world literature. What a deep and natural breath there was in Bjørnson in spite of his conflicts is nowhere revealed as in these songs. Here as before, there is almost always a battle. But usually the battle is won before the song comes, or it is just billowing like a dark ground swell, which makes the victory earnest and worth while. Even in the song "In a Dark Hour" the real outcome is no longer in doubt: "Be glad when danger presses Each power your soul possesses! In greater strain Your strength shall gain Till greater victory blesses!" Here is leisure for more than fighting: for dreams and longing, for the whispering of the twilight and the wordless song of the woods, for the wandering moods and ever unsatisfied yearnings of those who are young, for that sound and fresh romanticism which was also in Bjørnson. The climax of these personal poems is the morning songs, when "the gold of heaven is on the dust of earth," when the sailor climbs singing to the masthead "to clear the sail that shall swell more freely," and when the soul itself musters its powers of good and finds them to be unscathed:

> Day's coming up now, joy's returned,
> Sorrow's dark castles captured and burned;
> Over the mountaintops glowing
> Light-king his armies is throwing.
> "Up now, up now!" calls the bird,
> "Up now, up now!" child voice heard,
> Up now my hope in sunshine.

Rarely are these songs purely personal confessions, however. What they mostly express with striking directness is the common feeling of mankind towards its common problems. Even his most intimate outbursts usually are worded in such a way as to make them applicable to everyone. The form is as simple as it is elaborate, Wergeland's force in Welhaven's verse, a witness to what this rough-haired Teuton had really learned in the school of the classics. He does not sing within himself. He sings to those who listen and understand, and their recognition and participation is his highest reward.

Often he speaks directly on behalf of his audience. Surprisingly many of Bjørnson's poems were written for some occasion, tools for work and weapons in the fight. All the ideals of Norway's democracy rise before our eyes in these songs in monumental symbols: the promises of history, the burning issues of the day, and the great visions of the future. But the strongest of the poems speak of everyday life, without the banners of the platform. They carry a message that may seem almost prosaic: a praise of the plain existence and its simple heroism, a "love of the small and the near"; their challenge has a touch of resignation: "Give your strength and your deed Where you nearest see need." But the plain words and simple thoughts are filled with the might of experience and the spontaneous warmth of feeling, what Bjørnson himself once called "the clarity of the heart"; more than many pompous statements these songs reveal the real powers behind the cause he served. Here speaks a man to whom human companionship is not a thing of the festal days, but his very breath of life, closely connected with his Christian faith. He believes in "the recreative power of love" because he has seen it work in his own life; his confidence through night and dark, his morning hymns of the soul, are not for him alone, but for all fighting fellow beings. Even Wergeland lived in two worlds, although they were moved by the same power; there was always a far-away look in his eyes when he returned from his realm of fancy to the world of man. In Bjørnson no fissure is visible. The ideas he sings, the faces he lifts out of the crowd, the landscape which soughs and storms and whispers in dewy freshness through his verse, grow naturally from this common ground. The real strength and beauty of many of these poems is only revealed when they are sung in assembly, and the form is triumphantly filled by that for which it was made.

There are several national anthems in the collection: homages to the fathers who "brought order new with law and plough," songs for building site and workshop, proud statements of the conquests of present-day Norway: "each new plot reclaimed for harvest, each new ship running down the ways, each new child soul molded to manhood." One of these songs was soon adopted as the common expression of the nation's faith: "Yes, we love this land together Where the wild sea foams. . . ." It is a classical song, plain in style and subdued in words; it needs no oratory. It is "modern Norwegian," Bjørnson once said, "open and free as the day, rising without threats, self-assertive without ostentation, free from exaggeration and sentimentality," the anthem of a small, peace-loving nation. "But if it is sung in the hour of danger, then the self-assertion stands armored in every line."

About 1870, Bjørnson's future as a great national and Christian poet thus seemed to be staked out. But it proved otherwise.

From childhood on, he had felt religion as "the ground from which everything shoots," a Christianity glad and open as himself. He had been definitely hostile to the new wave of intellectual radicalism which surged over Europe. Toward the end of the 1870's this isolation was broken, and it was his own spirit of independence that urged him on. A long stay abroad had brought him in close contact with modern French literature; it had made him realize how hemmed in he was, with all his political and national programs of freedom. "There are more dogmas than mine," he wrote in self-reproach, "more forms, more sincere minds, more high aims, more paths to those things we all love." To work through these problems on the new ground became a challenge to his sincerity. Like Holberg, he found it to be a Christian duty to investigate before he believed; and before this investigation the whole system of dogma crumbled. The story of his conversion is pathetic. Each step was painful, he often felt as if he were uprooting his own heart; the pictures of him show the growing strain and restlessness almost from month to month. But his courage was unfailing; and he was rewarded by a new feeling of being on his own ground: "The truths that are bought with pain, also give the highest power to carry."

Bjørnson's break with Christianity was a far-reaching experience, not only to himself, but to his nation. Many contemporary authors went the same way; but Bjørnson's defection became much more important: he had been one of the great hopes of the creed he deserted. To many of his best followers his revolt could only appear as a betrayal, a pure loss. In longer perspective, however, the break is less important than the connection. The intellectual liberation of the 70's was as unavoidable as that of Holberg's time; and Bjørnson's fight for it had the same clear honesty as Holberg's. But like Holberg he was no revolutionary. He knew the values connected with the ideas he had to abandon; in tearing the old bonds, he tried to substitute others, in a new equilibrium. The spirit of his revolt was not anarchy or nihilism, but earnestness and responsibility; his great speech of conversion, "To Be in Truth," set the direction for a whole generation of youth, away from the tradition, and at the same time back to it.

He himself kept the channels open. There was "an eternal cry in his soul" for something to believe in; he "was not created for doubt." After the crisis had subsided, a new religion took form in him; again he could exclaim: "I believe, and I sing!" In this "earthly Christianity" much of his old creed was lost; impersonal Nature replaced the loving Father. But he felt that he had preserved the essentials: his belief in a creative and governing power, in God's presence in "all things great and noble," and in unbreakable Nemesis as the foundation of the moral world. He gave himself into the hands of "the law of order that all sustains" almost as confidently as he had once commended himself to the Lord's keeping. He was still "a link in the strong chain," he still felt himself increasing in the power of good, "more forgiving toward others, stronger in love." That he thus tried to bridge the gap, and to some extent succeeded, has meant more to the nation than the undisturbed faith of many believers.

The years of inner struggle did not leave him unchanged. He became more radical, more of a liberator: in one respect he had seen through the screen of conventional truth. More than before his art turned into a weapon. He mostly dropped the lyrical verse; in modern dramas and novels he turned to the problems of the day, often in aggressive closeness to realities. But his basic problem always remained the education of the will. His broad-mindedness did not change, neither did his understanding, or the heart behind it.

With increasing violence he threw himself into the political battle, more and more conceived as a frontal attack on the whole phalanx of intellectual reaction. After years of preparation, the crisis came in the 1880's, with a bitterness unheard of in Norway. Once in his youth Bjørnson had written that "of course there are many who don't like me, but enemies I have none." Now he could no longer stick to that optimistic judgment; and his sensitiveness made him vulnerable. During the worst storms he sometimes felt like a wounded wolf with blood in its tracks.

But his strength grew with the strain. Not for nothing was he the son of a giant father who sometimes for fun drew the plow himself; "I am of a vigorous nature, that can sleep off anything and wake up cheerful in the morning." He filled the faithful with his own laughing assurance: "I will live in Norway, I will beat and be beaten in Norway, I will sing and die in Norway, be sure of that!" Through his fighting humor his followers always felt his moral strength: "Victory belongs to those who have the strongest love, and therefore the strongest confidence in the future." His voice reached the most far-away corner in the country, and the masses arose. In 1881, he unveiled the statue of Wergeland in Oslo, under a storm of protest from the conservatives—"one of those statues which sing when touched by the rising sun"; he prophesied that Wergeland's summer was near. Three years later, political democracy won its definitive victory in Norway, not to be threatened again. In 1905 the union with Sweden was peacefully severed as well; no single man contributed more to this result.

But when triumph came, Bjørnson was already on his way to further goals. To him, "politics was practical altruism"; he formulated it splendidly when the full victory was won: "Now promise we each other: here Justice shall dwell with Peace, and Goodness reign supreme." Such a program could not be realized in a struggle of all against all; in the very thick of battle he was already busy rebuilding the foundations of a new community. Rather than kindle short-sighted hatreds, he wished to build the political will, the feeling of mutual responsibility, which could outlast the victories of the day; his work in creating this new attitude in the broad layers of Norway's population is perhaps his most important contribution to the country's political history. His program was symbolized in the children's flag parade which he organized on the national day and which soon became institutional throughout Norway: here a new fellowship would grow, unmarred by the struggles of the adults. His political dramas are not just weapons; they raise the broad moral issues which were often forgotten in the fray of battle, appealing to good will across the party lines. His great drama *Paul Lange and Tora Parsberg* is the moving tragedy and apologia of those who are undeservedly crushed in the political clash because they are noble and weak, too delicately organized for a world of unscrupulous struggle. There is an amazing lack of fanaticism in these plays, and a deep humanity; no short cut, however promising, can relieve us of our responsibility toward each other. "The pathetic grief of one single human being is enough to make all the inhuman ways to happiness incomprehensible, impossible, terrifying."

This broad conception of progress moved his goals forward, beyond political democracy, to the demands of the new classes of society: the workers, in countryside and town. They were no longer a problem of philanthropy; Bjørnson saw clearly their future role as a dominant force in society. His visit to the United States (1880–81) sharpened his eye. Through all disguising phrases he grasped the oppressive power of capital and the dangerous implications of its Nietzschean morality, that "pity is weakness"; above all, he saw the real conditions under which the workers were living. He warned of the consequences "if justice is not done in time": "God help us if our sense of fair play is not the strongest of all our feelings!" He solemnly declared himself a socialist; he wrote fiery songs for the workers, and was a supporter of the first Norwegian strike. Here, too, he pointed out the direction, a leader even to those who were bound to go much farther than he did. But he was no revolutionary; revolution was the thing he wished to avoid. In his great play on the social struggle he tried to show how both parts were overstrained in their claims, distorted by their absolute ideologies. He hoped for something in between, a workable compromise—"someone must begin to forgive"; he appealed to the moral forces that reach beyond the individual conflict. "Our future lies in our faith," he said in a speech to the striking women workers in the match mills. "We will have faith in what is good in the people; we will have faith that hearts will meet in understanding when they are called upon; we will have faith that even those who perhaps defy us today, will be with us tomorrow. We must!"

He became the great propagandist for the liberation of woman, beside Ibsen and even before him, not only in theory, but still more in his pictures of noble, freeborn womanhood, healthy, out-door Norwegian girls. This freedom included the liberation of the senses from religious asceticism and Victorian conventions, in the name of health: "the power of sensuality is also that of cour-age, of imagination, of color." In long novels (sometimes very long) he advocated a new education which prepared one for life instead of frightening one away from it. But to him, law was as much a part of health as was freedom; against the prophets of sexual anarchy he untiringly professed his belief in "self-mastery, vigilance, absorption in noble things, self-respect." In the midst of his sex campaigns he was not afraid to protest, once in a while, against the monomaniacs on his own side and their "everlasting love life—as if there were not also a life of work!" He chose the same difficult midway position in the feuds about morality and art roused by naturalism. He fought simultaneously the heralds of bigotry and the champions of "empty effeminacy," always guided by his instinct for the limits, softening the impact of the new standards, saving what could be saved.

Most one-track he might seem in his polemics against dogmatic Christianity. Down to his last years he wrote acid pamphlets against the theologians; his novels again and again lashed "the wrecks of forms from a passed existence." But his religious play *Beyond Our Power,* one of the masterpieces of dramatic literature, is filled with a different spirit. What frightened Bjørnson in the great religious personalities was their lack of "sound and straight humanity," their morbid tendency toward the impossible, which unsettled the balance of life on earth. He had felt the chilling breath of such idealism in Ibsen's *Brand;* in his own drama, the exaltation is crushed against the immutable laws of life. It is his most classical play, austere and merciless; and the very idea was close both to Greeks and Norse: whoever goes beyond his power is broken by the gods. But the persons who carry these over-strained ideas and sink under the burden are living human beings, seen with a tenderness and compassion which proves how deeply Bjørnson had himself shared the feelings he warned against. The moral nobility of the hero radiates both from the author and from the religion he attacks; and it remains when he himself has met his fate.

There is no hopelessness about it. In *The Wild Duck* Ibsen had shown the same destructive effect of an idealism beyond the power, leaving in the reader an impression of sad pity. Bjørnson's play is a sermon on the grandeur of good in man, even in delusion, a confession of the power of all who "walk God's ways" through the world of imperfection, attempting together that childlike and difficult thing: "to be good."

❊

This simple warmth of life gradually won the nation for Bjørnson, regardless of his disputed opinions.

He became an institution in Norway. After long sojourn abroad, he had gone home just before his religious crisis and bought a big farm in the heart of the country. He had never loved the barren mountains where nothing could grow; his own residence was in the broad and fertile valley, and it became a center of ideas unparalleled in Norway's history. He often escaped again to the great world, especially to France, sometimes for years; but always his roots pulled him back. From here he addressed the nation, and, with his growing fame, the world. From here he handled the daily "solar eclipse of letters"; here he summoned his staff and directed his campaigns; here he wrote books and planted forest, broke new ground, and held court; from here he concerned himself with everything that appealed to his interest or his heart, whether he was called on or not. Like his great predecessor, he could often provoke the patience of Job with his endless trouble-making, his pompous self-confidence, and his commanding voice. He could be inconsiderate, even brutal in his rightful eagerness; the hatred which followed him to his last years was not wholly unprovoked. But he captured the imagination by his dimensions, like a mountain in the landscape, visible from everywhere. Everyone had heard him or read him; everyone knew some colorful anecdote about him; everyone felt his influence. In good and bad he belonged to the nation, as a splendid expression of itself.

BJØRNSTJERNE BJØRNSON

As the battles subsided, moreover, and gave quiet for more unbiased observation, it became increasingly clear, even to his enemies, what kind of moral gold reserve Bjørnson really was to his nation, by his very existence. They realized how he had walked through a political fight of unheard-of violence as a symbol of sincerity, never hesitant to admit in public that he had been wrong, never afraid to tell a truth, even if it involved a loss of popularity. They saw the deep chivalry in him, what Ibsen called "his great, royal soul"—that he could fight the opinions of an adversary in violent attack and simultaneously defend him publicly against persecution for the same opinions, because he knew him to be sincere. Bjørnson once wrote that "if I fight for ideas of the future, it is because I see reality more acutely than you do"; overwhelmed by the results of his activity, even his opponents had to admit that he was right. But they also saw what kind of deep and cautious conservatism was hidden in his radicalism, how careful he was of life, how afraid that the nation should "overlook what it really has in fancy for what is unknown." They understood how sincere an urge for justice was behind his actions, how rare an objectivity, how even his ambition and self-assertion were just a part of his great, good strength.

Through his words and his actions they felt that warmheartedness that was his moving power. It is the unifying bond of his writing, not only in the analysis, but in the attitude toward his readers; again and again he expressed the hope that his books "might prove to be a help," give "strength and consolation" to many. But it is his letters which more than anything else show him as he was; they are wonderful prose and still more wonderful human documents. The whole man lives in these spontaneous outbursts, in his impetuosity and his openness, his naïveté and his wisdom, in his unending thought for others, his feeling of responsibility toward everyone who came in his path, and his boundless generosity of himself. As with Wergeland, nothing was too small, nothing insignificant, because it was part of a great unity. In his letters to the farm from abroad, the whole country is taken into his broad embrace: What about the cows? and how are the prospects for the elections? and have you read Robert Ingersoll's latest book on the Bible? and are the new maid's rooms really good? In his letters from home to his daughter in Paris, there is an essence of the fatherland in each little epistle, life and work and landscape, "sunshine and buzzing flies and cockcrow and silence and flags, and your father writing to you— Oh, how happy I feel in Norway!"

It was this surplus which overflowed into his public activity and really, in Ibsen's words, made his life his best poetry. He often expressed his fears that the Norwegians might become "a winter nation"; he himself went around among them for almost eighty years "radiating warmth like a great animal," teaching them how to keep warm. He did not know what parsimony was. His colleagues in poetry were always short of money; schoolboys wrote to him about their troubles; old widows were in straitened circumstances—he was always there, always willing to do something, to give, to make an appeal, to call attention, to stir consciences. His belief in the good in man made him sharp-sighted. Through his life runs a series of judicial murder cases, in and outside Norway, where he saw the truth through the clouds of mass suggestion, and in sensational campaigns made it prevail. But he was not less energetic in his articles on a thousand small problems of everyday life, railroads and housing, food and fashions, better working conditions for postmen and better care of schoolchildren's teeth, himself eager as a child, busy as a bee, indefatigable. "Verse-making is not the only form for poetry," he once wrote; "my poetry shall be a new and better Norway." It was this attitude which made him such a "gigantic creator of values" whenever he went in for something, and which again and again made him the rallying symbol of the nation in its great moments, beyond the limits of party and person. His break with religious dogma made no difference here. "I know that the Earth will sometime go to pieces," he wrote after his crisis. "But if there should be only a future of ten generations to work for, to make those few more happy than we are is a wonderful lot."

The center of his active love was Norway, not in the first place a state with its symbols, but the home of that people which he loved so much. There is a fruitful openness about his patriotism, which shows how sound it was. At the bottom lay his deep feeling of fellowship, beginning with his nearest relatives and expanding in growing circles to the great world of mankind. He once wrote that he could never understand a patriotism which did not "begin with the most heartfelt love for father and mother"; his own most natural sphere remained the family, where he went around "as the strong king in the fairy tale, turning everything into gold." His national anthem begins, not with history, but with "the land of the thousand homes"; it is "the carrying power of a father" that has carried the nation through. In all his creation, from the songs of his youth to the dramas of his seventies, the home is the obvious background and starting point, the place of organic growth, "where she stands bright amidst children's laughter," turning the wild forces into the furrow of joyful responsibility. Here, again, the secret of life is to begin with the nearest things; whoever does not manage to build his own house, "though victor from Moscow to Cartagena, he'll die alone at some St. Helena." One of his most profound national poems is that to the youth of his nation, "a youth which is strong and sound," thinking, fearless, growing characters, with the same light over their faces that emanated from himself.

This love of man, beginning in the small, consistently ended in embracing humanity. To Wergeland, starting in the universe, the problem had been to gain a foothold in his own soil. Bjørnson went the other way, with the natural growth of a tree.

His nationalism had always involved internationalism; barriers between the nations seemed to him not only foolish but sinful. Early he began advocating international conciliation, even in cases where it would involve sacrifice on the part of his own nation: "I will resign from the league of hatred!" But the work for the peace movement which filled his last decades was always marked by his realism. Civilization had not been built by letting everything loose, but by "setting bounds and holding them"; he was deeply disturbed by the Germans, who "break all possible bounds, and are not really in form except when they do so." Much more clearly than most of his contemporaries he saw the close connection between international order and real democracy. His task again was to arouse minds; toward the end of his life he gradually became the public conscience of Europe. He lifted his voice against all kinds of injustice, the subjugation of the peasants by Polish reactionaries, the judicial murder of Dreyfus, the danger to the world from Germany's unfree institutions and lack of "magnanimity, liberty, and beauty." The oppressed minorities of Europe came to regard him as their main spokesman; he called attention to the subjection of foreign-language groups in Hungary, he pleaded the cause of Croats and Ruthenians, of Finns under Russia, of Danes and Poles in Prussia, throwing his reputation into the scales in their support. To the Slovaks he became a kind of Lafayette; a monument of gratitude to him was unveiled in Czechoslovakia just before the German invasion.

He loved life so deeply; to part from it was hard. When in 1909, in his 77th year, his powers began to fail, he fought death as bravely as he had fought in life. His last poem, written after his first apoplectic stroke, still has the splendor of his imagination and the power of his thought, a description of the summer rain after drought, coming without violence and ravage, as a kind blessing from above. And he fought not only for himself; movingly his struggle was mingled with thoughts of those who needed him, fighting humanity all over the world: "Here I receive appeals from Croats, Slovaks, Rumanians, from distressed and wronged individuals in many countries for help—I, who cannot help myself. . . . Oh, how the life lines of the nations take clear shape before my eyes, and how I am in suspense every time that anything decisive happens! . . . Everything is fresh and radiant and fighting, I alone am not. But I cannot give up." When taken to Paris as the guest of the French Republic for the last, futile cure, he struggled in the clear moments of his long agony with a poem that should be dedicated to the poor Polish working girls, "who help and help, and carry around to all who starve and suffer." He managed to formulate only the title: "Good deeds save the world."

In his last delirium he believed that he was sailing homewards again, his face turned toward Norway. His dream came true when the battleship "Norway" carried his body home from France and up the Oslo fjord to a nation in awe and sorrow, greeted from the old castle of the Hákons by twenty-one guns, the salute reserved for kings.

❊

Toward the end of his life, Bjørnson himself defined his place in the history of his nation.

In his banquet speech on receiving the Nobel prize he outlined what literature should be to a people. It shall show "the consistency of life," give the secure feeling of its "beneficent surplus, that after the worst horror, the darkest devastation, the earth will again be irrigated by freshness welling forth from eternal springs"; it shall thus strengthen the courage to live. This "primeval experience of what is to advantage and what is to disadvantage, that is what I have tried to serve."

When he regarded Norway's intellectual history from this point of view he found that in his personal life he had fought the whole nation's fight. All through the traditions he saw a clash of two struggling forces: "a bright kind of people, building a social community, confident in the powers of life," and a dark stripe of individualistic protest from those who only, or mainly, see restriction in law and custom, and rise in defiance. This tension is sound: only so can freedom be kept vigilant; but the men of light must be in a great and cheerful majority. That is the case of Norway, as proved by its literature; as a whole it is sound and glad through its long history—the dark admixture is rarely more than one in twenty. Nothing had disgusted Bjørnson more than Wagner's "sea-sick" and sensual-sentimental "Nordic" plays, "signs of weakness which should be discouraged, not glorified." The real Norse tradition is different: no disconsolation and despondency, no sentimentality or dread of life, but healthy coolness and manly balance. It's all alike in the great authors, Holberg, "the laughing master builder," Petter Dass, "one of the brightest poets in world literature," Henrik Wergeland with his "white sails and flaming flag." And the contemporary poets as well are "sound as fishes and birds," their creation filled with healthy responsibility, the conscience of a plain, democratic people. "Still Thor with his red beard is the chief god of Norway."

In these words Bjørnson has not only sketched his historical background, but fitted himself into the picture. He gathered in him all the contrasts of the tradition, all the centrifugal forces, all the powers of lawless freedom. But still more he represented the power of centrality and unity, all that is constructive, sound and strong in the nation's history and its heritage, from the state builders of the Viking period to the common people of today, from Christianity to the Greeks, from Edda and Holberg to Wergeland and Ibsen, welding it into his own broad and healthy personality. He was once called "the sap of Norway's tree"; that he was. He has himself become the great expression of the consistency of the people, the confirmation of its beneficent surplus. He is himself the "chief god" of modern Norway.

Like Wergeland before him, he projected all his dreams and visions into a program of action. He wrote somewhere about the wonderful feeling of health and strength it gives to walk along "a well built road with its firm, ordered mass of stone"; he made his people feel like that about its future. What Wergeland sang with a lonely voice in the hesitant gray of dawn, Bjørnson carried into the clear daylight of work, the great, glad morning song of the nation. In the hour of trial, thirty years after his death, his people showed how closely that song was connected with their ideals of life, and how deep were its sources of strength.

ACCEPTING the HERITAGE

I

When in 1896 Bjørnson published in the American *Forum* a sketch of Norway's literature he described the poets of his country as an advancing fleet: "Something tight and solid about every ship, as if each had its own definite business to take care of. Not one single pleasure craft in the whole navy. No movement off the course. With one single exception no elegance about sails and hulls either; but a sure trustworthiness. Each vessel seemed to be a realm by itself. They came together, because they could not help it; but each was in its own way." This is still a fair description of Norse literature, and quite especially of the writers who were Ibsen's and Bjørnson's contemporaries. With all their variety of character and background they had a common direction and a unified command.

This does not imply that the group was uniform, not even within the wide range of possibilities presented by its leaders. There were strong trends of dogmatism and sectarianism in the ideology of the 70's and 80's, and important aspects of life found no expression at all. There was revolt and defection in the somber school of naturalism and in that scabby sheep of the movement, the "Bohemia," which specialized in sex liberation. Bjørnson thundered against the morbid hopelessness of the one and the distorted individualism of the other and comforted himself with the thought that such people had never been numerous in Norway. But this fact could not conceal that the problems they raised were real enough, in spite of life's basic soundness.

On the whole, however, unity prevailed, borne by those positive forces which were the strength of the generation. They were predominant even in the dissenting schools: behind the exaggerations and the monotonous sadness there was the same fanaticism for

truth, the same undaunted spirit of attack and the same terrible
earnestness. In the best representatives there was also that deep
feeling of human community which was the message of the age,
nowhere stronger than in the leader of the naturalists, Amalie
Skram (1847–1905). Her novels were born from a moralism of
almost shocking honesty, wild cries of revolt against the cruelty
of life, above all the sexual subjugation of woman; and her bitter
tale of human misery had an undercurrent of sobbing commisera-
tion which was the lifeblood of her art.

Even that literary yacht which Bjørnson singled out for its elegance followed the general course. Alexander Kielland (1849–
1906) was the dandy of Norse literature, a man of the world from
the cut of his waistcoat to the shading of his firm, playful prose.
His literary tradition was that of the eighteenth-century rational-
ists, and of Heine, "who scorned the grand attitudes and is therefore incomprehensible to the Germans." In his restrained poise he
really seems to be that extremely rare thing in Norway: a classic
by birth, not by struggle. But beneath his glittering surface the
same forces were at work: the severe moral idealism, the hatred of
fake and hypocrisy, the serious conception of freedom and fellowship. His ideal was to be a "useful" poet. He struggled with
the same general problems of life as did his comrades in arms; and
his light ironical style disguised no less holy indignation, or pity
and understanding, that fruitful common ground of the group.

The multiplicity of the generation and its bond of unity is strikingly brought out by Jonas Lie (1833–1908). He was a curiously
mingled soul, daydreamer and realist, "mole and butterfly," raptured by his grotesque power of fancy and terrified by his own
obscurity, always struggling for understanding and order; he was
born to be the man in the middle. He became the great chronicler
of his age; he filled its general ideas with the life of his truthful
and intimate vision, taking them his own way "from dimness up
into light and clarity." But his realism never grew dogmatic; and
he never lost his simple belief in the powers of good. In spite of
his radicalism, he never broke his allegiance to Jesus, "the freest
man on earth," who brought law into chaos; yet he was the only

one of the great authors to defend even the Bohemians, because through their senseless subjectivism he heard the cry of despair.

His novels are filled with deep and knowing sympathy for the common man, who was also the coming man. But no less did he struggle to do justice to the social groups which were unavoidably running to ruin, with a power of psychological divination which has been matched only in this century. And in the midst of modern realism he always kept alive the springs of spontaneity in himself, the emotional openness and that troll-like imagination which was the play form of his unshackled mind. It was this noble generosity which made Bjørnson, in his survey of the bright tradition in Norwegian life, call Jonas Lie "light all through," a pure representative of the golden era in the nation's literature.

II

The 90's brought a change of intellectual climate in the whole Western World.

By origin it was a sound and natural oscillation of the pendulum. For decades the poets had concentrated on general problems, with emphasis on their intellectual aspects. Now the stored-up interest turned to emotions and individuals again, seeking inspiration and support in the first romantic outburst at the beginning of the century. Sometimes the movement was connected with a wave of resurgent nationalism, and almost always with the intensified social struggle: the new ideals could be used as a means of escaping disagreeable realities, and of fighting them. But in most nations the established tradition easily absorbed the shock.

In Germany, however, special conditions gave the movement a revolutionary turn which proved to be fraught with fate. From the very beginning, German romanticism had a trend of convulsive self-assertion against the "foreign" influence from south and west; the neoromantic movement carried this tendency to excess, pushed on by Prussian nationalism and the reveries of Wagner and Nietzsche. The turgid and excessive traits of the Teutonic traditions were declared to be the "Gothic" heritage of the tribe and an expression of its real spirit, a painfully elaborated system of hero worship, instinct, blood-and-soil cult, vulgarized Darwinism in romantic disguise, which defiantly broke away from the main line of European culture. In the 90's, these theories were still in their heretic beginnings; but the stir never again subsided. There is an unbroken chain from these first ideologists of hate to that "Nordic" mixture of individualistic phrases and materialistic collectivism, of scholastic tricks and foggy emotional thinking which burst upon the world in the 1920's.

In Norway as well there was a definite change of atmosphere around 1890, and for the same general reasons. Norwegian literature had lived under high pressure for decades. Readers and writers began to weary of social problems and psychological test cases, of Ibsen's ethical intensity and even of Bjørnson's eternal healthiness; they would like some relaxation, and said so with considerable hubbub. In reality, however, the continuity was stronger than the change. In spite of some political disillusionments, most Norwegians were filled with victorious progressive ideals in national, political, and social life, and busy with immediate tasks; little space was left for hazy occultism and nostalgic longings for the past. The literary heritage called for no bloody revolution. Except for a few extremists, most Norwegian writers, regardless of school, still saw their ideal in the many-sidedness and the sound traditionalism which was personified in Wergeland. Authors like Ibsen, Bjørnson, and Jonas Lie certainly did not lack sound emotions or real respect for the individual. It is symptomatic that these elder poets, far from condemning the new currents, were considerably influenced by them in their own writing. A second time the romantic movement in Norwegian literature was felt as a supplement, not as a break.

The wave of emotion called forth a new flowering of lyric poetry which was to last deep into the following century, a new understanding of the subconscious in nation and individual, a new intimacy in the approach to landscape, and a new feeling of depth toward life itself; many strident slogans of the previous generation suddenly lost their meaning. In the first poets of the school there was a touch of romantic cliché and of decadent homelessness in life. But in most of them this literary fashion did not last long; their distinguishing mark was not a flight from reality, but a new approach to it. After the first flush they turned with new eagerness and new eyes to the immediate tasks, not as insurgents, but as workers in the nation's life. Many of the young ones openly declared their devotion to the elder generation. Even the most dreamy subjectivist among them, S. Obstfelder (1866–1900), a poet of mimosalike delicacy and truly cosmic emotion, did not feel himself a rebel against the tradition of the century.

The chief interest of poets and artists alike was the national life of the people, its "living tradition," conceived in a deeper way than in the 80's. But the enthusiasm of the new school had little of "Nordic" mysticism. The first national revival had a sound equilibrium of thought and feeling, combined with a strong realistic trend; and also in the new movement the main current both in scholars and poets was that of sober national self-knowledge, an endeavor to make the people feel more deeply at home in the country it had won for itself. The most important literary school was that of the "home-soil novelists," who went back to their own districts and pictured the life of their own folk, not so much their "problems" as their entire life, with a new and intimate understanding of its background. Even the vague dreamers usually ended there. They had little of "blood-and-earth" mythology and false romance, nor did they try to tear the hero out of his human surroundings; but they did have much faith in the sound forces of Norway's toilsome workaday, the undemonstrative endurance which through the centuries has vanquished the wilderness both around man and in him. Their traditions were those of the people itself, and their style was mostly close to the sources. Their psychology is penetrating, without making their persons a gallery of eccentrics; if they exalt a plain life, it is without coloring and simplification. The strongest expression of religious revival came from these circles—peasant-born hymnists, grown among the dangers and joys of a fighting life on shore and sea, praising the freedom of the common man as a part of their folk religion, singing their simple faith in the people's own tongue with the manful voice of Petter Dass.

There were other trends. But the main stream was strong enough to absorb them, most clearly in the keenest intelligence of the group, Hans E. Kinck (1865–1926). He was a rare brew of cynicism and subdued sympathy, of dreaminess and almost mephistophelic penetration; but the focus of his mind was Norway. It was the passion of his life to dig down unto "the mysterious underground" of the nation through all ages, "that small residue that can never be internationalized"; his vast literary work is one single attempt to define these fundamentals. In so doing, he often seemed to concentrate on what Bjørnson called the "dark stripe" in the nation's mind, the morbid powers of disorder and primitivism; and he supported his views by race speculations of dubious solidity. To him as to the Germans, Western influence in Norse history had often meant a contamination of the pure sources; his book on the period of Hákon Hákonson he called ironically "The Great Age."

But his conclusions pointed in a different direction. With all his burrowing skepticism he was a positive spirit. His guiding principle was not emotionalism, but intellectual honesty; at bottom he was a moralist. His search for the individuality of the nation had Ibsen's ethical earnestness; he probed the weaknesses in order to burn them out. Though he chastised modern civilization and feared its power of leveling down, he was far from being a primitivist. His cynicism did not affect his belief in the dignity of man and his faith in organic growth. He sharply dissociated himself from the German generalizations of the race theory, not to mention their race policy; being a profound student of Italian history, he greeted rising fascism with even more contempt than did the rest of his compatriots.

There was no strong trend of political or social reaction in the other neoromanticists either. Some of them bitterly lashed the excesses of Norwegian parliamentarism; but they followed Ibsen's and Bjørnson's line, their own allegiance to democratic principles was for the most part beyond doubt. The harshest critic, Gunnar Heiberg (1857–1929), was himself a burning spokesman of the radical and rational tradition. The few pale laments at modern times faded before the hopeful advance of new social forces, the cultural optimism of farm youth and the rising self-confidence of organized labor. Per Sivle (1857–1904) became the skald of this believing optimism, the writer of patriotic songs in which the great leaders of Old Norway lifted their voices in support of the nation's modern struggle.

The exception to confirm the rule was Knut Hamsun (born 1859). He was one of the leaders of the new movement, and not in Norway alone; his psychological subtlety, his flowering lyricism and his romantic heroes pitted against a dreamlike subarctic landscape were the thrill of his contemporaries. But his philosophy was completely German, anticipating far later developments. He loved the secret dynamics of the soul because he worshiped the primitive forces of life as a whole; at the bottom of him lay a savage self-assertion, revolting against the bonds of human fellowship and the core of human tradition. He hated "the modern spirit, railroads, and socialism, and American bellowing," as he hated the religion of mildness and humility. He was equally far from the pious Christians and the idealistic freethinkers of the 80's. There were few of the leading ideas of the nation's struggle which he did not ridicule; instead, he early called for "the born master, the natural despot, the great terrorist," the leader. But his influence remained purely literary in Norway. His compatriots enjoyed his witty artistry and liked to daydream with him; but it never occurred to them to build their own lives on his fancies.

The truest representatives of the 90's are two poets without world renown, Arne Garborg and Nils Collett Vogt.

Arne Garborg (1851–1924) came from a small western farm community, bright and cheerful till it was sombered by the tyranny of religious sectarianism. Through his youth and early manhood he fought a heroic struggle to break his bonds, guided by Ibsen and Bjørnson. But he left them far behind, until he stood as the great Leftist of the 80's, Norway's leading cosmopolite, the standardbearer of naturalism, close to the Bohemians, even to the anarchists. But this spirit of revolt in Garborg was mated with a painful sense of responsibility, a searching desire for truth which never left him in peace, and a concern over everything human which urged him to save and to rebuild. It was expressed throughout his life by a solidarity with the people of his western home district and a relentless fight for their genuine New Norse language. This fruitful feeling of obligation made him absorb the ideas of the 90's as intensively as he had those of the 80's. In many ways they meant to him a return to his own origins; after the struggle for liberation he dedicated his forces to the raising of new standards. But his aim was to reconcile, not to destroy. He broke away from the mechanistic ideology of the previous generation; he became a leader in the new school of lyricism and intimate psychology, singing in splendid verse and prose the beauty and traditions of his home country. He returned to a religious faith in the good will of man, connected with the simple Christian morals he remembered from his childhood. But he carried with him into this new world all that was strong and constructive in the world he left: its radicalism and intellectual sincerity, its feeling of social fellowship. He remained a cosmopolite and a man of freedom, a representative of "the rational line." His lyrics are unsentimental, fresh, and strong; there was no reaction in his social criticism, only an effort to bring the fight closer to the people he knew best. He wanted to preserve the values, and to a great extent he succeeded—the last great bridge builder of the century, and a living symbol of its continuous growth.

The pathos of his life, rescued over a purgatory of doubt, remained his belief in the common man, in his moral forces and "unmuddled humanity," as strong in his western home folk as in those of Homer. His creed had nothing of Hamsun's escapism and worship of the primitive; it was a belief in the nation's power of building standards in real life. The masterpiece of his creation is the narrative poem of a simple country girl who conquers the evil troll powers by her kind and pure heart, as did the heroines of the ballads, in a moral struggle of everyday life. He knew that his people were daily fighting and winning the same inconspicuous battle. In the prose of his later years he often returned to the farmers of Norway's eternal frontier, who again and again conquer the wintry mountain and make grain grow from the stony ridge. They have seen many crises and will see more without losing themselves.

What Garborg sang from the countryside, Nils Collett Vogt (1864–1937) echoed from the city. He, too, was born to real life under the banners of liberation, baptized by Wergeland's revolutionary fervor and initiated by the great radical believers of the 80's; and like Garborg he carried the intellectual faith of his youth through the new wave of emotion, because he never haughtily dissociated himself from the people. The romantic poet of Italy's joy and color also wrote the mighty battle song of Norwegian labor. He remained for the most part a lone fighter; but his solitary struggle for the continuity of tradition, for independence of thought and the rights of the young and the weak, was fought in behalf of the many.

He knew the emptiness of a liberty without obligations; to him as to Garborg the bond of unity was the country itself. He was a man of rugged honesty and of virile self-discipline. So was his Norway: serious and severe, not made for vanities and playfulness, a land of sincerity and immutable laws; and the people was molded in its picture. His great patriotic lyrics are void of insinuating melody and romantic phrase; they are filled with the austere and reticent feeling of fellowship grown from the land itself—the land of scanty smiles, "great, cold, and hard, poor, stern, and white, *our* land."

III

Nobody would be likely to call Norwegian literature in the twentieth century a close formation of any kind. There is a tremendous increase in the number of books and writers; and their inner variety is striking. Nevertheless, these four decades still appear as a whole. Most leading authors are active throughout the period and grapple with the same groups of problems; and there are common traits in their attitudes. It is an age of assimilation more than of revolt, open both to the future and the past.

ACCEPTING the HERITAGE

The First World War brought a deep shock to Norway, even if the country was not directly involved in the fighting. And the people suffered its full share in the aftermath: the disillusionment and decay of moral standards, the philosophical disintegration caused by modern physics, the revolution in psychology initiated by Freud, the economic crisis and unemployment with its wake of political and social unrest, and, from 1933, the increasing international war of nerves, leading up to the catastrophe. In Norway as elsewhere these feverish years changed the style and tempo of literature, partly under American influence. As yet, however, it seems dubious whether the incision was as deep as some contemporaries believed; in the merciless light of the 1940's the proportions of the past are swiftly changing. In many respects the First World War merely intensified tendencies which were already there; future generations may see the trends of connection still more strongly.

The interest in folk life is the dominating note in Norwegian literature after 1900 as it was in the 90's. Such extensive literary description of the authors' native parishes has sometimes narrowed the horizon; but there are many compensations. For centuries Norway was cut up into isolated valleys and fjords without a real national literature to tie them together; the present literary survey of the land continues the inevitable process of self-discovery begun in the 1830's. In everincreasing fullness counties and cities, classes and professions have been given their voices in literature, with inexhaustible variety of shade; and the competition of the country's two official languages has led the spoken dialects into the literary idioms to an unparalleled extent. Norway's national literature was still in the making, struggling toward unity through an extraordinary range of local and individual freedom. There was little of the refinement fostered by long academic cultivation. Instead, the literature has been instrumental in a national self-liberation and self-understanding which has few analogues in our time.

This trait is accentuated by the realistic trend of modern Norwegian writers. There is great difference between the literary description of the naturalists and the movielike technique of the 1930's. There is still a kinship in the approach: now as before the authors like to write about things they know, to see the characters in their real circle of life, struggling with their factual problems. They like to see things unflinchingly and express them soberly, in blunt words, preferably the proper, unshaven vocables of the people itself. This "neorealism," still more marked after the First World War, has sometimes made Norwegian literature earth-bound and myopic. But it has also kept the literary debate close to the ground and sharpened the feeling for values; traditions and innovations are probed within their real frame. There is little in Norway of sterile literary urbanism with its theoretical battles in the thin air of abstraction, and much of that deeper feeling for tradition which may well go together with fearless radicalism.

This realism is not one of chairs and tables, but of the soul. As psychologists, modern Norwegian writers proudly acknowledge their descent from Ibsen. They are not so engrossed by "problems"; often their aim is just to understand and make others understand. But in most of them, problem writers or not, there is at bottom a serious moralism, which may sometimes feel heavy and somber. Norse literature still draws its justification from life, not just from itself, and has a task in the human community. In this respect as well the modern writers accept the great tradition of the previous century, parallel to the general development of modern Norwegian society. Pleasure craft are still rare. There is great art, but little of artistry and over-decoration, little of spiritual rope dancing. The form is usually simple, strong, and clear; the author is not talking to connoisseurs, but gropes for plain expression accessible to everybody. And more often than not he carries a direct message for his day.

The struggle for freedom has moved into new fields.

The 90's were a lull, when the lines were reformed after the political victory. Then expanding industrialism caused the slogans of 1814 to rise once more in a sweeping demand for economic and social reform. Again, as in the political fight of the past, the program was supported by historical research, which tied the new issues to the great national tradition; and again literature took its part in the fighting. The lines were not so clear any more, and the grouping not so simple. But the pathos of justice was no less burning, and the urge for liberation no less spontaneous. The poetry of social struggle, formerly in the hands of outsiders, was now taken over by the fighters themselves, carried by a revolutionary strength unmatched since Wergeland sang against the tyrants, and expressed with the intellectual bluntness of the new era. Again the watchword was freedom; and hardly in any literature is the demand so focused on the individual and his right of personal development.

But this trend does not run counter to the tendency of organization which was inherent in the new form of social struggle. In few countries has the idea of team work been adopted more smoothly than in the homeland of Nordic individualism: to Norwegians the two principles have implied each other from of old. The sound traditionalism of the nation worked in the same direction; the aim of the social reform movement was not to break the national solidarity but to preserve it. The literary epic of Norwegian labor is not popular stories of railroad gangs, of the willful wanderers of industrial pioneering, romanticized in Hamsun's style, but the monumental novels of Kristofer Uppdal (born 1878), who follows his men through the jungle of the construction period into the slow building up of the National Federation of Labor within the framework of Norwegian democracy, never losing sight of the individual faces in the crowd and never forgetting their great common aims. The self-chosen symbol of his work is the mastered masses of a Gothic cathedral, with room both for farmer and worker, teeming with modern life and solemn with the spirit of national tradition.

Still more important than these writers is that literature which is "social" without being so labeled. It is not limited to any single class; some of the authors are radicals, others may be neutrals or even skeptics. But what they try to create is social consciousness and social conscience in the spirit of mutual understanding; and it is that spirit which has built modern Norway. Their influence has been deep. When, in the 20's and especially the 30's, the whole social atmosphere of the country became perhaps more promising than in any other nation, when an increasing number of Norwegians came to feel economic and social injustice not only as a problem of economic theory but as a personal challenge, it was partly due to political developments, but no less to that message of collaboration and good will which had been continuously carried to the nation by its writers through more than a century.

This trend of organized individualism may explain the way in which Norway and her poets reacted to the new mass movements of collectivism and dictatorship which followed in the wake of the First World War. Nazism never had a chance in Norway. The ideology did not take; the serum worked. Even Hamsun, who was proclaimed the main poet of Germanic resurrection by Alfred Rosenberg himself, was content with general statements of sympathy; a "brown" Norwegian poetry does not exist. Much deeper was the influence of Russia. Communism presented a connected system of thought, and could work on the strong social trend in the nation's political tradition; the small group of writers with communistic leanings was one of the literary storm centers of the 20's. But their main influence was not along the line of doctrinaire communism; in the long run, Norwegian literature proved to be as inaccessible to the mass spirit as was Norwegian labor. Their message was that flaming indignation which they threw into peaceful, reformist Norway; their cynical lack of courtesy toward accepted phrases, whether bourgeois or socialist; and their inexorable acuteness of logic, often sharpened by psychoanalysis. Like Norway's great writers of the past, they again called back to memory the fact that freedom is a challenge and a promise, not a good acquired for peaceful possession within *any* framework of social progress.

Almost as important was their influence in the international field. In spite of its closeness to the home soil, modern Norwegian literature has never lost its traditional openness to the world; the great exponent of this attitude in the 1920's was Fridtjof Nansen (1861–1930). From his early youth he had been the hero of the nation, a universal genius, outstanding even as a writer, "the man who lived the national anthem," felt as a symbol of the nation's strength in his complex role of scholar and dreamer, individualist and advocate of democratic unity, artist and man of action. After the First World War his patriotism, like that of Wergeland and Bjørnson, was naturally crowned by internationalism. In a world maddened by its unsolved problems he saw the single hope of regeneration in those ideals which had proved their power in the plain and severe life of his own little homeland. Again and again, in magnificent prose, he pointed to the simple human virtues of "altruism, reciprocity, helpfulness, and trust"; and his own heroic fight for the starving Russians and the millions of war prisoners and refugees regardless of race and creed proved to the world what his ideas really implied. In *his* spirit the authors of the 30's raised their warning against the resurging wave of barbarism, Christians, liberals, and communists alike, but most vigorously the radicals. Again it was not the political ideas of Arnulf Øverland (born 1889) and Nordahl Grieg (born 1902) which made their poems and plays stand out among the quiet psychological novels of their contemporaries. It was their capacity for human reactions, kept alive in a world callous of cruelty and blinded by blood, their feeling of joint responsibility for all human suffering, for things done and not done from Guernica to Peiping. Øverland's poem of 1936, "You Must Not Sleep," is one of the great, futile warnings of decent man against the rising powers of destruction. Through the uneasy half-heartedness of the late 30's, which had also its representatives in Norway, he again made the issues clear, guided by the same intuition of the heart which a hundred years before had made Wergeland lift his defiant voice in a world of slavery and lies.

The warnings were not generally heeded. No more than any other nation could the Norwegians see clearly the magnitude of the approaching danger. But if most writers were still preoccupied with inner problems, it did not mean a flight from reality. In the long run, their more inconspicuous work may have contributed no less to the building of real strength.

To a great extent these authors directly continued the struggle of previous generations for personal freedom. Progressive Norway still has a rich variety of standards, intellectual, moral, and religious. The writers of the new century fought against the drag of obsolete conventions, of prejudice and inert group mind no less indignantly than the men of the 80's attacked their ghosts. Even more than sex problems the religious oppression has remained a dominant subject; it is amazing how many Norwegian novels attack pietism with its somber laws and furtive freedoms, the plague of narrow communities. These books show the reverse side of Norwegian society, where the fight for individual independence may still have much of Ibsen's desperate bitterness.

The distinguishing mark of this radical literature, however, is a dissolution of the old slogans and a tremendous deepening of the problems, called forth by psychoanalysis. There is a good deal of provincial parroting in Norwegian authors of the analytic school; and there is a definite trend toward sexual anarchy, tending to break life up into disconnected parts. But far from promoting psychological disintegration, the main result has been a new understanding of human development as an unbroken whole; the flood of novels on childhood is significant. Psychoanalysis creates a new concept of freedom as an inner problem, conditioned less by theories and principles than by the entire relationship of the soul to its surroundings, consciously and unconsciously, from the very beginning of life. It lends new and ominous importance to the influences trying to mold the individual, from education, morality, and religion to the whole structure of society. Stronger than any other school of thought it emphasizes freedom of development as a prerequisite of the happiness and harmony of individuals and of their joint life. These ideas with their wide implications have proved fruitful in modern Norwegian literature, and the influence is not only negative. Through the first flush of doctrinairism the lines already emerge of a deepened conception even of law and responsibility; and it does not necessarily mean a break with the spirit of the past.

But there is a dissolution of old formulas from the opposite side as well, a deep-going critique of the whole ideology of the movements of liberation. This constructive conservatism also has its forerunners in tradition. The authors of the school are not necessarily reactionaries; but they warn against breaking up standards which in the long run may prove to be essential to progress itself. The chief representative is Sigrid Undset (born 1882). Her modern novels have their starting point in the problem of human happiness, which for centuries has been so closely associated with full individual self-realization; and her skeptical admonition is that even more important than liberty is law, which alone can give freedom its meaning. Like the psychoanalysts, but in a totally different way, she emphasizes the unity of life, in the individual and in the community, our unbreakable responsibility toward all its parts, quite especially in sexual love, and the futility of a happiness resting only in itself, detached from human fellowship and deprived of authority, self-sacrifice, and self-negation. Sigrid Undset's own development gradually led her into the Catholic church, a faith which is shared by few Norwegians. Her acrid attacks against trends of modern liberalism, especially the emancipation of women, have not been widely appreciated in her homeland. Such differences of opinion never impaired her real influence. Rightly the nation has recognized behind her personal solutions some of the main problems of its intellectual history, fought through in harrowing earnestness of conviction and with stunning penetration of the human soul.

She does not stand alone. There are parallel tendencies among her contemporaries, with different starting points and convergent aims. The great lyrical poets of the century, the pride of their generation, struggle with their problems on the same level, raising again and again the idea of a deeper independence against all mechanical conceptions of life. It is hard to point out in any contemporary literature a group of writers who make their artistic mastery serve more high intentions. Sometimes, these trends of thought curiously mingle with extreme radicalism; the most astounding expression of these underground cross-currents is the poetry of Arnulf Øverland. He is a revolutionary by profession, a communist and partisan of psychoanalysis in its extreme form, a virulent polemicist against the whole system of inherited standards, quite especially those of Christianity. But his poetry is one of mundane edification, which sometimes comes close to the creed he attacks. His cosmic visions are filled with manful resignation in the face of the chilling impassivity of the universe, expressed in a verse of lapidary self-discipline. But the main trend of his lyrics is an urgent appeal to the feeling of human community, the fellowship of the heart, an undogmatic religion of love, the single hope in a world of senseless brutality. In the whole literature between the great wars this poetry is the outstanding testimony to the fruitful complexity of the heritage.

Everywhere in this literature, the tradition of the nation is present as a background, more or less consciously, one part or another being emphasized or challenged, defended or defied. But the heritage is not only an arsenal of weapons in the battlefield of problems. It also has a life of its own, existing in the minds as an entity, obvious and secure; it knows not only struggle, but also fruitful possession. This feeling of underlying forces all through the nation's life has created the great historical novels which are the backbone of Norwegian literature during and after the First World War.

There are no chauvinistic rumblings in these authors, no repressed aggression and no cheap archaism. Their poetry is realistic, close to modern research. But what they try to present is not a colorful pageant of the externals of the past; the approach is that of ideas and morals, with the emphasis on peaceful, normal life. Here, as everywhere in modern Norse fiction, the background is the landscape—not the hazy dusk of the "Nordic" dreamers, but the country itself, with its poverty and its naked seriousness, loved for the things it has and has not, the eternal frame of the people's existence. It is not used as a pretext for primitivistic simplification. When Hamsun in *Growth of the Soil* would express the romanticism of a war-weary world, he made his hero a nameless savage without history, grown from the ground like a plant, unaffected by the great powers and problems in the nation's life. In the historic writers of today, nature is, to be sure, the soil from which the people grows, but only in order to embrace the problems of life in their full complexity. They tell how the nation has gradually approached these problems, and how in solving them it has built its kernel and drawn its line of growth through the centuries, in a huge interplay of soil and spirit, people, landscape, and world.

In this synopsis of the past, the country got for the first time a great modern religious fiction. In nineteenth-century authors, Christianity was present practically everywhere, from Wergeland on, often dominating the whole trend of thought and emotion; but for the most part it worked secretly, in disguise—the polemics are more conspicuous. The new historic novelists penetrate through the confessions and dogmas and human weaknesses down to those deep cravings of the soul which have through a millennium made Christianity one of the great constructive forces in Norway's growth.

The obvious master of the group is Sigrid Undset. In the first place her great novels from Norway's Middle Ages are the story of human beings, told with that earthy flight of fancy which is the wonder of her art. But through these individuals and their fate she builds the epic of Norway's spiritual rise from primitive life to European culture. In the center of the tale is the Catholic church: from her the light radiates into the spheres of life and the darkness of the hearts. But she also shows that the urge comes from within. She points to those constructive forces in the nation's own tradition which prepared for Christianity long before it came; she shows how the new ideals, far from being imported as foreign goods, grew naturally into the people's heavy struggle for life. Historians may discuss the distribution of emphasis in her novels;

but these are just variations of shade, in a picture of striking inner truth. To Sigrid Undset herself the balance of freedom and solidarity found in the Middle Ages is the eternal one, valid today as it was in the fourteenth century. What she really has shown, in the perplexing variety of life itself, is much more: the broad foundations of all Norway's culture.

No other author has tried his hand on a painting of corresponding audacity of proportions. But the main lines are carried on independently through the following periods of history by other novelists, writers of great art as well, even if their scope is more limited. In the saga by Inge Krokann (born 1893) picturing the mountain farmers of central Norway toward the end of the Middle Ages, in the monumental series of novels dedicated by Johan Falkberget (born 1879) to the eighteenth-century miners of the barren eastern mountain plains, in the tales of Gabriel Scott (born 1874) from the southern fishing districts toward the end of the period of union, human types and living conditions are immensely different from each other and from those of the world of Kristin Lavransdatter. But again from these works rises the picture of people who have turned their toilsome existence into moral strength, building their lives and struggling for their standards under the serious eyes of Norway's eternal landscape.

The strongest testimony of this intellectual metabolism is the great philosophical poems of Olav Aukrust (1883–1929). As he himself was a curious mixture of village sage and cosmopolite, modern artist and skald, so his magnificent work itself symbolizes the growth of the nation's culture from roots in the mold to the heights of philosophy, morals, and religion. With marvelous, intimate knowledge he shows how the very living conditions, the poverty of resources and the functionalism of purpose have fashioned the culture of Norwegian farmers from the first settlement on, have framed the tools of their hands and the trends of their mind in a constant interplay of necessity and human will, from the shape of a wooden spoon to the cadence of a folk song, till with increasing mastery of themselves and the world, they patiently built their edifice to reach up into the common atmosphere of human civilization. It was rightly said about his poetry, when it appeared, that it seemed to be contemporary with the Edda and contemporary with ourselves.

This feeling of a broad and secure undercurrent through all the vicissitudes of the people's existence carries over into modern fiction as well. It has nothing to do with idyll. Most often it comes forth in social literature; and here as before the tradition has more than one meaning. But again and again it suddenly breaks through, as a spontaneous confidence in what is built up in the nation, its mental reserves and resources, the "95 percent of health" which Vinje loved to talk about, that tradition of work and fellowship which made its endurance and its strength. It opens a long perspective behind the struggle of the day. In the plain existence of the simple man there is a depth of eternity, just because he belongs to Norway and always did:

> This is our land, our fatherland,
> From times of old belonging
> To Norway's working man.
>
> (Øverland)

All these trends, of the present and the past, are gathered with majestic finality in the work of Olav Duun (1876–1939).

His great series of novels, *The People of Juvik*, tells the saga of a farm family and a country community in northern Norway from the end of the eighteenth century down to our era; but within this short span of time it seems to comprise the entire growth of the nation. The motif is that of many of Duun's works: the sterility and the fruitfulness of freedom, self-assertion versus the heritage, the individual and the many, man and law. He follows the individual from the time when as yet he was hardly discernible in the group till he faces the world with clear eyes as a modern man; and behind the struggle for outer freedom Duun pictures his moral conflict, from primitive egotism to mature understanding of human fellowship. It is an epic of individualism, but an individualism which is fulfilled by self-sacrifice. The culmination of the work is the sunlit, stormy day when Odin, the hero, and his enemy, sailing alone together, capsize off the coast and Odin gives his life to save the other, leaving the wreck of the boat, which can carry only one of them. In a magnificent way Duun makes this individual fate symbolize the trend of a millennium. Everything plays together in his art: the people and their work, their thoughts and feelings, the cold and stern and magnificent landscape, ever changing and ever constant; and he makes this life grow out of this landscape as an unending force, taking what it needs everywhere but still remaining itself. Odin felt like that when he was drifting away from the boat, and for the last time took in with his eyes the land and the mountains over the smoking surf: it seemed to speak to him from out of eternity, and approve.

In the words of one of his characters, Duun has explicitly stated it: "This, he thought, was life—to extend one's roots back to what had been, and stretch ahead to what has never been, but which has slept within us just the same, from time immemorial."

The HOUR of TRIAL

There are histories of letters which make literature appear as a thing apart, where great spirits work, admire, and hate one another in an air-conditioned atmosphere, far from the sun and rain and sweat and tears of the common man.

This was never the case in Norway. From the very beginning, Norse literature has been written for the people and was a part of its life. For long periods its very preservation was dependent on its value to ordinary human beings, for it lived exclusively on the people's tongue. Even after the invention of printing, its main existence has been in the souls, not on the shelves. Men like Petter Dass, Holberg, and Wergeland were part of the national wealth long before they died; Bjørnson and Ibsen stirred the life of the average Norwegian more than any other contemporary. Foreigners sometimes teased the Norwegians about their "poetocracy." But if the nation was proud of its great writers, it was mostly because they meant so much to itself.

This close connection was not broken in the twentieth century. Still, in Norway before the German invasion, the "literary tradition" was no abstraction in the histories of letters, but a living power in the people's everyday life.

In few nations has literary interest been more developed and widespread. The production of books, periodicals, and newspapers was tremendous; and in great parts of the population literature was regarded with outright veneration. It was felt as a public interest, worthy of support out of the taxpayer's pocket. Writing can never be very profitable in a nation of three millions, except for a few best-sellers. For more than seventy years the Norwegian Parliament has therefore appropriated annual grants to outstanding authors, usually given while the recipients were still in their full power. The daily press devoted a space to literary matters hardly equaled anywhere. During the principal literary season, the months of November and December, it was no rare thing to see the new book of a prominent novelist advertised across the first page of the leading newspapers, and to find a review on the same page, under a headline competing with world news. The sale and distribution of books reached staggering proportions. Numerous novelists had a regular first year sale of their books which, translated into corresponding American figures, would range from 500,000 to 1,000,000 copies. This held equally good for the classics. The centenary edition of Bjørnson's Works (twelve volumes, 1932) in one year sold 70,000 copies, corresponding to an American sale of three millions—not to speak of those works (for example, the translation of Snorri's Royal Sagas) which were distributed in cheap popular editions directly subsidized by the state.

These books were really read, and not only by a literary elite. Wergeland's dream, to see a bookshelf in every Norwegian home, had long ago come true; and they were books for use. How much reading had come to mean in everyday life is proved by the records of the public libraries. The first among the Scandinavian states, Norway soon after 1900 adopted the American system of book distribution (no foreign nation has been so strongly represented in American library schools). In spite of limited allotments and obstacles of geography and communication, the figures of annual book circulation soon soared—ten volumes per inhabitant in the best towns. In the ship libraries of the merchant marine (paid for jointly by owner and state) the average number of books read by each crew member per year sometimes exceeded fifty. Behind the libraries and supporting them were the great educational movements built up in recent years by political and religious groups, labor and farm youth, which made books an instrument of daily work to a degree unknown before. The state operated broadcasting system by regular lectures and readings brought the treasures and history of the national literature into the most modest homes.

But tradition is more than books bought and used and appreciated. It is an atmosphere, a set of standards built up in the minds even of those who don't read much, a common ground without which higher literary interest remains limited and sterile. This basis in Norway was the broad democratic culture which the literature itself had been instrumental in building, and which in its turn carried the literary creations back to the nation.

The cells of this growth were the Norwegian homes. From time immemorial these homes had been the main carriers of the nation's heritage; and even in the age of rotary press and radio they still passed on the most intimate values of the tradition: the unconscious patterns of thought and feeling, picked up with the learning of the language, embodied in the behavior of parents and grownups, expressed in proverbs and jokes and fairy tales, hymns and prayers and Bible stories, nursery rhymes and commonplace quotations, hidden in the shade of a voice and the undertone of a song, and more ineradicable than any theoretical conviction. In these smallest units of society a national atmosphere was reborn with each new generation within the natural fellowship of family life.

On these foundations the school built its work, Norway's obligatory Lutheran elementary school, and its teachers, for generations the traditional vanguard of progressive democracy. Their modeling of good citizens rested on literary cornerstones: the Bible, the hymnbook of the church, and the Norse classics, from Edda and saga to modern times. There was an extensive children's literature of high quality supplementing the work, and the state subsidized libraries in all schools with more than twelve pupils, influencing the purchase effectively by price reductions on suitable literature. But the basic morale builders remained the fundamental books of the tradition. Especially important, because made for children, was the reader, one of the great molders of the nation. There were many of them, all through the century; the one that became leading dates back to the 1890's, in itself a monument to the new home feeling of that generation. It is a work of splendid realism. A fruit of the continued collaboration of educators, poets, and painters, its many volumes present to the child an up-to-date picture of the country and the nation through all ages in its endless variety of landscape and living conditions, of language and background. But through this complexity the work gradually builds up the great common things: the historic line through the nation's life, its growing unity of standards, political and social, secular and religious, its increasing common heritage of ideals and hopes and the simple feeling of fellowship behind it, expressed in the story of its heroes and in the words and lives of the great literary creators, from Snorri's saga to the tale about Henrik Wergeland. No child left elementary school in Norway (not to speak of higher education) without having thus met in poetic symbols what through the centuries the nation has tried to represent; and extensive memorization of poetry graved the essentials still more deeply into the mind. There are few Norwegians of the younger generation who have not a soft spot in their hearts for "Rolfsen's Reader"; much of what makes them feel themselves to be Norwegians was insensibly brought to them through its pages.

The impact was strengthened to an extraordinary extent by song. Most of Norway's composers have done their best things in vocal music; much of the country's great poetry has been set to tunes of high quality. To "swear allegiance to the flag" and corresponding ceremonies are unknown in Norway; the greater is the importance of these many songs in uniting the minds in common expressions of feeling. This joint heritage was carried over into adult life by the church, and quite especially by the national high schools for youth, where song is daily bread. No anthology of fastidious literary standard gives a more striking picture of Norway's living tradition than the book of song of these schools, which has also penetrated far and wide into the homes. The main stock comes from Bjørnson; and a glance through the selection is sufficient to understand his position in the people. But all the others are there as well, even poets of minor order, who are mentioned only in the biggest histories of literature, but have in one or two poems spoken out of the people's heart.

Most important, perhaps, was this core of tradition in the life of the countless organizations and associations which were the pride of modern Norway, political and social, educational, religious, and humanitarian. Their purposes were as different as those of a Y.M.C.A. and a trade union; and so were their battle songs.

But to an amazing extent their books of song built on common goods. In the different surroundings, adapted to different and even opposite aims, this treasure of joint wealth was a symbol of the basic unity of the nation, the standards which it was not necessary to emphasize because they were there all the time. This background of obvious knowledge, of common associations, and immediate understanding, gave its character both to the people's reading and to literary creation itself. In the tradition, vague and changeful in detail, clear and unambiguous in the essentials, the past was integrated into the present as a part of the people's attachment to home. "The literature of a nation," Wergeland said, "is the fatherland of its souls."

That fatherland, far more than the territory of visible Norway, was what the Germans attacked on April 9, 1940.

In spite of all warnings, to the great majority of Norwegians the blow fell as a paralyzing shock. There was little treason, but a widespread stupefaction, a momentary inability of adjustment. This was not merely due to the suddenness of the attack; the responsibility lies with the whole heritage of the people. Through more than a century the nation had built its life on confidence in good will and understanding, a faith warranted by its own development, but sadly inept for the world at large. Average Norwegians had come to take justice for granted and to regard sensible compromise as a matter of course; and they vaguely clung to the conviction that this development was general, that the humanity they saw growing in their own society, the veneration of peaceful, constructive work about which they sang in their songs, was still the universal aim of mankind, and the totalitarian ideologies just a temporary aberration. War and its instruments had been condemned consistently through generations by their most cherished intellectual leaders, had disappeared from poetry and fiction except as a subject of hatred and contempt, almost from the official ideology of the state, living a hidden life in a few lines of the national anthems. Overnight the invasion demanded from the Norwegians a set of intellectual and emotional reactions which most of them had willfully suppressed and many almost forgotten. No wonder, when the unthinkable suddenly became the single reality of importance that they were bewildered, that foreign correspondents mistook their petrified astonishment for indifference, that soldiers sometimes were hesitant in opening fire on "other human beings" and slow to blow up bridges, the construction of which had been the pride and enjoyment of their meandering valley.

But that the shock did not last long, that in the decisive circles the answer was spontaneous and immediate, and that after the first confusion peaceful Norway had to be conquered in hard fighting to the utter amazement of the Germans, this was to a great extent due to that same tradition and to what it had built up. The spontaneous sense of justice and the violent desire for freedom, the respect for constructive values and the belief in decency and humanity arose after the first blow in deep and bitter rage against those who triumphantly trampled all of it under their iron-studded boots. The real result of the attack was not a doubt about the principles of the nation, but a desperate resolution to defend them. The two months of wild fighting in Norway were no time for literature. But the unanimous decision of the Norwegian government on that bleak morning of April 9 to resist the Germans in spite of the hopeless military situation was not unworthy of Ibsen's people. There are no quotations in the terse proclamations of the king and the cabinet, no literary flowers in General Otto Ruge's monumental report of the fighting; but the spirit speaking through them is that of Norway's noblest heritage, in a style which needs not fear comparison with the saga. The behavior of the soldiers and the population in the war zones, their quiet courage and obvious humanity, their unlimited kindness toward the foreign refugees fleeing again before German invasion armies, gave proud evidence that the optimism of the poets about their nation had not been vain.

The representatives of the literary tradition itself did not fail. To be sure, Hamsun publicly hailed the invaders as helpers against the Anglo-Saxons who have "derailed the world"; but he remained alone. Sigrid Undset put herself at the disposal of the fighting gov-

ernment and went through the bomb hell of southern Norway
with them; as a soldier in the army, Nordahl Grieg read over the
radio on the seventeenth of May, Norway's national day, the first
of his magnificent war poems, calling up Norway's spiritual tradition against the powers of death, pointing again as had the great
poets before him to the eternal promise of 1814:

> Naked the flagstaff rises
> Through the green of the Eidsvoll trees,
> But now in this hour of peril
> We know what freedom is.
> A song from the land is rising,
> With victory's power it grows,
> Though whispered by lips tight fastened
> Under the gag of our foes.

The real ordeal began with the military defeat and the German
occupation, when the iron curtain was lowered between Norway
and the world, and the Wehrmacht and the Gestapo brought their
ideology experts and firing squads into the tiniest hamlet. Their
task was not only to turn Norway into a permanent fortress and
an economic colony of Germany; they were to incorporate it into
the new intellectual order, to break its traditions and conquer its
soul along with its body. Quisling took over his job with the ex-
plicit promise of "changing the mentality" of his nation. Newspapers and theater, church, school, and literature were gradually
brought under pressure to serve the grand idea of German propaganda: that after centuries of Western contamination Norway is
now at last finding its way back to its real self. He had not only
persuasion to apply, but all the methods and means of the Nazi
machine, from the bribe to the thumb screw.

In the silent trial of strength which thus began, and which has
now lasted for more than three years, all the imponderables in
Norway's intellectual endowment were put in the scales and
proved to be of full weight. On the surface traditions may seem

to be a subordinate power in the fight; people don't quote poetry before the Gestapo; there are no recitals at the meetings of the underground. But in the building of the spirit which makes them fight, and which holds them together in fighting and directs them toward a common goal, the traditions have proved to be an all-important force. In its extremity the people made a reckoning of those simple things in life which are worth dying for, and they discovered how fully they were expressed in the basic books of the nation. They turned to them for help and support—to the Christian texts in a new wave of religious fervor, to the secular traditions with a new kind of personal need; and these proved to be aspects of the same thing.

The men of letters showed the way. From the very morning of attack and as long as they managed to remain in their jobs, the Norwegian journalists turned their newspapers into anthologies of patriotic poetry, where the most innocent words have their allusions for those who understand. A few months after the occupation, the leading publishing houses brought out collections of Norwegian poetry of landscape and history, the purpose of which was obvious from the titles: "Yes, we love this land together," "Hard the night of our probation," lines from the national anthem. But mostly people found their own way; occupied Norway began reading as the nation had never read before. Relatively few books have yet been forbidden, chiefly political pamphlets and works by authors in exile; the Germans have probably not known where to begin with the poets. The bulk of literature is still free; and the nation has acquired it, during these years of war, literally to the last copy. There is a boom in books, old and new. The book shops are jammed through the winter season: "it is almost as hard to buy a book as to get hold of a bottle of brandy." The libraries have the heyday of their existence. This is not merely due to the curfew and the black-out and the theater boycott which limit the possibilities for pastime: "The great men of our intellectual life and our history speak directly to us today." People sing as never before. It is not organized; they just sit down, when they are together, and start the simple songs that everybody knows. They

The HOUR of TRIAL

bring out the old books of song: "We sing them from cover to cover; they have acquired new life this year."

What they look for and find in their books and their songs is strength, the "bright stripe" of confidence through the country's dark history, the urge for freedom and love for justice, the simple belief in good. It is borne out by the numerous quotations and references in their letters, as long as they still came out: one clear line through all the great names. There is the Bible, in terrifying actuality. There are the hymns, from Hans Nielsen Hauge's song in prison to the modern hymns of joyous freedom. There is Holberg with his dangerous smile, and Wergeland, mentioned and unmentioned, omnipresent—"the all in all of our literature, almost of our history." There are Aasen and Vinje with their granite patience, and Sivle's liberty songs from Old Norway, where one only needs to change the names. There are the great modern ones; above all, there is Bjørnson. He once expressed the hope that his songs might "in the hour of decision raise fighters for the fatherland"; now it has come true. No one is quoted so much, openly and in furtive allusions: his poems of liberty, his speeches of condemnation against the German oppressors of Europe, his letters with their deep and sound humanity. A father quietly tells about the deportation of his son (a young teacher) to a labor camp by the Arctic Ocean: "But, as the poet says, peace is not the best, but a will that never flinches." The boy's mother adds: "Please read B.B.'s poem of those who stand and wait for the day of deeds."

In such quotations dwells the strength of occupied Norway, its certainty and confidence, and its solidarity in the essential things. Now the nation gathers the fruits of its broad cultural democracy: everywhere there is a common basis to build on. There is nothing artificial or forced about this feeling of unity. Nobody could or would embrace all of the tradition, and there is no glossing-over of the differences; the pietist from the countryside and the labor leader from the manufacturing town do not put the emphasis in exactly the same place. But there is a new feeling of accord behind the dissension, a community of all forces of good will against those of willful evil. As a young intellectual put it, himself a believing Christian: "The more of Norway I feel myself fully identified with, the more faithful I shall prove to be."

The first result of this gathering of the forces has been the complete repudiation of Nazi propaganda. The nation was aware of its standards and needed only to compare. To people who realize the implications of their Christian faith, the ideology of Nazism does not present any problem of choice. To people who have lived with Edda and saga from their childhood as a part of the world of realities, the "Nordic" mixture of bullyism and subservience appears as the ugly day dream it really is. To people who have learned to laugh with the fairy tales and Holberg, who have loved Wergeland since their first Seventeenth of May and are imbued with the spirit of modern Norway, the whole philosophy of the goose step is just as revolting and ridiculous as Quisling's attempts to use Ibsen's poems as a prophecy of himself. Symptomatic is the reaction to Hamsun, before the war Norway's best-seller. A university professor who escaped to Sweden over the mountains of the High North a few weeks after the invasion found in a fisherman's cottage the twelve beautiful volumes of Hamsun's collected works under the kitchen stove, ready for their fate. At a recent auction in Oslo the same collection was with considerable difficulty sold for a quarter, the bids beginning at one cent.

But the strongest feeling drawn from the heritage is not that of negative repudiation, but of positive adherence. There is much primitive fighting back in all the tortured nations, much blind hatred and desire for revenge; and there must be. But stronger than the hatred of what they fight against, is in Norway the devotion to what they are fighting for—the promise of the past, which it is their responsibility to keep alive. Norwegians are not waiting for interpretations of the Atlantic Charter in order to understand what kind of life they are fighting for. They have lived it themselves. Their dream, in Sigrid Undset's words, is a "return to the future"; and their present sufferings have only made their ideals more clear to them, behind the war they are forced to fight. This feeling of growth in the midst of brutality and destruction gives the Norwegian home front its cheerful defiance, its note of hope and trust, sometimes almost of joy: "When we discount the purely extrinsic things and remember all the great and good which is happening in our people now, it is impossible to hang one's head"; "We would not wish to be anywhere but here." It has transformed spontaneous reactions into that tough and elastic power of endurance which is indispensable in a long underground war; and it has turned the tradition from defensive to attack. In a new and unexpected way the nation has realized the truth of Bjørnson's words, when he donated most of the books he owned to a public library in the countryside: they are going to be no dead treasure, but "a strong weapon in the hand of the people against intellectual oppression."

Again the men of letters showed the way. The Germans had hoped to support their propaganda by a new Norwegian literature in the Nazi spirit; the lenient censorship in the beginning may have been intended to promote this beneficial development. The miscarriage was conspicuous. In addition to Hamsun, who is eighty-four and does not write any more, the Nazis have succeeded in winning, after three years of threats and promises, seven authors, only two of whom have any reputation; this manpower problem has postponed the birth of a Norwegian Nazi literature indefinitely. They have met the same resistance with the publishers. Even as late as 1943 there was still no censorship in advance on Norwegian fiction, because of the threat of the publishers to discontinue all publication of books if further restrictions were established; and the Germans have been equally unable to cope with the quiet boycott organized by the booksellers.

Instead of assisting the Nazis, the men of letters, writers, and scholars unflinchingly dedicated their power to emphasizing the real traditions and turning them into the fight. The educational institutions all over the country, from elementary schools to colleges, became intellectual war academies, with Norwegian literature as one of the main subjects. In the University of Oslo lecturing and research concentrated with sudden interest on the monuments from previous periods of invasion and national distress; in a public speech the president of the University declared it to be the task of the institution "to defend the positions of Norwegian intellectual life." Norway's leading periodical remained a camouflaged arsenal of democracy till its voluntary discontinuation in 1942, after the second editor in turn had escaped from the country. To their last faithful journalist the newspapers continued to tell what Norway really stands for. When one of the Quisling poets in a great anthology of Norwegian lyrics tried to point out a Nazi line through the nation's literature, an outstanding critic did not hesitate to tell the nation what kind of fake the book was, although, as had to be expected, the review turned out to be his last article. The theaters continued to play those classics which it is difficult to forbid, but which to Norwegians today are fraught with double meaning. The manager of the theater in Trondheim was executed as a hostage on the morning of the day he was to present Ibsen's *Wild Duck*, a perfect contrast of two worlds at war.

The novelists did not speak up less clearly, and again as so often before they made the country itself the strongest ally in the nation's fight. Here is the conclusion of a novel describing the moment when the news of the German invasion was reported over the radio to a fleet of fishing boats in the North, and the feeling of the youngster going ashore to join his detachment:

He stood looking toward the land under the rising dawn. High and hard it mounted from the ocean. In there, on the shores between mountains and sea, the people had lived and suffered and fought . . . men battling storm and ocean for livelihood and life, women looking after their homes in quivering anxiety through days and nights of storm. But the marks of their work will never be wiped out. Here we have been through the change of times as long as man has lived in this land. Here on these shores the history is written of a patriotism that carried us through years of distress and of ease, through the long night of alien rule, and the short day of freedom. It shall carry us through new times of stress, if they have to come.

This was printed and published under the German domination by one of the leading Norwegian publishing houses in the fall of 1941. And it is no isolated case.

But mightier than any words was the example of those literary men who paid with their freedom for Norway's cause: the professors and teachers, writers, publishers, and journalists tortured and killed in concentration camps in Norway and Germany. The very symbol of the spirit of endurance became Arnulf Øverland, who long ago has disappeared in German prisons, but not till his new poems of Norway's battle had penetrated into the most far-away corners of the country, easily recognizable from their incisive emphasis and flaming indignation.

After 1941–42 the battle grew in violence. Large-scale attacks on cultural institutions forced intellectual life into the catacombs, and the tortures and reprisals, the bestial persecution of Norwegian Jews, and the wholesale execution of hostages turned the passive resistance into open war once more. The great traditions of the past became the rallying symbol, not only to men of letters, but to the common man. The two first labor leaders picked out at random and executed in September, 1941, went to their death singing Bjørnson's national anthem. In the schools, as long as they remained open, the reader became the gospel of defiance; escaped teachers tell moving stories about the unsolicited demonstrations of their classes, when the students turned an old, innocent-looking text into a flaming manifesto of their hope and faith, many of them already veterans of the underground. In the great sermons of the church leaders who denounced Nazism in the face of the German authorities, the classics were quoted along with the Bible; on the day when Nazi storm troopers closed the doors of Trondheim Cathedral, place of sepulture of St. Olaf, and thus provoked an open break, the massed congregation outside the church spontaneously raised Luther's old battle song against the Turks and the Norwegian national hymn, the quietest and strongest song in the world. When the teachers refused to indoctrinate the children with Nazi ideology, and five hundred of them were deported to the Arctic Coast, it was a matter of course that in their joint declaration of faith they should refer to the aim of their educational work in Bjørnson's words. Out of the concentration camps escaped Norwegians bring the word of imprisoned college professors, lecturing to their fellow prisoners in the dark of night about that sacred common heritage of poetry which even the Gestapo is unable to take away from them.

These links not only unite the Norwegians at home; they also draw into community those thousands of Norwegians who today fight for their country far away from it. The letters smuggled out of Norway refer to this secret fellowship spanning the whole world: "When the day draws to a close and the stars twinkle here at home, we hope that you and we gather around Norwegian words." The same prophetic verses quoted in the mimeographed underground papers in Norway, are those referred to for encouragement and support in the newspapers of Fighting Norway in London and New York. The songs which the merchant sailors sing together in the seamen's churches in Durban or Buenos Aires, Bristol or Halifax before they go to sea again are the same which resound behind the blacked-out windows of the folk at home. A journalist who recently sailed on a Norwegian destroyer in action on the North Sea, tells of how, when again they were in smooth waters and the sailors gathered in the wardroom for the inevitable cup of coffee, the captain read poems to them (he himself had Ibsen, Bjørnson, and Garborg on the shelf in his cabin). In conclusion he reminded them that "We fight for even more than a liberated Norway: we fight for a free intellectual life in a free fatherland."

One of the highlights of the celebration of May Seventeenth in Oslo, besides the flag parade of the children, was always the placing of flowers on the graves of Wergeland, Aasen, Ibsen, and Bjørnson in the Cemetery of Our Saviour. These last years there have been no children's parade and no placing of flowers; the graves have been under heavy German guard, dangerous as they are. Nevertheless, there have always been some flowers before evening: modest bundles with home-made poems attached to them, or quotations from the works. Above all has this been true of Wergeland's grave, on the monument erected by grateful Jews to whom he opened the country, inscribed "To the indefatigable fighter for the freedom and right of men and citizens." Perhaps more Norwegians than the Germans realize remember on that day his words about "the voice of truth which cannot die." Perhaps there are also those who remember what he once wrote about the work of Snorri Sturluson: "With national enthusiasm, with the gigantic promises and dreams of old he will man an invisible rampart, which in the hour of battle shall be revealed behind the betrayed fortifications."

The chief expression of this spirit of survival is the Norwegian war poetry. It was born during the battles on Norway's soil; it is carried on anonymously and underground in the occupied country, and in the open by exiled Norwegians all over the globe. There are important prose works as well, especially those published by Sigrid Undset in her exile in the United States. But the kernel is in the lyrics, and the leading poets are Arnulf Øverland and Nordahl Grieg. It could all be comprised into one not too fat volume; but these few songs are the living stones that span the gap of war in Norway's literature.

It is a fighting poetry, and carries the scars of battle. All the agonies of total war are in it: the horror of destruction and death, the desperation in the face of those who cannot be helped, the sob of the exiled toward all that is irretrievably lost, the cry of defiance and self-assertion, the triumphant pride and hope, and the rightful and devastating hatred. But the warmth that softens the austere form is not the arid heat of hate. It draws its strength from a vision: a Norway "unseen by the foe," for which the battle is really fought; in these songs, written in face of the utter destruction of all that seemed to be Norway, its heritage is victoriously reborn. It is *that* Norway which has struggled through a millennium to build a realm of decency, good will, and reason, *that* Norway which defiantly took its pride in respect and tenderness for life and is going to do so again, the Norway where the days are still white and the nights are blue to memory because of the life that was lived there. To fight for it is not only to fight for a national tradition, but for the dignity of man.

All through this poetry runs an anxious promise: that the ideals shall not be distorted and lost in the holocaust of brutality; "Violence itself must be homeless when we find our way home." But the strongest feeling is that of confidence—of fellowship across the frontiers of fighting humanity, and of faith in things greater than individuals and nations:

> If many of us fall
> And others still will fall,
> Inner strength remains.
> We shall live through all.
> The light of faith with sacred glow
> Gives patience and peace of heart.
> Spirit we know endures
> And always life will grow. (Øverland)

The magnificent symbol of this connection of old and new is Nordahl Grieg's song for the children of occupied Norway, written to the tune of Wergeland's "National Anthem of the Children" and born from the same spirit. It is filled with all the brutality of war, the cold and the hunger, devastation and death, with the reticent solidarity of the underground and the grim determination to fight back. But what the children fight for in their mute battle is not revenge; it is the standards of their hearts, built up in them from times of old. They don't hate the German soldiers as much as they scorn them, as morbid examples of what Norwegian children shall never be, not even in fighting them. "They trample the weak under their heel, they torture body and soul, they live to kill." Even in the fray of battle Norwegians will remember that *their* task is to be different, to build and rebuild, to heal the wounds; that, too, is victory. "We will be strong, even hard. But inside our strength we have a soul, we have a peace, we have a soil to cultivate. We have a land where the mountain wind goes pure and free in the starlight; and if there is hatred in our minds, it is because we love."

In these verses Norwegian literature of the past hands the torch to the generations of the future. Today, more than ever, we know that it is going to be carried on.

ACKNOWLEDGMENTS

The authors wish to acknowledge their indebtedness to all their unnamed fellow scholars in Norwegian humanities, who have made it possible to write this book. The author of the literary section wants to express his special feeling of gratitude toward the leading men of contemporary Norwegian literary research: Professor Fredrik Paasche (died in exile in Sweden in 1943), Professor Francis Bull (in a German concentration camp since 1941), and Professor A. H. Winsnes (exiled in Great Britain since 1942). This sketch of Norwegian literary development draws from their ideas much more than can be acknowledged in detail. Many of the quotations as well are taken from their works.

Translations of Norse texts have been borrowed or adapted from *The Poetic Edda*, translated by H. A. Bellows (1923); *The King's Mirror*, translated by L. M. Larson (1917); *Anthology of Norwegian Lyrics*, translated by C. W. Stork (1942); B. Bjørnson: *Poems and Songs*, translated by A. H. Palmer (1915); A. Øverland: "We shall live through all," translated by H. Naeseth (1941; all published by the American-Scandinavian Foundation, the latter in the *American-Scandinavian Review*), and I. Grøndahl's contributions to H. Wergeland: *Poems*, ed. G. M. Gathorne-Hardy (Gyldendal, Oslo; Hodder & Stoughton, Ltd., London, 1929).

The authors express their deep-felt gratitude to Dr. Guy Stanton Ford (Washington, D.C.), who has read part of the manuscript, and especially to Professor Einar Haugen (University of Wisconsin), who has worked through the whole book and tried to level the rocky English of the original. If inequalities still remain, these kind helpers are not to blame.

INDEX

Aasen, Ivar, 223, 289, 294; language
movement, 219, 222; writings, 220
Abel, Niels Henrik, 91
Absalon Pederssøn, 169, 177
Absolute monarchy established, 46;
see also Kings
Adams, John Quincy, 72
Æthelstane, King, 7
Agriculture, 5; see Farmers
Alfred the Great, 7
Althing, 2
America, spirit of, represented by
Norway, 72; see also United States
American Revolution, 54, 65, 67, 193
Amund Sigurdson, 33
Amundsen, Roald, 91
Anthem, see National anthem
Arbitration, international, 111, 115
Arbitration laws and courts, 102
Archbishopric in Trondheim, 23, 28,
32, 34; western islands under juris-
diction of, 32
Area of Norway, 4
Arendal, city of, 53, 57
Armenians, homeless, 114
Army, created, 45; democratized, 86
Arnljot Gelline (Bjørnson), 240
Art of Love (Ovid), 159
Asbjørn, peasant leader, 151
Aslak Bolt, Archbishop, 33
Assembly, forbidden, 59; freedom of,
90
Assembly, national (Riksforsamling),
meeting of 1814, at Eidsvoll, 64 ff.;
constitution adopted, 66; classes
represented, 66, 67-69; constitu-
tional provisions governing elec-
tion, character, and powers of, 66 f.;
political democracy, personal lib-
erty, 67; nature and influence of
the "generation of," 193, 198
Assembly of Estates, Danish, 34
Aukrust, Olav, 278

Balder, "the white God," 134
Ballad or folk song; origin, 170; anal-
ysis of, 171-74; diction, style, 173;
replaced by lyric songs, 176; redis-
covered, 216, 217
Banks, state bank demanded, 55, 61;
serving farmers, 83, 94, 100; labor,
100; industry, 105; deposits taxed,
106
Barons, feudal character of relations
with king, 28; see also Nobility;
Officials
Beam of Light, 154
Bergen, city, 41, 42, 43, 53, 92
Bersi, skald, 137
Beyond Our Power (Bjørnson), 252
Bjarni, skald, 162
Bjerknes, Vilhelm, 91
Bjørnson, Bjørnstjerne, 78, 81, 91, 223,
262, 263, 265, 266, 281, 284, 291, 293,
294; quoted, 5, 21, 81; champion of
national self-assertion and international peace, 110 ff., 256; character
and life work, 235-59; similarities
between Wergeland and, 235-40,
244, 246, 247, 254, 256; appearance
and personality, 235-39; sympathy
and sense of responsibility, 237,
254; formative influences, 239; capacity for action in all fields: main
task that of poet: first creations,
240; peasant novels, 240-42; religion,
241, 247, 252, 255; vision the future
of a whole nation: resulting activities, 242 ff.; greatest orator, 243;
enormous correspondence, 243,
253, 254; political services, 244 f.,
249 ff.; work in creating new attitude in the people most important
contribution to political history:
his program, 250; position in relation to Christianity, 241, 247; support of labor and socialism, 251;

INDEX

INDEX

in, 113; Holberg's close connection with, 184; Wergeland's admiration for, 199, 211; social backwardness attacked, 222
English Pilot, The (Wergeland), 211
Equality before the law, 67, 90
Erasmus Montanus (Holberg), 190
Erling Skjalgson, 142, 151
Ermengard, Viscountess, 141
Estates of the Realm, 44, 45, 46
Europe, Viking conquests, 1 f.; widespread Scandinavian influence, 2 f.; Norway's entry into family of nations, 25; Nansen's services for war victims in, 114, 273; Bjørnson as main spokesman for oppressed minorities, 257
Expropriation rights, 17, 105
Eystein, King, 22, 139
Eyvind, court poet, 140

Factory control law, 101, 104
Fairy tales, 174-76, 216
Falkberget, Johan, 278
Falkvord Lommansson, 171
Falsen, Christian Magnus, 58, 65
Falsen, Christian Magnus, II, 65, 71
Falsen, Envold, 58, 65
Family, kinship obligations, 16; changes in rights of, by state and church, 17; *see also* Odal, right of
Family sagas, 145 f.
Farmers, freedom of, 14, 15; right of odal, 17, 36, 47, 68; new lands cleared, farms acquired, 23, 49, 105; struggle for their rights against nobility, 32-40 *passim;* age of hardship, 36; leaders among: uprisings, 37 ff., 57-59; peace treaties, 39; ascendency of burghers over: resulting struggles, 42 ff., 48 f., 56, 68, 76; taxes, 44, 49, 57; interests furthered by governors, 47; development of a farmers' democracy, 48 ff.; numbers of tenants and, 49; aristocracy arising among, 50; seen in light of physiocratic thinking as basis of a new national freedom, 56; influence at Eidsvoll assembly and in drafting of constitution, 67-69; suffrage, 69; fight for full social

equality, 77 ff.; new orientation, 81; banks, 83, 94, 100; lost dominating part in national economy, 92; increase in number of farms, decrease in size: effect of industry upon conditions of, 93; relations with labor, 93, 100, 104; coöperative movement, 94; anti-capitalism, 100; increasing organization, economic and political, 103; organizations to aid sales, adjust prices and profits, 105; Eddic picture of the ideal, 125; effect upon, of Dano-Norwegian union, 169; clung to heritage of the past, 170; development of ballad or folk song by, 170 ff.; fairy tales, 174 f.; characteristics shown in cherished literature, 176; fight for political power aided by Wergeland, 201; reading habits encouraged, 203; effect of national renaissance upon: reforms sought, language movement, 219
"Farmers' Friends, The," 83
Farmers' Party, 78, 83, 84, 93; support of Labor Government, 104
Faroe Islands, 1, 2, 31
Feudalism, 27, 35
Fines, system of, 10, 12, 15, 47
Fisheries, 5, 42; exports, 25, 41, 53; organizations, 105
Flag parade, children's, 107, 250, 294
Folk culture, ballad or folk song, 170-74; fairy tales, 174-76; replaced by lyric songs, 176; again a dominating interest, 216, 217, 264, 269
Foreign affairs, demand for control of, 87, 111; efforts in behalf of peace and international justice, 110-16, 200, 256, 272 f.
Foreign culture: inflow of, and its influence upon medieval life and literature, 159-68; fiction of chivalry introduced, 160; resulting losses and gains, 161; elements coalesced into original poetic creation, 170
Forests, 4, 5, 48, 56
For the Working Class, periodical, 204
Fram expedition, Nansen's, 113
France, Vikings in, 2, 3; ideas, and their influence, 54, 67, 76, 110, 184,

INDEX

Heritage, *see* Odal

Heroship, in the Edda, 121; Christ imaged, 157; in ballad or folk song, 171, 172; *see also* Kings

High One, Eddic diety, 125, 126, 129, 134, 140, 155, 174; *Songs of the . . .*, 124, 128, 164, 165

Historians, sagas by, 145-51; *see* Sagas

Historical novels during and after First World War, 276

Historiography, Norwegian: Snorri the founder of, 148

History, scholarly research in, 216, 244, 270

Holberg, Ludvig, 54, 180, 193, 198, 205, 208, 215, 220, 221, 227, 248, 259, 281, 289, 290; the man and his activities, 181-92; comedies, 181, 188-90; mentality and writings, 182-90; European alliances and influence, 183 f.; political conservatism, 185; novel that won world fame: essays and epistles: moral nucleus of work, 186; religion, 187; his master stroke, 189; influence, 190-92

Holiday, national, 69, 201, 207, 250, 294

Holidays with pay, 104

Holland, shipping, 53; commerce with: ideas, 54

Homer, 132, 146, 223

"Home-soil novelists," 264

Horace, Sigvat compared to, 141

Hours of labor, 98, 101

Housing, of workers, 92 f.; public, 98; bank for, 100

Hugo, Victor, 111, 244

Ibsen, Henrik, 4, 78, 91, 160, 223, 238, 251, 252, 253, 254, 255, 263, 265, 266, 270, 281, 292, 294; conflict of law and freedom the crucial problem of existence: ethical earnestness and urge for independence: why his worldwide influence, 224; early life and activities: revolutionary forces in, 225 f.; spirit of protest against lax bourgeois society, 226 ff.; power of raising questions: dramas that at once became classics: belief in and preparation for, a God-imposed task, 228 f.; the at-

tack and its fruits: later dramas, 229-33; period of doubts and uncertainties, 231-33; culmination in his masterpiece, 232; work and influence appraised, 233 f.

Iceland, 1, 2, 25, 31; books and newspapers read, 108; manuscript of Edda, 121; skalds, 137, 141; predominance of verse making: use of Norse language and traditions, 140; the storehouse of tradition: unparalleled art of story telling, 145; family sagas, 145 f.; Royal Sagas, 146-51; Snorri's influence in union with Norway, 147; religious influence in literature, 154, 156; ballads took no root in, 170

Ideas, *see* Intellectual life

Incomes, average: in different nations, 108

Income taxes, 106

Independence re-won in 1814, 64-69

India, 200

Industry, growth and effects, 41 ff.; lumber, 43, 48, 53, 76; minerals, 43; water-power, 43, 92, 99, 100, 105; development, 92; effect upon conditions of agriculture, 93; capital and labor problems created by, 95 ff.

Ingersoll, Robert, 255

Inheritability, royal: principle of, 25, 28, 45

Insurance, social, 101, 104

Insurrections, 37, 38, 57

Intellectual life, influence of foreign ideas, 54 (see also England: France); evidences of independence and new life, 55; Norway's elevated standards, 108

Intellectual reactionaries, generation of, 215, 221, 222

International justice and peace, efforts in behalf of, 110-16, 200, 256, 272 f.

Interparliamentary Conference, 111

Interparliamentary Union, 112

Isle of Man, 2, 20, 31

Italy, 268

Jaabæk, Søren, 83, 98

Jeppe, the Transfigured Peasant (Holberg), 189

INDEX

Jews, Norway opened to, 79, 211; German persecutions, 293; monument to Wergeland, 294
Jones, S. Shepard, quoted, 115
Judges, 16, 36, 166; four rules governing decisions of, 26
Judicial development under national kingdom, 47
Julian the Apostate, play about, 231
Jury system introduced, 86
Justice, ideal of, 110; international, 110-16

Kant, Immanuel, 110
Kiel, Treaty of, 61, 62
Kielland, Alexander, 261
Kinck, Hans E., 265
Kings and kingship, early organizers and law makers, 7, 8, 9, 19-29 *passim;* obligation to obey and defend law, 12; administration of law, 15, 16; traditions about honor and bravery of, 19 ff.; those who were poets, 22, 137; relations with church, 23, 152; changes in status of, 24; rules for royal succession, 25, 28, 45; relations with nobility, 28, 30; Norway's kings in common with Sweden, 30, 61, 62 f.; with Denmark, 31, 46, 62; authority increased by Reformation, 34; people's conception of, 39; assemblies for acknowledgment of, 44; struggle to restore power as supreme ruler, 45; enlargement of royal activities as to government and legislation, 27, 46; decreasing confidence in, as defender of law, 58; foreign affairs only left to king, 72; struggles between Storthing and, 74 f.; attitude on cabinet question, 85; crown declared forfeited, 87; why monarchical government continued, 88; focus of intellectual endeavor, 136; homage to, in skaldic poetry, 136-44; Royal Sagas about, 146-51, 239, 282; development from arrogated power to authority of law, 150; open to foreign ideas, 159; development of new culture a policy of: ideals of chivalry introduced, 160; as focus of the new

culture, 166, 169; prayer written for, 166 f.; correct dress and behavior in presence of, 167
King's Mirror (Einar Gunnarson?), 163-68, 169, 172
Kinship, 16; relation to land, 17; right of odal, 17, 36, 47, 68
"Knight's sagas," 161
Konungr, Eddic hero, 136
Kristin Lavransdatter (S. Undset), 278
Krokann, Inge, 278
Kyrvestad Ketil, 176

Labor, increase of, in farming and lumber districts, 50; movement of 1848: first efforts to organize crushed by force: effects, 79 f., 81, 220; homes: effects of capitalistic industry, 92; relations with farmers, 93, 100, 104; trade unions, 95, 101; problems of capital and, 95; legislation, 96-109 *passim;* question of public interference in conflicts, 101; high economic standards, 108; Wergeland's efforts for: his periodical, 204; other poets supporting, 220, 225; Bjørnson's aid, 251; Uppdal's novels, 271; National Federation of Labor, 271
Labor court, 102
Labor Party, established, 95; socialistic program, 95, 107; seats in Storthing: influence, 96, 103; governments, 98, 104 ff., 107; joined by small holders, 100; strongest party in Storthing: measures adopted, 103 ff.
Lagthing (Law *Thing*), 2, 14; maintained as courts, 16, 26; local assemblies: limited powers, 27; acknowledgment of king at, 28, 33; attendance of governor, 45; maintained as part of Storthing, 66, 76, 90
Lamartine, A. de, 85
Land, right of odal, 17, 36, 47, 68; expropriation, 17, 105; cleared, cultivated, 23, 52, 105; rents and taxes, 32, 36, 37, 49; crown lands allotted to nobles, 34 f.; bought up by capitalists, 48 f., 56; crown land sales,

INDEX

INDEX

Literature (*Continued*)
twentieth century, 268 ff.; trend of
organized individualism in new
form of social struggle, 271 f.; influence in international field, 272;
great historical novels during and
after First World War: underlying
forces, 276-80; written for the people: a living power in everyday
life: support by government, 281;
during Nazi occupation, 286-96;
war poetry, 295; *see also works,
e. g.,* Edda; Sagas; *and names of
writers, e. g.,* Bjørnson, B.; Wergeland, H.
Local government, *see* Municipalities
Lofthuus, Christian J., 57, 58
Loki, mephistophelic deity, 132, 134
Louis IX of France, 25
Love, community of: a moving force
in medieval life, 156; Wergeland's
religion of, 197
Love's Comedy (Ibsen), 227
Lumber industry, 43, 48, 53, 76
Luther, Martin, battle song, 293

Magnus I (the Good), King, 8, 11,
20, 22, 143
Magnus Bareleg, King, 20, 22, 141;
queen of, 22
Magnus the Law Mender, King, 25;
law revision, 25-27, 166; constitution of, 27; Code of the *Hird,* 27-
29; provinces lost by, 31
Margaret, Queen, 31
Matthaeus Parisiensis, 24, 160
May Seventeenth, national festival,
69, 201, 207, 250, 294
Mazzini, Giuseppe, 81
Mercantilism, 46, 47, 54, 55
Merchant marine, 53, 92; libraries:
books read, 282, 294
Merchants, German, 25, 41-44, 169;
native, 41, 43; *see also* Burgher class
Military establishment, position of
barons, 28; conscription, 28, 68, 76,
82; organization of army and navy,
45; army democratized, 86
Minerals, 43
Minorities, protection of, 89 f.
Mirabeau, 193
Monarchy, *see* Kings and kingship

Monroe, President, 72
Montesquieu, 65
Mountains, 4 f.
Munch, Edvard, 91
Municipalities, self-government, 51,
69, 75, 78, 87; elections, 69, 90, 95,
96; population, 53, 92; reform meas-
ures, 98; state credits for enter-
prises of, 104; measure to equalize
taxes of, 106; *see also names, e. g.,*
Bergen
Music, *see* Songs

Nansen, Fridtjof, 91; character: back-
ground; hero, 113, 272 f.; public
services, 114-16, 273
Napoleonic Wars, 61
National anthem, 55, 247, 288, 293
National Broadcasting System, 107,
282
National character, varied, 6, 21, 39,
48, 110, 119
National Coöperative, 99
National Federation of Labor, 271
National Federation of Trade Unions,
95
National holiday, 69, 201, 207, 250,
294
National Industrial Bank, 105
Nationalism, labor legislation and
social reforms strengthened by con-
sciousness of, 96
Navy, Royal, 45
Nazis, *see* German Nazis
Neergaard, John, 77, 78
Neorealism, 270
Neoromanticism, 262 ff.
Netherlands, 2; commercial compe-
tition, 43; immigrants from, 44
Neutrality, 111
New Norse language, 219 f., 267
Newspapers, 55, 108, 204, 222, 239;
freedom of the press, 67, 90; space
devoted to literary matters, 282;
during Nazi occupation, 288, 292,
294
Niels Klim's Journey . . . (Hol-
berg), 186
Nietzschean morality, 251, 262
Nobel, Alfred, peace prize, 112
Nobel prize awarded Bjørnson, 258
Nobility, foundation of new, 24;

INDEX

feudal character of relations with king: power organized: no jurisdiction over tenants or cotters, 28; struggles for power, 30-40 *passim;* denationalized, 30, 48, 169; influx of Danish: small national party within, 34; burghers a counterbalance to, 44, 45; becomes secondary, 48; practically extinct, 61; abolishment of privileges and titles, 74 f.

Nordskog, J. E., 98*n*

Normandy, duchy of, 2, 3, 9

Northern War, 51, 53

North Pole, expedition to, 113

Norwegians, lands settled by, 1 f.; race, 6; varied national character, 6, 21, 39, 48, 110, 119, 171, 175; in U.S., 73, 92, 282; emigration, 93; characteristics as depicted in the Edda, 121 ff.; in the sagas, 145; paralyzing shock of German attack, 285; conquered only by hard fighting, 286; during Nazi occupation, 109, 116, 287-96

Norwegian Society, Copenhagen, 192

Oath, royal, 27

Obstfelder, S., 264

Odal (heritage), right of, 17, 36, 47, 68

Odelsthing, 66, 90

Odin, Eddic deity, 124, 125, 126

Official class, influence in drafting of constitution, 67, 68; liberalism: backbone of intellectuals, 77; generation of intellectual reactionaries, 215, 221, 222

Officials, functions of royal, 14; their judicial authority, 26; feudal character of barons' relations with king, 28; sheriffs, 32, 36, 37, 38, 46, 57, 172; new bureaucracy developed, 37, 46; intellectuals in bureaucracy, 55; transfer of functions to elected bodies, 78; conflict over royal counselors' admission to Storthing, 84-86

Olaf I Trygvason, King, 8, 19

Olaf II, King (Saint Olaf), 8, 9 f., 11, 19, 20, 22, 24, 152, 176, 241, 293; laws of, 10, 11, 21, 35; relations of

skalds with, 137, 141-43; love songs by, 140; center of Snorri's sagas, 149; interpretation of, as a Christian character, 157 f.

Olaf III, King, 22

Old age pensions, 98, 104

Old Norse language, 140, 178; dialects a homogeneous idiom descended from, 219

Orators, great, 82, 243

Ore reduction, 43

Organization, tendency of, in new form of social struggle, 94-97, 109, 271, 272

Orkney Islands, 1, 31

Oskeladden (the Cinder Lad), 174

Oslo, 42, 43, 44, 53, 92, 98; rechristened Christiania, 45

"Oslo breakfast," 98

Outlawry, 13, 17, 47

Øverland, Arnulf, 273, 276, 293, 295; quoted, 279, 296

Oxford University, Bodleian Library, 184

Parliamentary government accomplished, 81, 86; *see* Storthing

Parties, political: beginnings of organized, 78, 80, 81, 83, 95; period of disintegration, 102; *see also under* Farmers' Party; Labor; Left

Paul Lange and Tora Parsberg (Bjørnson), 250

Peace, celebrated in sagas of the kings, 22; desire for: "farmers' peace treaties," 39; long periods of, 52, 91; efforts in behalf of international justice and, 110-16, 200, 256, 272 f.

Peace Conference, Hague, 112

Peace prize, Nobel, 112, 258

Peasants, serfdom, 10, 14, 61; liberation in Denmark, 22, 56; struggle with nobility, 32, 38

Peder Paars (Holberg), 185

Peer Gynt (Ibsen), 228, 232, 233

People of Juvik, The (O. Duun), 279

Personal and family rights, changes made by state and church, 17; *see also* Odal, right of

Peter the Great, 186

Philip Augustus of France, 24

INDEX

INDEX

eral trends: search for truth, 147; Snorri Sturluson and his influence, 147-51; foundation of Norwegian historiography, 148; religious influences, 154, 157; court literature of "knight's sagas," 161; popular editions, 282

Saint Olaf, *see* Olaf II, King

Saint-Simonists, 110

Sars, J. E., 244

Scandinavian countries, law the basic principle in, 1, 2; establishments abroad, 1; influence, 3; geography, 4; political unions: kings in common, 30 (*see also* Kings); meaning of Lutheran Reformation (*q.v.*), 34; idea of freedom spread by people from, 56; standard of living, 108; attitude toward League of Nations, 115

Schøning, Gerhard, 191

Schools, 86, 107, 169; decrees establishing, 51; social legislation for, 98; established by Wergeland, 204; books of song, 284 f., 293; during Nazi occupation, 293

Scotland, 1, 31; treaty re shipping, 24; immigrants from, 44

Scott, Gabriel, 278

Self-government, 51, 69, 75, 78, 87; interdependence of democracy and, 84; *see also* Municipalities

Serfdom, 10, 14, 61; *see also* Peasants

Seventeenth of May, *see* May seventeenth

Sex campaigns, of Wergeland, 206; of Ibsen, 230; of Bjørnson, 252, 260; *see also* Women

Sexual anarchy, 260, 274

Shakespeare, 189, 208

Shays' Rebellion, 57

Sheriffs, 32, 36, 37, 38, 46, 57, 172

Shetland Islands, 1, 31

Shipping, treaties securing, 24; and exporting interests, 53, 54 f.; Norway's ascendency, 77, 92

Sigrun and Helgi, 122, 123, 128, 172

Sigurd and Brynhild, 130

Sigurd Slembe, 140

Sigurd the Crusader, King, 21 f., 24

Sigvat Thordson, skald, 10, 141-44,

168, 199; relations with King Olaf: political influence, 141 ff., 150

"Silhouettes, generation of," 215

Sivle, Per, 266, 289

Skaldic poetry and the kings, 136-44; position of the skald, 136; his independence, 137; form and subject matter, 138; taken over by Icelanders, 140; political influence, 141, 143

Skram, Amalie, 261

Slovaks and Bjørnson, 257

Snorri Sturluson and his sagas, 147-51, 152, 165, 168, 191, 239; influence on future, 151; interpretation of Olaf as a Christian, 157 f.; Wergeland's tribute to, 294; extensive distribution of his sagas, 282

Social and economic, *see under* Economic

Socialism, preached to workmen, 80; in America, 81; program adopted by Labor Party, 95, 107; ideas adopted by Storthing, 96; highly different types of social results: creation of law the essence of, 107; support by Bjørnson, 251

Social security measures, 101 f., 104 ff.

Social set up, medieval: pictured in *King's Mirror*, 165 ff.

Society of Sciences and Letters, 55

Songs, national anthems, 55, 293, 296; for children, 207, 284, 296; extent and importance, 284, 288, 296; books of, 284, 285, 289; *see also* Edda

Songs of the High One, 124, 128, 164, 165

Sovereignty of the people, *see* Popular Sovereignty

Spain, civil war, 200

Spanish constitution, 65

Speculum Regale (*King's Mirror*), 163-68, 169, 172

Speech, freedom of, 77, 90

Standard of living, 108

State, *see* Government

State credits, 104

Stiklestad, battle of, 8, 150, 152, 158

Storthing (Great *Thing*), name of general assembly, 67; class representation in, 69; meeting to consider union with Sweden: consti-

INDEX